Critical Essays on Dante

Critical Essays on
World Literature

Robert Lecker, General Editor
McGill University

Critical Essays on Dante

Giuseppe Mazzotta

G. K. Hall & Co. • Boston, Massachusetts

First published 1991.
10 9 8 7 6 5 4 3 2 1

Library of Congress Cataloging-in-Publication Data

Critical essays on Dante / Giuseppe Mazzotta [editor].
      p.   cm. -- (Critical essays on world literature)
    Includes bibliographical references and index.
    ISBN 0-8161-8849-1
    1. Dante Alighieri, 1265–1321. Divina commedia. I. Maz-
zotta, Giuseppe, 1942–   . II. Series.
PQ4390.C788   1991
    851'.1--dc20   90-20307

The paper used in this publication meets the minimum requirements of American National Standard for Information Sciences—
Permanence of Paper for Printed Library Materials, ANSI Z39.48-
1984. ∞ ™

Printed and bound in the United States of America

CONTENTS

PREFACE

The essays collected here deal exclusively with the *Divine Comedy*, and they chart the major lines of the history of Dante criticism from Dante's own self-exegesis to our own times. As is clear from the texts, this history is punctuated by a remarkable variety of views and by an equally remarkable degree of continuity in interpretive perspectives.

The selection in no way seeks to give an exhaustive picture of the heterogeneity of critical theses the *Divine Comedy* has elicited since its publication. The omissions are glaring. The purists and anti-Dantists—who are the prolongation of Petrarch's position—are not represented; there is no sample of the exacting scholarship produced at the turn of the century by textual critics and by the adherents to philological positivism. Nor are any esoteric readings of the *Divine Comedy* included. These omissions are accountable in two ways. One is the strictly technical—and intellectually less compelling—demand of space. The other is the conviction that the philological and esoteric strains of Dante criticism survive, with considerable adjustments, respectively, in the historicist approaches to the poem and the allegorical readings current in more recent times.

All quotations from the *Divine Comedy* are taken from *La Commedia secondo l'antica vulgata*, ed. Giorgio Petrocchi, 4 vols. (Milan: Mondadori, 1966–67). In essays translated specifically for this volume, passages are taken from *The Divine Comedy*, trans. Charles S. Singleton (Princeton: Princton University Press, 1970).

INTRODUCTION

In the history of Western literature, few other texts have engendered as much critical discourse as the *Divine Comedy*. A sign of the power of this poem to disseminate itself in scholarly argument and to shape debates on aesthetic values over a span of almost seven centuries is evident from the metacritical practice that has come to be known as *la fortuna di Dante*. The subject matter of this substantial chapter of Italian literary history is the investigation of Dante's poetic influence, as well as the assessment of ongoing commentaries, erudite glosses, controversies, and polemics that have been flourishing since the earliest appearance of the *Divine Comedy*.

This well-established scholarly tradition of taking stock of the poem's reception across the shifting tastes and concerns of seven centuries will possibly bring to mind the work of the recent school of hermeneutics that goes under the awkward label "aesthetics of reception." To be sure, the theoretical links between the two strains of scholarship are nonexistent, just as their practical aims are entirely different from each other. Whereas the aesthetics of reception is chiefly oriented toward theoretical speculations in pursuit of general laws of interpretation, the *fortuna di Dante* deals with the history of specific texts. It considers the poem as the focus of contingent, episodic questions of history, and it documents historically the intellectual temper underlying and generating a certain interpretation of the poem. Unlike the latter-day hermeneuts, whom in a way it may recall, the genre of the *fortuna di Dante* never aims at determining the transcendent meaning of the poem within the horizon of the reader's expectations.

This collection of critical essays on Dante, selected from the Middle Ages to the present, does not pretend to be either another episode in the *fortuna di Dante* sequel or a study in the aesthetics of Dante's reception in time. Unavoidably the structure of the book may bear the traces of the two modes; nonetheless the primary objective in collecting this material is simply to make available a wide array of the major critical perspectives Dante's poetry and thought have elicited in the long history of their commentary.

The works included here have been selected either because they have been central in shaping the exegetical tradition of the *Divine Comedy* or because they sharply reflect and crystallize the broad intellectual issues of a particular period. In either case these pieces constitute veritable paradigms of the poem. That statement, however, should not be construed to imply that, taken collectively in the contradictory plurality of their outlooks and emphases, these essays exhaust all possible critical perspectives on the *Divine Comedy* or (much the same thing) that they end up disclosing the total transcendent meaning of Dante's extraordinary vision. It can be said that the claim that a text's meaning lies in the sum total of the readings it has produced is the pitfall inherent in the aesthetics of reception. Such a claim of a totalized and transcendent meaning, however fictional the assumption of totality may be, short-circuits the radical contingency of each reading. The notion of totality preempts the possibility of future readings capable of altering the contours of the existing discourses of the text.

The claim of contingency carries with it several implications. One is the possibility of radically new readings of the poem; Vico's discoveries of the poem's principles are genuinely new. The second is that, as the views contained in this book make clear, there are no perspectives on the poem that are fixed and final. On the contrary, together they exemplify the nature of understanding as a cumulative pattern in the sense that each perspective grows out of or in reaction to preceding ones. This does not mean that there is a movement of progressive clarification of the poem's difficulties. One should hardly stress that the discovery of a new perspective usually takes place at the expense of traditional ones. Nonetheless, it is clear that, for instance, Vico capitalizes on the rhetorical-philosophical insights of Renaissance thought. A third implication in the claim of the contingency of the various perspectives is that the poem effectively becomes the mirror of the ages, a pretext for articulating the spiritual-aesthetic perplexities peculiar to each age.

Viewed as a whole, this collection of essays, arranged in chronological order, is inescapably caught within the predicament of any work that wants to be simultaneously history and criticism of a poem. The double bind of such an enterprise can be quickly formulated: do the temporal shifts in the understanding of the *Divine Comedy* depend on the changing cultural temper? If so, can one legitimately maintain that the links between a text and its interpretation are logical and necessary? And to what extent do the various interpretive theories figure and reinscribe meanings that, though partial, are immanent to the poem? And, finally, are there any constant concerns in the multiple and spirited historical debates? The questions are in no way arbitrary, and some light can be shed on them by looking briefly at features of the *Divine Comedy* retrieved by the larger generality of the essays included here.

It is an almost worn-out cliché of literary criticism that the *Divine Comedy* is an encyclopedic poem. Its narrative, as countless generations of readers know, focuses on the journey of a historical man, Dante, through the land of the dead to heaven, where it is granted to him to see God face to face. At the same time, this pilgrim's quest for a spiritual redemption involves the poet in a complex confrontation with a heterogeneity of poetic traditions, philosophical systems, and political realities—the vast provinces of the encyclopedic order. Such are the intricacy and power of Dante's construction that readers of the *Divine Comedy* historically confront it as if to measure the limitations of their own visions. The reading of the *Divine Comedy* in history is, by and large, the parable of its inevitable fragmentation. Thus, Cristoforo Landino, a Renaissance Neoplatonist, reads the poem in terms of the Platonic allegory of the soul as it strives to unchain itself from the shadows of ignorance and reach the sun-lit plain of truth. Similarly Iacopo Mazzoni, a neo-Aristotelean, emphasizes the importance of the scientific doctrines of the Stagirite.

These various clusters of ideas and themes are certainly present in the *Divine Comedy*. They are the material made malleable and melted down in the crucible of Dante's imagination. Yet these abstract conceptual systems, which are variously played down or highlighted by scholars, are balanced by a question that permanently abides at the center of the poem, to emerge only occasionally in the critical analyses: the nature of poetry and its relationship to theology. The common response to this fundamental problem is that Dante bridges the gap between and harmonizes the disjunctive assumptions of a rhetorical-humanistic tradition and a biblical, theological standpoint. The harmonization Dante produces, however, cannot blunt the radical quality of his questions.

A number of essays (for example, Varchi's and Gilson's) emphasize that Dante pushes the conclusions of all the sciences he absorbs in his poem to their theological limits and that he draws all forms of knowledge under the sway of vision. And many of them, especially in the last century, obliquely focus on how Dante rethinks the lexical sedimentation of language, its depth and obliterated resonances (the technical registers of the hierocrats, of the mystics, of Vergil, Aquinas, and others) in order to restore, by an act of authority that edges toward sublime madness, the spiritual order of the world. The real sense of these formulations, I believe, is that in the *Divine Comedy* theology is the standpoint for a critique of the sciences; at the same time, rhetoric is the perspective from which the claims of theological language itself are questioned.

The exact relationship between theology and poetry, as the two foci of an ellipsis around which the poem's movement is figured, emerges from the first essay in this book. This exceptional text is commonly known as the epistle Dante wrote to Cangrande della Scala. Although the letter's authorship continues to be contested, its conceptual energy, the clarity and vigilance with which the grid of the poem is configured, and the complex of insights into its structure and finalities are such that most subsequent readers, especially in the fourteenth century, have been drawn within the horizon of concerns the epistle maps.

Its immediate aim was to serve as an introduction to *Paradiso* (and, in fact, it glosses the first 12 lines of that canticle), but it also marks the general terms and the exegetical method employed in the construction and, consequently, in the interpretation of the poem. The *Divine Comedy*, we are told, is written according to the principles of theological allegory; specifically, it is patterned on the biblical account of Exodus. The historical events of Exodus—the epic experience of the Jews who journey from Egypt through the desert to Jerusalem—lie under both the four senses of the biblical exegesis and the polysemy of the *Divine Comedy* (its four senses are the literal, the allegorical, the moral, and the anagogical). This biblical-theological scheme was revived in the second half of the century by Auerbach, Singleton, and their epigons in the guise of attention to what is known as biblical typology and figuralism.

This theological rationale is unquestionably central to the *Divine Comedy*, although some critics (in the wake of Croce) inexplicably persist writing about the poem as if the theology were irrelevant to its understanding. Yet it is true that in the letter to Cangrande, the attention to theology is balanced by the lucid awareness of formal and rhetorical questions, which Auerbach, Singleton, and their followers tend to neglect. Sundry issues such as the literary genre of the poem; classification of genre according to Horace's *Ars Poetica;* the role of exordium as is understood by Aristotle's *Rhetoric;* overt definitions of the form of treatment of the poem as poetic, fictive, digressive, or something else; unequivocal assertions that the poem belongs to the general category of ethics; remarks on the sublime (which in the Middle Ages is known as *admiratio*): all these are some of the elements that thematize rhetoric not just as a series of technical or ornamental precepts. Rhetoric is a veritable epistemology, a discipline with unique claims about truth and knowledge and their links with persuasion and artifice. From this standpoint, the poem is the imaginative domain where a threatening and mutual interrogation between theology and poetry steadily occurs.

Finally, the epistle to Cangrande faces another issue that contemporary critical debates have been reluctant to explore in its full implication: that the poem is placed within a visionary-mystical tradition. Texts by the pseudo-Dionysius, St. Augustine, St. Bernard, Richard of St. Victor, and St. John's Apocalypse are explicitly recalled by Dante in order to convey a visionary claim for his own poem. Bruno Nardi and Gian Roberto Sarolli have seized on Dante's statement in order to argue for the prophetic substance of the *Divine Comedy*, which indeed features riddles about the future and passionate pleas for the spiritual reform of the world. This dimension of meaning is absolutely correct, but it is partial. The question of vision is so crucial to the unfolding of *Paradise*, for instance, that one would have to consider the textual allusions to St. Paul's rapture, the sequence of dreams with which the *Inferno* begins and ends and which punctuate *Purgatory*, the emphasis on faith as a mode of vision, the cantos of the contemplatives, and, ultimately, the beatific vision recorded in *Paradiso* XXXIII in order to grasp the value of vision. Dante's apocalyptic discourse, one suspects, is the recognition of the predicament and hermeneutical tension of the poem: the poet's difficulty in saying what the pilgrim has seen, as well as the difficulty for us to see what the poet says.

I have chosen to spend quite some time on the elaborate content of the epistle to Cangrande because of its powerful exegesis of the poem and because it establishes the paradigms of interpretation taking place in the fourteenth century. It is impossible to do justice here to the earliest commentaries to the *Divine Comedy*. Suffice it to say that the barest outline of the commentary—beginning with the glosses by the poet's son, Iacopo Alighieri, through the comments by Graziolo de' Bambaglioli, Iacopo della Lana, the Ottimo, and Guido da Pisa, to mention only some of them—would show the strong traces of the letter's impact.

Iacopo's glosses, for instance, with their emphasis on the various levels of style (elegiac, tragic, and comical) and genre, are obviously indebted to the letter. These, as well as those by Graziolo, stress the didactic, moral quality of Dante's voice. There is a good reason for the moral, allegorical urgency claimed by them: this is the time when Dante's political subversiveness, as it appears in *Monarchia*, was fiercely denounced by Guido Vernani and, a bit later, by Cardinal Bertrando del Poggetto.

The influence of the letter is also evident in Guido da Pisa's commentary. Guido acknowledges, as does the letter, the allegorical structure of the poem; as in the letter, there is in Guido close attention to the rhetorical structure and form of the text. But the unmistakable influence of the letter should not be seen as a mechanical doubling of the insight voiced by it. Actually, with Guido da Pisa's commentary, a drastic turn takes place in Dante criticism. Guido knows all the works of Dante; he refers to them and makes an effort to capture a global view of the poet's convictions. In exegetical terms, moreover, a new perspective is developed for the *accessus* to the poem: Guido da Pisa treats the self of the poet, or the poet's autobiographical focus, as a central thematic element of the story. "The agent or author of this work is Dante," we are told, and Dante is represented as a man well versed in many arts who revives dead poetry just as Boethius in earlier times revived dead philosophy. Guido da Pisa's insight into the autobiographical structure of the poem prefigures the hermeneutics of the self, on which in our time, John Freccero has focused in a number of studies. Guido's remark about the self, however, leads him to the heart of the poem's poetic-theological predicament: what is the status, he lucidly wonders in the earlier *Declaration*, what is the status of the poet's own assertions, which manifestly deviate from the body of common theological beliefs? Guido's answer lies in the view of theology and poetry as two distinct spheres of activity. Simply, he claims that poetry can do what theology does not do. Undoubtedly Guido da Pisa's aim in separating poetry from theology is to safeguard poetry from facile condemnations by censors, and in the *Expositions*—the prologue of which is reprinted here— poetry is said to accord with theology. The poem is said to be visionary and is related to Ezekiel's vision; its structure is figured through the trichambered ark of Noah. At the same time, theology does not have a univocal definition but is said to have a variety of expressions: the poetic theology St. Augustine discusses in his *City of God*, the natural theology upheld by the philosophers, and the theology of the multitudes.

If Guido da Pisa's brilliant commentary touches on but does not come to terms with the problematical core of Dante's text, with Boccaccio and Petrarch we enter a different phase of the *fortuna di Dante*. Boccaccio's attitude to Dante certainly signals the recognition of Dante as both a popular figure and a classic, whose poem becomes the object of public lectures to a large audience. The commentator sees his role as the eclectic transmitter of the learned traditions of the past, and to this end he mixes pedagogical fervor with mechanical repetition. Because the memory of the historical Dante is receding, Boccaccio writes his biography to retrieve the solid, substantial reality of the poet, which turns out to be a veritable legend. In substantive terms, in the reading of the *Divine Comedy* Boccaccio never renounces the primacy of the theological impulse animating the poem. For him Dante is a poet, and, by that very fact, he is a theologian because poets are the first theologians of humanity who conceal the truth under fabulous veils. Such a view, which reflects the concerns of the flowering Italian humanism, is decidedly not shared by Petrarch.

Nothing underscores Boccaccio's devotion to the poetry of Dante more than his effort to persuade his great interlocutor, Petrarch, to read Dante's poem. Petrarch, as the excerpt from his letter makes clear, does not share Boccaccio's judgment. Dante is the poet for the crowds in taverns and marketplaces, one from whose work Petrarch decided to stay away while writing his own poetry in Italian. Philological analyses of Petrarch's poetry have long shown—his disclaimers notwithstanding—his familiarity with Dante's poetry, but it is clear that Petrarch would never accede to Boccaccio's wish of acknowledging Dante's mastery and stature as a classic. There are several reasons for his posture; a certain amount of "anxiety,"— which the critical temper of our times tends to exaggerate, probably accounts for it. But there is a more compelling historical reason for it: the fact is that with Petrarch we are in an entirely different intellectual climate. He entertains no illusions about political or religious utopias, and he sees with a clarity that was unmatched in his own day that the Middle Ages lay waste (or better: he disapproves of the emergent hybrid cultural forces visible in the West) and that a new poetic imagination was needed to remake the world.

Petrarch's anti-Dantism will reemerge in successive centuries. For the time being, however, Boccaccio's formulations became the point of departure for Benvenuto da Imola's commentary. As he writes his textual explications around 1380, after the death of both Petrarch and Boccaccio, Benvenuto keeps both of them in mind and calls Boccaccio "my venerable master," while quoting Petrarch. There is more to this procedure than a mere humanistic, proud acknowledgment of discipleship. The spiritual focus of the *Divine Comedy* actually shifts in Benvenuto's commentary, and the references he makes to Boccaccio and Petrarch are the stylistic symptom of such a shift.

The interpretive scheme advanced in the letter to Cangrande is still observed by Benvenuto. Dante is a most Christian poet seeking to bring poetry back to theology ("Christianissimus poeta Dantes poetriam ad theologiam studuit revocare"). Even Benvenuto's splendid sense that the heterogeneity of knowledge—all the diverse sciences in the cycle of education—had to be brought to bear on the poem echoes Iacopo della Lana's earlier perception. In the middle of these continuities of exegetical method, however, Benvenuto inserts concrete references to the life and history of Dante's times: papacy and empire, the crisis of the cities, and the devastation caused by civil wars. There is also evidence of complex ideological valorizations. Before Benvenuto da Imola, Caesar, who is listed as one of the spirits dwelling in Limbo, is understood as the embodiment of the majesty and providentiality of the Roman Empire. For Benvenuto, on the contrary, Caesar is the oppressor of freedom.

This shift in the political-moral judgment of Caesar is a sign that the cultural nomenclature of Florentine life is being fundamentally reassessed. Coluccio Salutati's text on tyranny and Bruni's defense of civic liberties as the very foundation of moral life, among others, exemplify what Hans Baron has called "the crisis of the Italian cities." The compelling reality of the crisis in one's own immediate world made the abstract universality of the empire no longer viable as a myth. With the waning of the myth of the empire, Dante's star, if not completely eclipsed, starts to wane. His vast doctrine is now contested, and because he did not write his poem in Latin, and elegance (generally defined as Latin) is the canon of current aesthetic values, Petrarch, not Dante, is the favorite poet.

It was only at the court of the Medici in the later part of the fifteenth century that the *Divine Comedy* came to enjoy a renewed prestige and a renewed centrality in the intellectual debates. The revival of interest in Dante had clearly to do with Lorenzo's political designs and with the hegemony of the Platonic discourse promoted by Ficino. In such a context where politics and a universalizing culture mingle, Dante appears as the great precursor whose vision is the crucible of rich imaginative and conceptual experiences foreshadowing those favored by the Medici. The universality of Dante is now a model refracted in a number of actual Florentine concerns. Cristoforo Landino, as I said earlier, platonizes Dante in his commentary, which was published in 1481. His edition of the *Divine Comedy*, it might be added, is the one that Leonardo, Raphael, and Michelangelo used. In other circles, Dante is hailed as a religious prophet; in still others, he is the man who yokes together science and theology.

These various facets in the critical perception of Dante were triggered by Landino's Platonic parable whereby the pilgrim Dante is what Aeneas was to the Platonic allegorizers of the Middle Ages, such as Bernard Sylvester. There is no doubt that there is a Neoplatonic strain in the poem. Landino's interpretation, however, resulted in a questionable overhauling of a number of motifs punctuating the old commentaries. Because the Aristotelean universe of reference, to which Benvenuto da Imola still subscribes, is supplanted by a Platonic one, the whole Scholastic system of doctrine is now bracketed; the four levels of exegesis are discarded in favor of a generalized, abstract, philosophical allegory; the practice of identifying historical figures and reading the poem as a Florentine chronicle is equally abandoned. If the disinterest in the dogmatic coherence of the poem strikes one as a loss, Landino's belief that the essence of the poem is vision and that poetry itself is a divine madness can be seen to prepare Vico's insight in the eighteenth century.

Landino's commentary opens up the text to the fierce quarrels that characterize the intellectual life of the Renaissance. The *Divine Comedy*, as Iacopo Mazzoni remarks, is now explicitly considered within the larger horizon of general poetics. On the one hand, the impact of Aristotle's *Poetics* on all literary arguments and, on the other, the abiding concern with the "questione della lingua"—two issues in which most men of letters participate—account for the emergence of linguistic interest and interest in general poetics in Dante scholarship. Further, Landino's Neoplatonic reading of the poem brings about an Aristotelean reaction traditionally identified with the aims of the Florentine Academy instituted in 1540. Its double overarching aim is to provide a literal interpretation of the poem and to determine its moral substance in terms of Aristotelean thought. Among the many intellectuals who adhered to the academy, one finds Varchi and Mazzoni.

Benedetto Varchi is a protagonist in the systematic critical revision of Dante the academy pursues. He believes in the existence of a unified philosophical theory controlling Dante's poetic practice: philosophy, rather than theology is the substantial unifying principle of the poem. For Varchi this philosophy includes Plato, but it is eminently embodied by Aristotle. He is the perspective from which Averroes, Galen, and Avicenna (above all his reading of *Purgatorio* XXV) are eclectically gathered and the epistemological conflicts between their systems are harmonized. In so doing Varchi is convinced that he is miming Dante's own practice of harmonizing disparate philosophical traditions, and because Dante for Varchi is a philosopher, it follows that he views poetry as occupying a place hierarchically inferior to philosophy.

Because poetry for him is nothing more than an ornament to philosophical speculations, Varchi intuits how poetry has the negative power of obfuscating the sense of utility philosophy pursues. Varchi's aesthetics is certainly negligible, yet his commentary is still valuable because it upholds an encyclopedic ideal: the belief that a periplus through the vast provinces of knowledge (the seven liberal arts) is essential to grasping the complex doctrine contained in the *Divine Comedy*. There is even the acknowledgment of the importance of philology, which Varchi understood as the work of retrieving the traditions and texts that flow into Dante's poem. These positions are continued by Iacopo Mazzoni who, in effect, contributes to putting an end to the supremacy of Landino's Neoplatonism.

Varchi's and Mazzoni's perspectives produced a luxuriant flowering of disputes throughout the sixteenth century. The character of Dante the man, which clearly was the pretext of deciding whether to invest the poet's voice with a privileged moral authority, is once again the focus of controversies. Of central concern is the question of the appropriateness of the pagan myths to the religious truths of the poem: the perplexities of the Counter-Reformation are being directly felt. There are now efforts, for instance, to correct Dante's theological doctrines, such as his views on vows articulated in *Paradiso* V, as well as the "inadequate" proofs on the immortality of the soul given in *Paradiso* VII. The flip side of this theological censorship is the pedantic inventory of rhetorical tropes, of rare locutions, descriptions, and comparisons figuring in the text. These traits of Dante scholarship in this baroque period deserve to be noted, however summarily, because they enable one to appreciate the radical break Giambattista Vico in the eighteenth century makes from his predecessors.

In order to gauge the originality of Vico's interpretation, his piece in this collection is preceded by the musings on Dante by Gian Vincenzo Gravina. The excerpt, taken from his general treatise on poetics, shows Gravina's effort to rescue the poetry of the *Divine Comedy* from the desiccated quibbles and fastidious postmortems of the baroque postilers and pedants. Gian Vincenzo Gravina, who works in the wake of the Dominican Tommaso Campanella, is above all a classical theorist forever mindful of rules of versification and canons of decorum. Still, he seeks to come to grips with the divine substance of the poem in which technical questions of philosophy, locution, and theological inspiration converge. In a move that Vico will turn and develop into a key element in his own speculation, Gravina even links Homer to Dante. The link merely introduces Gravina's notion that the *Divine Comedy* is a repository of wisdom and eloquence and, more generally, the principle that it is a dramatic text in the sense that it is the parable of the tensions and of a spiritual drama involving all the characters. For all his attention to Dante's theological passion, however, Gravina remains caught within a classical conception of poetry as order and balance.

Vico, who knew Gravina personally, can in no way accept the Cartesian structure of his thought—his constant demand that rational limits harness the poetic imagination. Vico, the philosopher of the imagination, acknowledges this faculty's power to produce and to receive unbridled images, dreams, and nightmares—the shadowy domain of unreason—that threaten the stability of reflective judgments. His insight into the power of poetry and the imagination allows him to discover in Dante a kindred spirit, the sublime poet who grasps the extent to which all rational practices are encroached upon and are constituted by the imagination. From this standpoint, Vico enunciates critical principles that mark a genuine watershed in the history of the interpretation of the poem.

Vico believes that the visionariness made available by the poetic imagination is more than just an element of the poem; it is the poem's essence. This visionariness shapes and binds together rhetoric, history, and theology. The novelty of this conception is readily apparent. The fatal error of Renaissance treatises on poetry—to which Vico refers in the *New Science*—and a fortiori of Dante commentaries—is to assume that poetry gives expression to Aristotelian and Platonic doctrines. Indeed, to this very day most commentaries on Dante end up casting the *Divine Comedy* as a poetic rendition of existing Thomistic, Averroistic, or Augustinian systems of thought. As they do so, knowingly or not, these contemporary commentaries reenact the drama of Plato's *Republic* where poetry is said to be the inferior copy of philosophy. Vico goes beyond such things.

By making poetry the foundation of all knowledge, he recaptures the vital depths—the pulsation—as it were, of Dante's mythopoeia. Like Homer, Dante is the poet who absorbs and thereby forges the language of the people; his poetry is both history and divination, and it fully deserves to be called sublime poetry. The "sublime," which Vico considers to be the distinctive trait of Dante's severe imaginings, is never purely a question of grandiloquence or an artifice of style. It designates, rather, a world of ruthless passions, effulgences, and bewildering excesses. In a way, one can perceive in Vico's noble speculation, which transcends Platonic and Aristotelean categories of knowledge, the glimmers of the critical reflections by Guido da Pisa, Boccaccio, and Landino that in Vico flare up into a powerful vision.

The later part of the eighteenth century (for example, the case of Bettinelli) largely ignores Vico's thought. Toward the end of that century a romantic cult of Dante, promoted by a number of romantic poets, establishes itself. In this mythical view, which becomes the pretext for ideological confrontations between conservatives and liberals (say, Gioberti and Rossetti), Dante is the moral voice chastising clerical abuses, the political exile, and the sublime poet. It is only with the work of Francesco De Sanctis that the original burden of Vico's intuition was to be recuperated.

De Sanctis addresses the spiritual substance of Dante's poetry, which is said "to embrace all life, heaven and earth, time and eternity, the human and the divine." This spiritual form of life is what Dante's art conveys in profundity. De Sanctis's emphasis on poetry as the core of Dante's text clearly plays down the importance of theological, ethical, and philosophical discourses. No doubt he had a sharp sense of the European intellectual ideologies in his own days (Hegel, particularly). Yet his representation of Dante appears as a domesticated, tame version of Vico's insights. More than the powerful fabulist and the prodigious seer of the totality of discourses heralded by Vico, De Sanctis understands Dante's poem as disclosing a mind incapable of leaving on anything the imprint of his own thought.

De Sanctis's view was harshly contested by the troops of positivists and philologists (D'Ancona, Carducci, and Scartazzini, among others) who, beginning anew in those years, were busy tracking down the sources and analogues of the poem, compiling dictionaries and manuals, producing critical editions that would quantify or at least account for Dante's imaginative construction. But De Sanctis's lesson withstood the onslaught of the philologists and was destined to be revived in different ways in our century by Croce and Auerbach.

Croce's essay on Dante's poetry (1921) seeks to define Dante's essence—something he distinguishes from the poem's theological structure. This distinction echoes De Sanctis's own notion of the organic form intertwined with and yet separable from the material contents of a text. Even the power of Croce's critical description of the poem, I would suggest, matches the brilliance and energy of De Sanctis's critical prose; it is an analysis of the rich manifestations of the passions animating Dante's fictional representation, but it bypasses the historical specificity of Dante's vision and thought. As is well known, Croce's style of aesthetic appreciation ushered in a critical fashion that thwarts the very possibility of interaction between poetry and all the other forms of discourse. More than Croce, Auerbach, who was a reader of Vico, closely follows De Sanctis's aesthetics and, like De Sanctis, translates Dante's poetry into the mimetic represen- tation of reality. But his work also crystallizes the concerns of a number of romance philologists (Spitzer, Curtius, and Schiaffini, for example) in that it retrieves a specific linguistic, historical, and poetic background for the *Divine Comedy*.

If the horizon of theological and philosophical questions is ob- scured in the work of these three historicists, it reemerges forcefully in the research conducted by two brilliant historians of medieval philosophy, Etienne Gilson and Bruno Nardi. Their studies descend directly from the historical-philological scholarship of the nineteenth century, and because of the illusion of objectivity produced by the rigor of their findings, they have profoundly affected our understand- ing of the Middle Ages. Because of their labors, the myth of the Middle Ages, projected by the early philologists of the nineteenth century and by the romantic novelists and poets as an age of spiritual unity and untroubled harmony, has collapsed. Nardi documented the persistent vitality of philosophical dissidence in the guise of Averroism and its prolongation in Dante's works; Gilson, a neo-Thomist, pro- ceeded to map what he intuited to be the limits of Dante's Thomism. One cannot expect from either Gilson or Nardi a definition of poetry as a specific mode of knowledge. This area of concerns, understandably enough, falls outside the sphere of their interests.

Nonetheless, it is clear that their theological and philosophical formulations lie behind Charles S. Singleton's original perspective on the *Divine Comedy* as a theological allegory reenacting the biblical story of Exodus. This decisive structure of the poem, which had first figured in the letter to Cangrande, logically entails for Singleton a crucial corollary: the literal sense of the poem (the pilgrim's journey to the beyond and the representation of the souls in the afterlife) cannot be taken as a mere fiction. On the contrary, it is to be taken as an actual historical event. Such an allegorical view, which makes Dante simultaneously a daring and a theologically orthodox poet (the theology Singleton mentions is generally Thomistic), has provided an overarching, unified structure within which the large articulation of the narrative—the pilgrim's journey to God—and the number of textual details are made intelligible.

Singleton's view has remained a hegemonic form of analysis at least among academics until recently, although it overlooks the text's problematics of rhetoric and poetics. In our century the dividing line between academic and nonacademic critics (Ungaretti, Eliot, Mandelstam, Borges, Penn Warren, and others) is fairly sharp, just as it was sharp between Boccaccio and, say, Benvenuto da Imola. Nonacademic readers clearly tend to be daring in their insights and thereby force on us new perceptions of the complexities of the poem. Academic critics, such as Singleton, on the other hand, read in the light of theories elaborated by the culture of their own times. The most glaring shortcoming in Singleton's theory is highlighted by his myth of the transparency of language, possibly derived from Poulet's phenomenological criticism. The poem, Singleton states, "exceeds metaphor," and it comes across with the irreducibility of reality itself. Because of this premise, obvious facts, such as Dante's relation to language and to his own craft, are neglected; no attention is paid to the way in which the ambivalences of the nonempirical imagination are constitutive of knowledge; nor is there ever any inquiry into the possible discrepancies within the spectrum of theological sources Dante deploys. I have argued elsewhere that behind Singleton stands Emerson's radical vision. Yet Singleton swerves away from Emerson's sublime imaginings.[1]

These shortcomings notwithstanding, it is clear that the critical legacy engendered by Singleton's theoretical formula is incomparably rich. Two scholars, Gian Roberto Sarolli and John Freccero, have taken Singleton's lead as a point of departure; they have refined and, in the process, much altered the configuration of problems originally elaborated by their forerunner. Gian Roberto Sarolli has grafted onto the rational theological scheme of Gilson, Nardi, and Singleton a philological taste for exegetical, symbolic, and literary parallels and sources. Sarolli's interpretive outlook, as the brief excerpt included here from one of his books shows, can be seen as an updating of conventional notions of political theology as the ground of Dante's vision. Yet his scholarship, his systematic delving into what can be called the archeology of history, is a brilliant and decisive contribution to the current debates on Dante.

The power of John Freccero's work, on the other hand, lies in the unity of poetics and theology it steadily pursues. If Singleton displayed a certain indifference to the literary aspects of the *Divine*

Comedy, Freccero's criticism has isolated the autobiographical structure of the poem, which Guido da Pisa had perceived, as the central
narrative trajectory. And if Singleton's understanding of Dante's theology is largely derived from Busnelli's findings, Freccero has read
Dante in terms of Neoplatonic and Augustinian theology of interiority.
From the standpoint of Augustinian Christianity, unquestionably a
central strain of the poem, Freccero has made education the chief
plot of the narrative. In effect, Freccero is the counterpoint to Sarolli.
Whereas Sarolli investigates Dante's abstract encyclopedism, Freccero
focuses on the conceptual and moral growth of the self, even if the
self is not treated as an empirical entity. One wishes, in effect, that
Dante's sense of exteriority—which is to be taken as Dante's radical
sense of exile—figured more openly as the central value of Dante's
vision. The essay by Giuseppe Mazzotta, which closes this anthology,
addresses the question of Dante's poetry in relation to theology and
philosophy. Poetry is viewed as the locus of history, as the space of
exile wherein rhetoric and theology are steadily entangled with each
other. Dante's visionariness, as Vico and Emerson had understood, is
the scandal of commonplace knowledge, for it challenges us to a
radical rethinking of all values.

The highlights of the concluding section of this book are the
essays by two creative writers, Ungaretti and Borges. Their inclusion
is primarily a tribute to the modernity of Dante's value among
imaginative writers. The *Divine Comedy*, in fact, has been constantly
quarried by poets—one thinks of Petrarch, Shelley, Mandelstam, and
Pound—for their imaginative ends. The essays by Ungaretti and
Borges are particularly striking because they point toward other,
elusive, unpredictable directions. These two essays are, above all,
readings—in the strong sense of the word, the sense that academicians
do not really understand—and not commentaries or erudite glosses,
though Borges manifestly plays with the genre of glossing the text.
The essays by Ungaretti and Borges address, respectively, *Inferno* I
and *Inferno* XXXIV. Both pieces affirm, in their different cadences
but with an uncanny convergence of poetic intuition, which recalls
Vico's incandescent phantasmagoria, the enigmatic economy of dreams,
theology, and history that together make up the *Divine Comedy*. In
the space delineated by their vision lies the future possibility of Dante
criticism and the *fortuna di Dante*.

Yale University   GIUSEPPE MAZZOTTA

Note

1. Giuseppe Mazzotta, "Dante nella critica americana di Charles Singleton,"
Letture classensi 18 (1989): 195–209.

ESSAYS

Epistle to Cangrande

Dante Alighieri°

To the magnificent and most victorious Lord, the Lord Can Grande della Scala. . . .

1. The illustrious renown of your Magnificence, which wakeful Fame spreads abroad as she flies, affects divers persons in divers ways, so that some it uplifts with the hope of good fortune, while others it casts down with the dread of destruction. The report whereof, overtopping all deeds of recent times, I erstwhile did deem extravagant, as going beyond the appearance of truth. But that continued uncertainty might not keep me longer in suspense, even as the Queen of the South sought Jerusalem, and as Pallas sought Helicon, so did I seek Verona, in order to examine with my own trusty eyes the things of which I had heard. And there was I witness of your splendour, there was I witness and partaker of your bounty; and whereas I had formerly suspected the reports to be somewhat unmeasured, I afterwards recognized that it was the facts themselves that were beyond measure. Whence it came to pass that whereas through hearsay alone, with a certain subjection of mind, I had previously become well disposed towards you, at the first sight of you I became your most devoted servant and friend.

2. Nor do I think that in assuming the name of friend I shall lay myself open to a charge of presumption, as some perchance might object; inasmuch as unequals no less than equals are united by the sacred tie of friendship. For if one should examine friendships which have been pleasant and profitable, it will be evident that in many cases the bond has been between persons of superior station and their inferiors. And if our attention be directed to true friendship for its own sake, shall we not find that the friends of illustrious and mighty princes have many a time been men obscure in condition but of distinguished virtue? Why not? since even the friendship of God and man is in no wise impeded by the disparity between them. But

° From *The Letters of Dante*, ed. and trans. Paget Toynbee (Oxford: Clarendon Press, 1920), 195–211.

if any man consider this assertion unseemly, let him hearken to the Holy Spirit when it declares that certain men have been partakers of its friendship. For in Wisdom we read, concerning wisdom: "For she is a treasure unto men that never faileth; which they that use are made partakers of the friendship of God." But the common herd in their ignorance judge without discernment; and even as they imagine the sun to be a foot across, so they judge with regard to questions of conduct; and they are deceived by their foolish credulity with regard to both the one and the other matter. But it does not become us, to whom it has been given to know what is best in our nature, but follow in the footsteps of the common herd; nay, rather are we bound to oppose their errors. For those who have vigour of intellect and reason, being endowed with a certain divine liberty, are not restricted by precedent. Nor is this to be wondered at, for it is not they who receive direction from the laws, but rather the laws from them. It is manifest, therefore, that what I said above, namely that I was your most devoted servant and friend, in no wise savours of presumption.

3. Esteeming, then, your friendship as a most precious treasure, I desire to preserve it with assiduous forethought and anxious care. Therefore, since it is a doctrine of ethics that friendship is equalized and preserved by reciprocity, it is my wish to preserve due reciprocity in making a return for the bounty more than once conferred upon me. For which reason I have often and long examined such poor gifts as I can offer, and have set them out separately, and scrutinized each in turn, in order to decide which would be the most worthy and the most acceptable to you. And I have found nothing more suitable even for your exalted station than the sublime cantica of the *Comedy* which is adorned with the title of *Paradise;* this, then, dedicated to yourself, with the present letter to serve as its super-scription, I inscribe, offer, and in fine commend to you.

4. Nor does the simple ardour of my affection permit me to pass over in silence the consideration that in this offering there may seem to be greater honour and fame conferred on the patron than on the gift; the rather that in the address I shall appear to such as read with attention to have given utterance to a forecast as to the increase of the glory of your name—and this of set purpose. But eagerness for your favour, for which I thirst, heedless of envy, will urge me forward to the goal which was my aim from the first. And so, having made an end of what I had to say in epistolary form, I will now in the capacity of commentator essay a few words by way of introduction to the work which is offered for your acceptance.

5. As the Philosopher says in the second book of the *Metaphysics,* "as a thing is in respect of being, so is it in respect of truth"; the reason of which is, that the truth concerning a thing, which consists

in the truth as in its subject, is the perfect likeness of the thing as it is. Now of things which exist, some are such as to have absolute being in themselves; while others are such as to have their being dependent upon something else, by virtue of a certain relation, as being in existence at the same time, or having respect to some other thing, as in the case of correlatives, such as father and son, master and servant, double and half, the whole and part, and other similar things, in so far as they are related. Inasmuch, then, as the being of such things depends upon something else, it follows that the truth of these things likewise depends upon something else; for if the half is unknown, its double cannot be known; and so of the rest.

6. If any one, therefore, is desirous of offering any sort of introduction to part of a work, it behoves him to furnish some notion of the whole of which it is a part. Wherefore I, too, being desirous of offering something by way of introduction to the above-mentioned part of the whole *Comedy,* thought it incumbent on me in the first place to say something concerning the work as a whole, in order that access to the part might be the easier and the more perfect. There are six points, then, as to which inquiry must be made at the beginning of every didactic work; namely, the subject, the author, the form, the aim, the title of the book, and the branch of philosophy to which it belongs. Now of these six points there are three in respect of which the part which I have had in mind to address to you differs from the whole work; namely, the subject, the form, and the title; whereas in respect of the others there is no difference, as is obvious to any one who considers the matter. Consequently, in an examination of the whole, these three points must be made the subject of a separate inquiry; which being done, the way will be sufficiently clear for the introduction to the part. Later we will examine the other three points, not only with reference to the whole work, but also with reference to the particular part which is offered to you.

7. For the elucidation, therefore, of what we have to say, it must be understood that the meaning of this work is not of one kind only; rather the work may be described as "polysemous," that is, having several meanings; for the first meaning is that which is conveyed by the letter, and the next is that which is conveyed by what the letter signifies; the former of which is called literal, while the latter is called allegorical, or mystical. And for the better illustration of this method of exposition we may apply it to the following verses: "When Israel went out of Egypt, the house of Jacob from a people of strange language; Judah was his sanctuary, and Israel his dominion." For if we consider the letter alone, the thing signified to us is the going out of the children of Israel from Egypt in the time of Moses; if the allegory, our redemption through Christ is signified; if the moral sense, the conversion of the soul from the sorrow and misery of sin

to a state of grace is signified; if the anagogical, the passing of the sanctified soul from the bondage of the corruption of this world to the liberty of everlasting glory is signified. And although these mystical meanings are called by various names, they may one and all in a general sense be termed allegorical, inasmuch as they are different *(diversi)* from the literal or historical; for the word "allegory" is so called from the Greek *alleon,* which in Latin is *alienum* (strange) or *diversum* (different).

8. This being understood, it is clear that the subject, with regard to which the alternative meanings are brought into play, must be twofold. And therefore the subject of this work must be considered in the first place from the point of view of the literal meaning, and next from that of the allegorical interpretation. The subject, then, of the whole work, taken in the literal sense only, is the state of souls after death, pure and simple. For on and about that the argument of the whole work turns. If, however, the work be regarded from the allegorical point of view, the subject is man according as by his merits or demerits in the exercise of his free will he is deserving of reward or punishment by justice.

9. And the form is twofold—the form of the treatise, and the form of the treatment. The form of the treatise is threefold, according to the threefold division. The first division is that whereby the whole work is divided into three cantiche; the second, whereby each cantica is divided into cantos; and the third, whereby each canto is divided into rhymed lines. The form or manner of treatment is poetic, fictive, descriptive, digressive, and figurative; and further, it is definitive, analytical, probative, refutative, and exemplificative.

10. The title of the book is "Here begins the *Comedy* of Dante Alighieri, a Florentine by birth, not by disposition." For the understanding of which it must be noted that "comedy" is so called from *comos,* a village, and *oda,* a song; whence comedy is as it were a "rustic song." Now comedy is a certain kind of poetical narration which differs from all others. It differs, then, from tragedy in its subject-matter, in that tragedy at the beginning is admirable and placid, but at the end or issue is foul and horrible. And tragedy is so called from *tragos,* a goat, and *oda;* as it were a "goat song," that is to say foul like a goat, as appears from the tragedies of Seneca. Whereas comedy begins with sundry adverse conditions, but ends happily, as appears from the comedies of Terence. And for this reason it is the custom of some writers in their salutation to say by way of greeting: "a tragic beginning and a comic ending to you!" Tragedy and comedy differ likewise in their style of language; for that of tragedy is high-flown and sublime, while that of comedy is unstudied and lowly. And this is implied by Horace in the *Art of Poetry,* where

he grants that the comedian may on occasion use the language of tragedy, and vice versa:

> Yet sometimes comedy her voice will raise,
> And angry Chremes scold with swelling phrase;
> And prosy periods oft our ears assail
> When Telephus and Peleus tell their tragic tale.

And from this it is clear that the present work is to be described as a comedy. For if we consider the subject-matter, at the beginning it is horrible and foul, as being *Hell;* but at the close it is happy, desirable, and pleasing, as being *Paradise.* As regards the style of language, the style is unstudied and lowly, as being in the vulgar tongue, in which even women-folk hold their talk. And hence it is evident why the work is called a comedy. And there are other kinds of poetical narration, such as the pastoral poem, the elegy, the satire, and the votive song, as may also be gathered from Horace in the *Art of Poetry;* but of these we need say nothing at present.

11. It can now be shown in what manner the subject of the part offered to you is to be determined. For if the subject of the whole work taken in the literal sense is the state of souls after death, pure and simple, without limitation; it is evident that in this part the same state is the subject, but with a limitation, namely the state of blessed souls after death. And if the subject of the whole work from the allegorical point of view is man according as by his merits or demerits in the exercise of his free will he is deserving of reward or punishment by justice, it is evident that in this part this subject has a limitation, and that it is man according as by his merits he is deserving of reward by justice.

12. In like manner the form of the part is determined by that of the whole work. For if the form of the treatise as a whole is threefold, in this part it is twofold only, the division being that of the cantica and of the cantos. The first division (into cantiche) cannot be applicable to the form of the part, since the cantica is itself a part under the first division.

13. The title of the book also is clear. For the title of the whole book is "Here begins the *Comedy*," etc., as above; but the title of the part is "Here begins the third cantica of the *Comedy* of Dante, which is called *Paradise.*"

14. These three points, in which the part differs from the whole, having been examined, we may now turn our attention to the other three, in respect of which there is no difference between the part and the whole. The author, then, of the whole and of the part is the person mentioned above, who is seen to be such throughout.

15. The aim of the whole and of the part might be manifold; as, for instance, immediate and remote. But leaving aside any minute

examination of this question, it may be stated briefly that the aim of the whole and of the part is to remove those living in this life from a state of misery, and to bring them to a state of happiness.

16. The branch of philosophy to which the work is subject, in the whole as in the part, is that of morals or ethics; inasmuch as the whole as well as the part was conceived, not for speculation, but with a practical object. For if in certain parts or passages the treatment is after the manner of speculative philosophy, that is not for the sake of speculation, but for a practical purpose; since, as the Philosopher says in the second book of the *Metaphysics:* "practical men occasionally speculate on things in their particular and temporal relations."

17. Having therefore premised these matters, we may now apply ourselves to the exposition of the literal meaning, by way of sample; as to which it must first be understood that the exposition of the letter is in effect but a demonstration of the form of the work. The part in question then, that is, this third cantica which is called *Paradise,* falls by its main division into two parts, namely the prologue, and the executive part; which second part begins:

> Surge ai mortali per diverse foci.

> [The lamp of the world] rises on mortals by different portals.

18. As regards the first part, it should be noted that although in common parlance it might be termed an exordium, yet, properly speaking, it can only be termed a prologue; as the Philosopher seems to indicate in the third book of his *Rhetoric,* where he says that "the proem in a rhetorical oration answers to the prologue in poetry, and to the prelude in flute-playing." It must further be observed that this preamble, which may ordinarily be termed an exordium, is one thing in the hands of a poet, and another in those of an orator. For orators are wont to give a forecast of what they are about to say, in order to gain the attention of their hearers. Now poets not only do this, but in addition they make use of some sort of invocation afterwards. And this is fitting in their case, for they have need of invocation in a large measure, inasmuch as they have to petition the superior beings for something beyond the ordinary range of human powers, something almost in the nature of a divine gift. Therefore the present prologue is divided into two parts: in the first is given a forecast of what is to follow; in the second is an invocation to Apollo; which second part begins:

> O buon Apollo, all'ultimo lavoro, . . .
> O good Apollo, for the last labor. . . .

19. With reference to the first part it must be observed that to make a good exordium three things are requisite, as Tully says in his

New Rhetoric; that the hearer, namely, should be rendered favourably disposed, attentive, and willing to learn; and this is especially needful in the case of a subject which is out of the common, as Tully himself remarks. Inasmuch, then, as the subject dealt with in the present work is out of the common, it is the aim of the first part of the exordium or prologue to bring about the above-mentioned three results with regard to this out-of-the-way subject. For the author declares that he will relate such things as he who beheld them in the first heaven was able to retain. In which statement all those three things are comprised; for the profitableness of what he is about to be told begets a favourable disposition in the hearer; its being out of the common engages his attention; and its being within the range of possibility renders him willing to learn. Its profitableness he gives to be understood when he says that he shall tell of that which above all things excites the longing of mankind, namely the joys of Paradise; its uncommon nature is indicated when he promises to treat of such exalted and sublime matters as the conditions of the celestial kingdom; its being within the range of possibility is demonstrated when he says that he will tell of those things which he was able to retain in his mind—for if he was able, so will others be also. All this is indicated in the passage where he declares that he had been in the first heaven, and that he purposes to relate concerning the celestial kingdom whatsoever he was able to store up, like a treasure, in his mind. Having thus noted the excellence and perfection of the first part of the prologue, we may now proceed to the literal exposition.

20. He says, then, that "the glory of the First Mover," which is God, "shines forth in every part of the universe," but in such wise that it shines "in one part more and in another less." That it shines in every part both reason and authority declare. Reason thus: Everything which exists has its being either from itself, or from some other thing. But it is plain that self-existence can be the attribute of one being only, namely the First or Beginning, which is God, since to have being does not argue necessary self-existence, and necessary self-existence appertains to one being only, namely the First or Beginning, which is the cause of all things; therefore everything which exists, except that One itself, has its being from some other thing. If, then, we take, not any thing whatsoever, but that thing which is the most remote in the universe, it is manifest that this has its being from something; and that from which it derives either has its being from itself, or from something else. If from itself, then it is primal; if from something else, then that again must either be self-existent, or derive from something else. But in this way we should go on to infinity in the chain of effective causes, as is shown in the second book of the *Metaphysics.* So we must come to a primal existence, which is God. Hence, mediately or immediately, everything

that exists has its being from Him, because, inasmuch as the second cause has its effect from the first, its influence on what it acts upon is like that of a body which receives and reflects a ray; since the first cause is the more effective cause. And this is stated in the book *On Causes*, namely, that "every primary cause has influence in a greater degree on what it acts upon than any second cause." So much with regard to being.

21. With regard to essence I argue in this wise: Every essence, except the first, is caused; otherwise there would be more than one necessarily self-existent being, which is impossible. For what it causes is the effect either of nature or of intellect; and what is of nature is, consequently, caused by intellect, inasmuch as nature is the work of intelligence. Everything, then, which is caused is the effect, mediately or immediately, of some intellect. Since, then, virtue follows the essence whose virtue it is, if the essence is of intellect, the virtue is wholly and solely of the intellectual essence whose effect it is. And so, just as we had to go back to a first cause in the case of being, so now we must do so in the case of essence and of virtue. Whence it is evident that every essence and every virtue proceeds from a primal one; and that the lower intelligences have their effect as it were from a radiating body, and, after the fashion of mirrors, reflect the rays of the higher to the one below them. Which matter appears to be discussed clearly enough by Dionysius in his work *On the Celestial Hierarchy*. And therefore it is stated in the book *On Causes* that "every intelligence is full of forms." Reason, then, as we have seen, demonstrates that the divine light, that is to say the divine goodness, wisdom, and virtue, shines in every part.

22. Authority likewise declares the same, but with more knowledge. For the Holy Spirit says by the mouth of Jeremiah: "Do not I fill heaven and earth?" And in the Psalm: "Whither shall I go from thy Spirit: and whither shall I flee from thy Presence? If I ascend up into heaven, thou art there; if I descend into hell, thou art there also. If I take my wings," etc. And Wisdom says: "The Spirit of the Lord hath filled the whole world." And Ecclesiasticus, in the forty-second chapter: "His work is full of the glory of the Lord." To which also the writings of the pagans bear witness; for Lucan says in his ninth book: "Jupiter is whatever thou seest, wherever thou goest."

23. He says well, then, when he says that the divine ray, or divine glory, "penetrates and shines through the universe"; penetrates, as to essence; shines forth, as to being. And what he adds as to "more or less" is manifestly true, since we see that one essence exists in a more excellent degree, and another in a less; as is clearly the case with regard to the heaven and the elements, the former being incorruptible, while the latter are corruptible.

24. And having premised this truth, he next goes on to indicate

Paradise by a circumlocution; and says that he was in that heaven which receives the glory of God, or his light, in most bountiful measure. As to which it must be understood that that heaven is the highest heaven, which contains all the bodies of the universe, and is contained by none, within which all bodies move (itself remaining everlastingly at rest), and which receives virtue from no corporeal substance. And it is called the Empyrean, which is as much as to say, the heaven glowing with fire or heat; not that there is material fire or heat therein, but spiritual, which is holy love, or charity.

25. Now that this heaven receives more of the divine light than any other can be proved by two things. Firstly, by its containing all things, and being contained by none; secondly, by its state of everlasting rest or peace. As to the first the proof is as follows: The containing body stands in the same relation to the content in natural position as the formative does to the formable, as we are told in the fourth book of the *Physics*. But in the natural position of the whole universe the first heaven is the heaven which contains all things; consequently it is related to all things as the formative to the formable, which is to be in the relation of cause to effect. And since every causative force is in the nature of a ray emanating from the first cause, which is God, it is manifest that that heaven which is in the highest degree causative receives most of the divine light.

26. As to the second the proof is this: Everything which has motion moves because of something which it has not, and which is the terminus of its motion. The heaven of the moon, for instance, moves because of some part of itself which has not attained the station towards which it is moving; and because no part whatsoever of it has attained any terminus whatsoever (as indeed it never can), it moves to another station, and thus is always in motion, and is never at rest, which is what it desires. And what I say of the heaven of the moon applies to all the other heavens, except the first. Everything, then, which has motion is in some respect defective, and has not its whole being complete. That heaven, therefore, which is subject to no movement, in itself and in every part whatsoever of itself has whatever it is capable of having in perfect measure, to that it has no need of motion for its perfection. And since every perfection is a ray of the Primal One, inasmuch as He is perfection in the highest degree, it is manifest that the first heaven receives more than any other of the light of the Primal One, which is God. This reasoning, however, has the appearance of an argument based on the denial of the antecedent, in that it is not a direct proof and according to syllogistic form. But if we consider its content it is a good proof, because it deals with a thing eternal, and assumes it to be capable of being eternally defective; so that, if God did not give that heaven motion, it is evident that He did not give it material in any respect

defective. And on this supposition the argument holds good by reason of the content; and this form of argument is much the same as though we should reason: "if he is man, he is able to laugh"; for in every convertible proposition a like reasoning holds good by virtue of the content. Hence it is clear that when the author says "in that heaven which receives more of the light of God," he intends by a circumlocution to indicate Paradise, or the heaven of the Empyrean.

27. And in agreement with the foregoing is what the Philosopher says in the first book *On Heaven,* namely that "a heaven has so much the more honourable material than those below it as it is the further removed from terrestrial things." In addition to which might be adduced what the Apostle says to the Ephesians of Christ: "Who ascended up far above all heavens, that He might fill all things." This is the heaven of the delights of the Lord; of which delights it is said by Ezekiel against Lucifer: "Thou, the seal of similitude, full of wisdom, beautiful in perfection, wast in the delights of the Paradise of God."

28. And after he has said that he was in that place of Paradise which he describes by circumlocution, he goes on to say that he saw certain things which he who descends therefrom is powerless to relate. And he gives the reason, saying that "the intellect plunges itself to such depth" in its very longing, which is for God, "that the memory cannot follow." For the understanding of which it must be noted that the human intellect in this life, by reason of its connaturality and affinity to the separate intellectual substance, when in exaltation, reaches such a height of exaltation that after its return to itself memory fails, since it has transcended the range of human faculty. And this is conveyed to us by the Apostle where he says, addressing the Corinthians: "I know a man (whether in the body, or out of the body, I cannot tell; God knoweth) how that he was caught up to the third heaven, and heard unspeakable words, which it is not lawful for a man to utter." Behold, after the intellect had passed beyond the bounds of human faculty in its exaltation, it could not recall what took place outside of its range. This again is conveyed to us in Matthew, where we read that the three disciples fell on their faces, and record nothing thereafter, as though memory had failed them. And in Ezekiel it is written: "And when I saw it, I fell upon my face." And should these not satisfy the cavillers, let them read Richard of St. Victor in his book *On Contemplation;* let them read Bernard in his book *On Consideration;* let them read Augustine in his book *On the Consideration;* let them read Augustine in his book *On the Capacity of the Soul;* and they will cease from their cavilling. But if on account of the sinfulness of the speaker they should cry out against the claim to have reached such a height of exaltation, let them read Daniel, where they will find that even Nebuchadnezzar by divine

permission beheld certain things as a warning to sinners, and straight-way forgot them. For He "who maketh his sun to shine on the good and on the evil, and sendeth rain on the just and on the unjust," sometimes in compassion for their conversion, sometimes in wrath for their chastisement, in greater or lesser measure, according as He wills, manifests his glory to evil-doers, be they never so evil.

29. He says, then, as he says, certain things "which he who returns has neither knowledge nor power to relate." Now it must be carefully noted that he says "has neither knowledge nor power"—knowledge he has not, because he has forgotten; power he has not, because even if he remembers, and retains it thereafter, nevertheless speech fails him. For we perceive many things by the intellect for which language has no terms—a fact which Plato indicates plainly enough in his books by his employment of metaphors; for he perceived many things by the light of the intellect which his everyday language was inadequate to express.

30. Afterwards the author says that he will relate concerning the celestial kingdom such things as he was able to retain; and he says that this is the subject of his work; the nature and extent of which things will be shown in the executive part.

31. Then when he says: "O buono Apollo," etc., he makes his invocation. And this part is divided into two parts—in the first, he invokes the deity and makes a petition; in the second, he inclines Apollo to the granting of his petition by the promise of a certain recompense; which second part begins: "O divina virtù." The first part again is divided into two parts—in the first, he prays for divine aid; in the second, he adverts to the necessity for his petition, whereby he justifies it; and this part begins: "Infino a qui l'un giogo di Parnaso, etc." [Thus far the one peak of Parnasus, etc.] "

32. This is the general meaning of the second part of the prologue; the particular meaning I shall not expound on the present occasion; for anxiety as to my domestic affairs presses so heavily upon me that I must perforce abandon this and other tasks of public utility. I trust, however, that your Magnificence may afford me the opportunity to continue this useful exposition at some other time.

33. With regard to the executive part of the work, which was divided after the same manner as the prologue taken as a whole, I shall say nothing either as to its divisions or its interpretation at present; save only that the process of the narrative will be by ascent from heaven to heaven, and that an account will be given of the blessed spirits who are met with in each sphere; and that their true blessedness consists in the apprehension of Him who is the beginning of truth, as appears from what John says: "This is life eternal, to know thee the true God," etc.; and from what Boethius says in his third book *On Consolation:* "To behold thee is the end." Hence it

is that, in order to reveal the glory of the blessedness of those spirits, many things which have great profit and delight will be asked of them, as of those who behold the fullness of truth. And since, when the Beginning or First, which is God, as been reached, there is nought to be sought for beyond, inasmuch as He is Alpha and Omega, that is, the Beginning and the End, as the Vision of John tells us, the work ends in God Himself, who is blessed for evermore, world without end.

Prologue to the Commentary   Guido da Pisa*

PROLOGUE

Expositions and glosses on Dante's Comedy, made by Friar Guido Pisanus, of the Order of Blessed Mary of Mount Carmel, for the nobleman Lucano Spinola of Genoa.

Here Begins the Prologue

It is written in the fifth chapter of Daniel that while Balthasar king of Babylon was sitting at his table, there appeared opposite him a hand writing of the wall: *Mane, Thechel, Phares*. This hand is our new poet Dante, who wrote, that is composed, this most lofty and most penetrating Comedy, which is divided into three parts: the first is called *Hell*, the second *Purgatory*, the third *Paradise*. Those three words which were written on the wall correspond to these three parts. For *Mane* corresponds to *Hell*, since *Mane* is interpreted as "number"; and this poet in the first part of his Comedy numbers the places, punishments, and wicked deeds of the damned. *Thechel* corresponds to *Purgatory*, for *Thechel* is interpreted as "weighing" or "ponderation"; and in the second part of his Comedy he weighs and ponders the penances of those who are to be purged. *Phares* then corresponds to *Paradise*, for *Phares* is interpreted as "division"; and this poet in the third part of his Comedy separates, that is distinguishes, the order of the blessed and the angelic hierarchies. Hand, then, that is, Dante; for by hand we mean Dante. Indeed *manus* (hand) comes from *mano, manas* (to pour forth), and Dante comes from *do, das* (to give); because just as from the hand comes forth a gift, so from Dante there is given to us this most lofty work.

He wrote, as I say, on the wall, that is openly and publicly, for

* From "The Prologue to the Commentary of Guido da Pisa," trans. Vincenzo Cioffari and Francesco Mazzoni, *Dante Studies* 90 (1972): 126–37.

the benefit of all: *Mane*, namely *Hell*, whose punishments and places he enumerated; *Thechel*, namely *Purgatory*, whose penances he weighed and pondered; *Phares*, namely *Paradise*, whose site he showed to be elevated from the lowest depths, and whose degrees of blessedness he differentiated in an orderly manner. For according to what is written in the ninth *Book of Wisdom*, this distinguished one among poets placed all of these things "in number, weight and measure." For this poet placed *Hell* in number, because he enumerates sins and punishments; *Purgatory* in weight, because he ponders and weighs penances; *Paradise* in measure, because he measures the heavens and differentiates the orders of the blessed. Certainly to this poet and to his Comedy can be related that vision which Ezechiel the prophet saw; of which vision the same prophet writes thus: "Behold the hand sent to me in which there was a book written within and without; and there were written therein *Lamentations, Song,* and *Woe.*" This hand is this poet. The book of this hand is his most lofty Comedy, which thereafter is said to be written within and without, because it contains not only the letter, but also the allegory. Moreover three things are written in this book, namely *Lamentations, Song,* and *Woe. Woe,* which is an interjection of one who is suffering and despairing, refers to *Hell,* for woe in the Sacred Scriptures denotes eternal damnation, as the saints say commenting on that word: "Woe to the man through whom the Son of man shall be betrayed"; and the meaning is, he shall be lost forever. *Lamentations,* which are notes of voluntary and adopted grief, refer to *Purgatory.* And *Song,* which is the same as glory and jubilation, refers to *Paradise.*

In fact, this Comedy can also be seen represented in Noah's ark, which was tri-chambered; for in the lower chamber there were wild animals and serpents; in the middle one there were domestic and tame animals; and in the upper one there were men and birds. But the first chamber we can understand *Hell,* in which there are wild and undomesticated animals, that is damned human beings and serpents, namely demons. By the second chamber we can understand *Purgatory,* in which there are mild animals, that is mild souls who patiently bear sufferings. And by the third chamber we can understand *Paradise,* in which there are men and birds, that is saints and angels exalted in glory.

Having seen these things, let us explore briefly six points in this Comedy: first the subject, namely the material cause; second the form, namely the formal cause; third the author, that is the efficient cause (the agent); fourth the aim, that is the final cause; fifth the branch of philosophy, that is under which branch of philosophy this Comedy might be included or might proceed; sixth and last, the title of the book, that is by what title this book should be entitled. As regards the first, note that the subject of this book is twofold, namely literal and allegorical. For if taken literally, I say that the subject of this work is the state of souls after death, taken pure and simple; in fact this state is divided into three parts, just as the condition of those souls is threefold. The first state or condition is of those souls which are eternally damned and which dwell in punishments without any hope whatever of escaping from them; and this part is called *Hell*. The second state or condition is of those souls which voluntarily remain in punishments so that they may satisfy God for acts committed, and they are in those very punishments with the hope of ascending to glory; and this part is called *Purgatory*. The third state or condition is of those souls which are in blessed glory, joined to that highest and eternal good for eternity, that is without end; and this part is called *Paradise*. And thus it becomes clear how the subject of this work is the state of souls after death taken pure and simple; because on this theme and about it the course of this whole work proceeds. If indeed the subject is taken allegorically, I say that the subject or subject matter is man himself according as by deserving merit or not, through his free will, he is subject to the justice of being rewarded or punished, on account of which merit or fault there is assigned glory or punishment to said man. For the intention of the author is devoted to narrating or explaining to us regarding the punishment or glory attributed to man himself. And thus becomes clear what is the subject of this work or the material cause. Regarding the second, moreover, that is, regarding the formal cause, not that the formal cause in this work is twofold, namely the form of that which is treated and the form of treatment. The form of the subject treated is threefold, following the triple division which this book receives or contains. The first division is that whereby the whole work is divided into *cantiche* and these are three. The second, that whereby each *cantica* is divided into cantos; for the first *cantica* is divided into thirty-four cantos, the second into thirty-three, and the third into a like number. And thus the whole work contains one hundred cantos.

Moreover the third division is that whereby each canto is divided into rhymed lines. And the rhymed line is a certain type of verses whose endings are alternately coupled with each other, and by means of matching syllables are linked together in a concordant manner. And this is one of three extremely sweet sounds which most delight and soothe the spirit of the listener; and it comes from music, whose parts are three, namely harmony, rhythm, and meter, as blessed Isidor tells us in the third book of the *Etymologies*. Three indeed are the types of rhymed verses in respect to the present Comedy. First is that one whose rhymed verse contains only ten syllables; and this is the one whose last syllable is long and accented, as in: "D'Abel su' fillio et quella di Noe" [That (i.e., shade) of his son Abel and that of Noah]; likewise in: "Abraham patriarca et David re" [Abraham the patriarch and King David]; likewise in" "Et con Rachele per cui tanto fe" [And with Rachael, for whom he did so much]; likewise in the third cantica: "Osanna sanctus Deus Sabaoth" [Hosanna, holy God of hosts]. For these rhymed verses take only ten syllables. The second type is the one whose rhymed verses have twelve syllables, and this is the one whose next-to-the-last syllable is short, as in: "Ch'era ronchioso, stretto et malagevole" [Which was rocky, narrow, and difficult]; likewise in: "Parlando andava per non parer fievole" [He went on talking so as not to appear worn out]; likewise in: "A parole formar disconvenevole" [Unable to formulate words]. The third type indeed is the one whose rhymed verse has eleven syllables; and this is the one whose next-to-the-last syllable is long, as its common use shows, as in: "Nel mezzo del cammin di nostra vita" [Midway through the path of our life].

At this point note, Lucano Spinola, to whom I dedicate this exposition, that the rhymed verses of the first type need rhyme on only one syllable or letter, namely on the last one; the second ones, however, need to rhyme on three syllables, that is, on the next-to-the-last ones and the last one: and the third ones on two, namely on the last two, as the letters very clearly show. And thus the form of that which is treated is clear.

The form indeed or manner of treatment is poetic, fictive, descriptive, digressive, and figurative; and further it is definitive, analytical, probative, refutative, and exemplificative. And thus the form or mode of treatment becomes clear.

Regarding the third, however, namely regarding the efficient cause, note that the agent or author of this work is Dante. Dante, I say, was Florentine by birth, born of noble and ancient blood, descending from those glorious Romans who founded the city of Florence after Fiesole was destroyed; distinguished in his manners and clearly well versed in many arts, and especially in the arts of the poets. For he it was who brought back dead poetry from the shadows to the light; and in this he imitated Boethius, who in his time revived dead philosophy. Regarding the fourth, namely the final cause, note that the author composed this work primarily with the following aim, although many other aims can be assigned to it; it is, I say, his principal aim to remove the living from a state of misery, leaving sins behind, and so he composed the *Hell;* to lead them back toward virtues, and so he composed the *Purgatory;* thus so he composed the *Paradise.* As for other aims which can be assigned to this work, there are three: first, that men might learn to speak elegantly and masterfully; indeed no mortal can be compared to him in the glory of language. In fact he himself can well be called the word of the prophet who says: "God gave me a learned tongue." And this: "My tongue is the pen of a scribe writing speedily." For he was indeed the pen of the Holy Spirit, with which pen the Holy Spirit wrote speedily for us both the penalties of the damned and the glory of the blessed. Likewise the Holy Spirit itself, through this man, openly confuted the wicked deeds of prelates and kings and princes of the earth. A second aim is that he might restore the books of poets, which had been totally forsaken and abandoned to oblivion, as it were, in which books there are many useful precepts necessary for good living, because without them we cannot achieve a thorough understanding of his Comedy. A third aim is that he might condemn by examples the wretched life or evil men, and most of all the prelates and princes, while on the other hand he might commend all the more the life of the good and the virtuous through the examples which he sets forth. And thus the final cause in this work is made clear.

Regarding the fifth, namely under what branch of philosophy this Comedy proceeds, note that the branch is morals or ethics, inasmuch as the whole as well as the part was conceived and composed for a practical and not for a speculative purpose. For although in certain places or passages the treatment is in the manner of speculative philosophy, that is not for the sake of speculation primarily, but for a practical purpose, since, as the Philosopher says in the second book of the *Metaphysics*, "Practical men at times speculate on things in their particular and temporal relations." And thus it becomes clear under what philosophy this most lofty Comedy belongs. Regarding the sixth and last point, namely the title, note that the title of the book is as follows: "Here begins the intensely profound and supremely lofty Comedy of Dante, a most excellent poet." This Comedy is divided into three *cantiche:* the first is called Hell, the second Purgatory, and the third Paradise. It is called intensely profound because it treats of the lower regions; supremely lofty because it treats of the regions above. Moreover it is called Comedy because in the beginning it is horrifying and in the end delightful. For greater clarity on this matter I want you to know, Lucano, that four are the kinds of poets, of which any one of the types has its own art. Some indeed are called lyric poets, namely those who in their works include all varieties of songs; and they are called lyric poets from the Greek *apotulirin,* which means from the variety of songs; the lyre likewise is so called because it has many strings. David used this type of songs in composing the *Psalter.* Whence Arator, cardinal of the Holy Roman Church, commenting on the *Acts of the Apostles,* says: "Lyric feet composed the Psalter." Some are called satirists because they are full of fecundity, or from fullness or abundance. For they speak of various things at the same time, and they are called satirical or satirists from a certain poetic art which is called satire. And as a certain gloss on Persius remarks: "Satire is a sumptuous table replete with many kinds of produce which at one time was offered to Venus as a sacrifice." For that reason this second kind of poetic narration is called satire, because it abounds in the reprehension of vice and the commendation of virtue; or satire is so called from Satyr, god of the forests. For satyrs are certain animals having the form of a man from the navel up, but from the navel down they have a caprine form; on their head they have two horns and a beaked nose. These satyrs are light and saltatory, blunt and sarcastic, and deriders of everything. Likewise this art of the poets is light because it skips quickly from vice to virtue and from virtue to vice; it is called blunt and sarcastic because it openly reprehends vices; it is derisive because it derides the wicked.

Some are called tragic poets, and their art is called tragedy. Tragedy is in fact a certain poetical narration which in the beginning is admirable and pleasant, but in the end or outcome, it is foul and horrible; and because of this it receives its name from *tragos*, which is goat, and *oda*, which is son; hence tragedy, as if it were a goat-song, that is foul in the manner of a goat, as is evident through Seneca in his tragedies. Or, as blessed Isidor says in the eighth book of the *Etymologies:* "They are called tragedians because of the fact that, in the beginning, for those who sang the prize was a goat, which the Greeks called *tragos.*" Likewise Horace: "Who in tragic song competed for a vile goat." Some indeed are called comic writers, and their art comedy. Comedy is in fact a certain poetical narration which in the beginning has the harshness of someone's misery; but its subject ends favorably, as is evident through Terence in his comedies. And so this book is called Comedy because in the beginning of its narration or description it has harshness and horror, in that it treats of the penalties of Hell; toward the end, however, it contains joy and delight, because it treats of the joys of Paradise.

Among the lyric poets Boethius and Symonides hold the first place; among the satirists, Horace and Persius; among the tragedians, Homer and Virgil; and among the comic writers, Plautus and Terence. Thus Dante can be called not only a comic writer because of his Comedy, but also a lyric poet because of the diversity of his rhymes and because of the very sweet and mellifluous sound which they render; and satirist because of the reprehension of vices and commendation of virtues which he makes; and tragedian because of the great deeds which he narrates of sublime personages. And this is shown by two verses for his epitaph which I constructed in his memory:

> Here lies Dante the lofty comic
>   poet,
> And satiric, lyric, and tragic poet

as well.
And thus the title of the book is clear.

After those six points which are to be sought in any doctrinal work have been manifested, we must realize that this Comedy contains four senses, as well as the knowledge of sacred theology. For in this work poetry accords with theology, because each one of these sciences can be explained in a fourfold manner: all the more because by the ancient doctors poetry is included under theology. For blessed Augustine writes in the seventh book of the *City of God* that Marcus Varro postulated three types of theology: one, of course, full of fables, which the poets use; another natural, which the philosophers use, and the third civil, which the multitude uses. For the first meaning or sense which the Comedy contains is called historical, the second allegorical, the third tropological, the fourth and last is called anagogical. The first meaning, I say, is historical. This meaning extends only to the letter, as when we consider Minos as the judge and assessor of Hell, who classifies the fallen souls. The second meaning is allegorical, by which I mean that the letter or history has one meaning on the outer surface and another in the marrow; and according to this allegorical meaning, Minos stands for divine justice. The third meaning is tropological, or moral, by which I mean how I must judge myself. And according to this meaning, Minos stands for human reason, which should rule every man, or the remorse of conscience, which should correct evil deeds. And the fourth and last meaning is anagogical, through which I must hope to receive rewards for things I have done, and according to this meaning Minos stands for hope, through which we must expect punishments for our sins and glory for our virtues. Now as for those people whom he places there, understand this meaning, that we must not believe they are actually there, but we must understand them as examples, because when he treats of some vice, in order that we might better understand that vice he cites as an example some man who has steeped in that vice. Having considered all of these things, let us proceed to a sort of literal exposition. This Comedy, as has been mentioned, is divided into three *cantiche:* the first is called *Hell*, the second *Purgatory*, and the third *Paradise*. But first let us discuss the first one, whose title is given: "Here begins the first *Cantica* of Dante's Comedy."

[From *Life of Dante*]   Giovanni Boccaccio[*]

HIS APPEARANCE, HABITS AND CHARACTER

Such as has been set forth above was the end of Dante's life, worn out by varied studies. And in as much as I think I have adequately related his flames, his domestic and public cares, his miserable exile and his end, according to my promise, I judge it well to go on to an account of his bodily stature, his dress, and generally the most notable ways that he observed in his life, proceeding thence at once to the noteworthy works that were composed by him in his day, troubled by so fierce a whirlwind as hath been briefly shewn above.

This our poet, then, was of middle height; and when he had reached maturity he went somewhat bowed, his gait grave and gentle, and ever clad in most seemly apparel, in such garb as befitted his ripe years. His face was long, his nose aquiline, and his eyes rather large than small; his jaws big, and the underlip protruding beyond the upper. His complexion was dark, his hair and beard thick, black, and curling, and his expression was ever melancholy and thoughtful. Hence it chanced one day in Verona (when the fame of his works had spread abroad everywhere, and especially that part of his Comedy which he entitles Hell; and when he himself was known by sight to many, both men and women), that as he passed by a gateway where sat a group of women, one of them said to the others, softly, yet so that she was heard well enough by him and by his company: "Do you see the man who goes to Hell, and comes again, at his pleasure; and brings tidings up here of them that be below?" To that which one of the others answered in all good faith: "In truth it must needs be as thou sayest. Seest thou not how his beard is crisped and his skin darkened by the heat and smoke that are there below?" And hearing these words spoken behind him and perceiving that they sprang from the perfect belief of the women, he was pleased, and as though content that they should be of such opinion, he passed on, smiling a little. In his private and public manners he was wondrous orderly and composed, and in all things was he courteous and polished beyond any other. In food and drink he was most moderate, both in taking them at the appointed hours and in never going beyond the limit of necessity; nor did he ever shew any nicety in one thing rather than another. Delicate viands he complimented, and for the most part fed on plain ones, blaming beyond measure such as bestow great part of their study on getting choice things and having them prepared

[*] This section is taken from *The Early Lives of Dante*, trans. Philip H. Wicksteed (London: Alexander Morings Press, 1904), 53–59, 67–76.

with extremest diligence; declaring that the likes of these do not eat
to live, but rather live to eat. No man kept vigil more than he,
whether in studies or in any such other concern as might assail him;
in so much that many a time both his household and his wife were
grieved thereat, until they grew used to his ways, and took no further
note of it. Seldom did he speak save when questioned, and that
deliberately and with voice suited to the matter of discourse; not but
what, when occasion rose, he was most eloquent and copious, and
with excellent and ready delivery.

In his youth he took the greatest delight in music and song; and
with all the best singers and musicians of those times he was in
friendship and familiarity; and many a poem was he drawn on by
this delight to compose, which he then caused to be clothed in
pleasing and commanding melody by these his friends. How fervently
he was subject to love hath been already set forth clearly enough;
and, in the firm belief of all, this love it was that moved his genius
to vernacular poetry, first in the way of imitation; then through
longing to set forth his emotions more expressly, and to win glory,
he eagerly exercised himself therein till he not only excelled all his
contemporaries, but so clarified and beautified the vernacular that
then and thenceforth, he made and shall make many others desirous
to become expert therein. In like manner he delighted to be alone
and far removed from all folk, that his contemplations might not be
broken in upon; and if some thought that pleased him well should
come upon him when in company, howsoever he should be questioned
about aught he would answer his questioner never a word until he
had either accepted or rejected this his imagination. And many times
this chanced to him as he sat at table, or was journeying with
companions, and elsewhere, too, when questioned.

In his studies he was most assiduous, during such time as he
assigned to them; in so much that nothing, however startling to hear,
could distract him from them. And as concerning this giving himself
up wholly to the thing that pleased him, there are certain, worthy
of faith, who relate how one of the times when he was in Siena he
chanced to be at an apothecary's shop, and there a little book that
had been promised him before was placed in his hand, which book
was of much fame amongst men of worth, and had never yet been
seen of him; and, as it befell, not having opportunity to take it to
some other place he lay with his breast upon the bench that stood
before the apothecary's and set the book before him and began most
eagerly to examine it; and although soon after, in that very district,
right before him, by occasion of some general festival of the Sienese,
a great tournament was begun and carried through by certain young
gentlemen, and therewith the mightiest din of them around—as in
like cases is wont to come about, with various instruments and with

applauding shouts—and although many other things took place such as might draw one to look on them, as dances of fair ladies, and sundry sports of youth, yet was there never a one that saw him stir thence, nor once raise his eyes from the book; nay rather, he having placed himself there about the hour of noon, it was past vespers, and he had examined it all and as it were taken a general survey thereof, ere he raised himself up from it; declaring afterwards, to certain who asked him how he could hold himself from looking upon so fair festivities as had been done before him, that he had perceived naught at all of them; whereat for his questioners a second wonder was not unduly added to the first.

Moreover, this poet was of marvelous capacity and firmness of memory, and of piercing intellect, in so much that when he was in Paris, and in a disputation *de quolibet* held there in the schools of theology fourteen theses had been maintained by divers men of worth on divers matters, he straightway gathered all together, with the arguments for and against urged by the opponents, and in due sequence, as they had been produced, recited them without break, following the same order, subtly solving and refuting the counter arguments; the which thing was reputed all but a miracle by them that stood by. Of most exalted genius was he likewise, and subtle invention, as his works make far more manifest to such as understand than could by letters. He longed most ardently for honour and glory; perchance more than befitted his illustrious virtue. But what then! what life so humble that it is not touched by the sweetness of glory? And by reason of this longing I suppose it was that he loved poetry beyond all other study, seeing that albeit philosophy transcends all others in nobility, yet her excellence can be communicated only to a few, and there are many who have fame therein throughout the world; whereas poetry is more conspicuous and giveth more delight to each and all, and poets are exceeding few. And therefore, hoping that by poesy he might achieve the unwonted and imposing honour of the crown of laurel, he gave himself all to her, both in study and composition. And of a surety his desire would have come to pass had fortune been so gracious to him as to suffer him ever to return to Florence; for in her alone, and over the font of San Giovanni was he disposed to take the crown, to the end that where he had taken his first name by baptism, in that same place he might take his second name by coronation. But it came so to pass that, albeit his merit was great, even such that in whatsoever place he would he might have had the honour of the laurel (which, though it increase not knowledge, yet is the most certain token and adornment of its acquisition) yet because he awaited just that return which was never to come about, he would receive it in no other place. And in so much as the question is often raised by readers, what poetry and the poet are, and whence this name has come, and wherefore poets be crowned with laurel; and few, methinks, have shewn it forth; therefore I think fit here to make a certain digression wherein somewhat to explain all this, returning so soon as I may to the purpose.

THE DIFFERENCE BETWEEN POESY AND THEOLOGY

It is the purpose of divine Scripture (which is what we mean by Theology), now under figure of some history, now by the meaning of some vision, now by the purport of some lamentation, and in many another fashion, to set forth to us the high mystery of the incarnation of the divine Word, his life, the things that chanced at his death, his victorious resurrection, his marvelous ascension, and every other act of his; instructed whereby we may come to that glory which he revealed to us, both in his death and in his resurrection, after it had long been barred against us by the sin of the first man. And in like manner the poets in their words (which are what we mean by Poesy), now under the fictions of diverse gods, now under the transformations of men into vain forms, and now with winsome pleadings, set forth to us the causes of things, the results of virtues and of vices, what we are to flee and what pursue, in order that by virtuous doing we may come to that goal which they, who had no right knowledge of the true God, regarded as the highest blessedness. The Holy Spirit was minded to set forth in that greenest bush wherein Moses beheld God, as under fashion of a burning flame, that her virginity who was pure beyond every other creature, and who was destined to become the abode and receptacle of the Lord of nature, should receive no attaint by conceiving, nor by bearing the Word of the Father. He was minded, by the vision seen by Nebuchadnezzar in the statue composed of many metals, shattered by a stone that turned into a mountain, to set forth how all the preceding ages should be submerged by the death of Christ, who was and is a living stone, and how the Christian religion, born from this stone, should come to be unmovable and perpetual like as we see the mountains. He was minded in the Lamentations of Jeremiah to declare the coming fall of Jerusalem.

In like fashion our poets, feigning that Saturn had many children and that he devoured them all save four, were minded to signify naught else to us by Saturn save time, wherein everything is produced, and like as everything is produced in it, so it is the destroyer of all things, and reduces all things to naught. As for his four sons whom he devoured not, the first is Jove, to wit the element of fire; the second is Juno, wife and sister of Jove, to wit the air, through the mediation of which fire accomplishes all its effects down here; the third is Neptune, god of the sea, to wit the element of water; the fourth and last is Pluto, god of hell, to wit earth, lowest of all the elements. In like manner our poets feigned that Hercules was transformed from a man to a god, and Lycaon to a wolf; giving us to understand, in the moral order, that by doing virtuously, as did Hercules, man becomes a god by participating in heaven, and by doing viciously, as did Lycaon, albeit he seem to be a man, he may in truth be called that beast which by common consent is characterized by doings most akin to his special vice; just as Lyacoan by reason of his rapacity and avarice, which are wholly fitting to the wolf, is feigned to have been changed into one. In like fashion our poets invented the beauty of the Elysian fields, by which I understand the sweetness of heaven; and the darkness of Dis, whereby I understand the bitterness of hell; in order that, attracted by the joy of the one and terrified by the affliction of the other, we might pursue the virtues which will lead us to Elysium, and flee the vices which would make us cross the bank to Dis. I will grind these things no finer in detailed exposition, because had I a mind to explain them at the fitting length to which they could be stretched, albeit they would themselves grow in attractiveness and my argument would be further strengthened thereby, I doubt they would draw me much further on than my main theme demands, or than I am willing to go.

And surely were no more said than what has already been set forth, there should be no difficulty in understanding that Theology and Poesy agree in the way in which they go to work. But in their subject matter I affirm that they are not only quite diverse, but also in some sort adverse; because the subject of sacred Theology is the divine truth, that of ancient Poetry the gods of the Gentiles and men. They are opposed to each other in as much as Theology presupposes naught save what is true, whereas Poesy supposes certain things as true which are most false and erroneous and counter to the Christian religion. But inasmuch as certain witless ones lift themselves up against the poets, declaring that they have composed foul and evil stories, which conform to no kind of truth, and that they ought to have shown their talent and given instruction to the lay world in some other way than by their stories, I am minded to go somewhat further with the present discourse.

Let those then of whom I speak consider the visions of Daniel, of Isaiah, of Ezekiel, and of the others in the Old Testament; visions endited with divine pen, and revealed by him who had no beginning and shall have no end. Let them further consider, in the New Testament, the visions of the Evangelist, full of marvelous truth to whoso understandeth, and if they can find any poetic fiction as remote from truth or verisimilitude as these visions in many parts appear to be on the surface, then let it be granted that the Poets, and they alone, have uttered fables which can give neither pleasure nor profit. I might now pass on without saying another word to repel their attack upon the Poets for setting forth their teaching in fables, or under the guise of fables; knowing that whilst they madly rebuke the Poets in this matter they fall unawares into reviling that Spirit which is no other than the Way, the Life, and the Truth. But I purpose, for all that, to say something to meet their objections.

It is a thing plain to see that whatever is gained by toil hath a certain sweetness over and above that which cometh without effort; so that the plain truth, in as much as it is swiftly understood, gives delight and passes into memory with but little force. Wherefore, in order that being gained with toil it should be the more loved and therefore the better preserved, the Poets concealed it under things quite counter to it in appearance; and so they composed their fables in preference to any other disguise, that their beauties might draw such as neither the demonstrations of philosophy nor her persuasions would have been able to attract. What then shall we say of the Poets? Are we to hold them for the witless wights, which they who themselves lack with in our own day and talk of they know not what declare them to be? Nay verily! Rather was there profoundest meaning in what they did, as concerns the hidden fruit, and most excellent and ornate eloquence as concerns the bark and leaves that outwardly appear. But let us return to the point we had reached.

I say that Theology and Poesy may be considered to be almost one and the same thing, in such parts wherein their subject is one; nay, I say further that Theology is naught else than a certain Poesy of God. And what else than a poetic fiction is it in Scripture to say now that Christ is a lion, and now a lamb, and now a worm, and now a dragon, and now a rock, and many other figures which to attempt to enumerate were long indeed? What else do the words of the Saviour, uttered in the Gospel pronounce, save a discourse remote from the sense, which kind of speech we are wont to call allegory? Wherefore it doth well appear not only that Poesy is Theology, but also that Theology is Poesy. And truly if my words should deserve but little faith in so great a matter I shall not be troubled thereat; but let faith be given to Aristotle, a most worthy witness in any matter of great import, who affirms that he has found the Poets to have been the first Theologians. And let this suffice for this part, and let us turn to the demonstrations why to the Poets alone, amongst men of knowledge, the honour of the laurel crown was granted.

Amongst all the many nations on the circuit of the earth, the Greeks are held to have been the first to whom Philosophy revealed herself and her secrets; and from her treasures they drew military science political organization, and many other precious things whereby they became famous and revered beyond every other nation. Now amongst the rest that they drew from her treasure was that most sacred opinion of Solon set at the beginning of this work; and in order that their Commonwealth, which in those days flourished above all others, should go and stand erect upon its two feet they made and observed majestic ordinances concerning the punishment of the guilty and rewarding of the worthy. And amongst the other rewards established by them for whoso should have done well, this was the chief: to crown with laurel leaves in public and with public assent, Poets, when their toil had been triumphant, and Commanders, when they had victoriously strengthened their Commonwealth; judging that equal glory was due to him by whose valour human things were preserved and enlarged, and him by whom divine things were handled. And albeit the Greeks were the inventors of this honour, it afterwards passed to the Latins, when alike the glory and the arms of all the world made way for the Roman name. And as to the crowning of Poets, at least (though it very rarely comes to pass), the custom yet abides with them. But why the laurel more than any other leaf should be chosen for this coronation it will not be unpleasing to consider.

There are some who, in as much as they know that Daphne was loved of Phoebus and was transformed into a laurel, hold that since Phoebus was the first patron and fosterer of poets, and since he likewise had his triumphs, he was moved by the love that he bore to these leaves to crown his lyres and his triumphs with them; and that men took example hence, so that what Phoebus did in the first instance, was the cause of this crowning, and of the use of these leaves, for Poets and Commanders, even to this day. And truly I have naught to say against this opinion, nor do I deny that so it may have been; but none the less there is another account of it which rather appeals to me, which is the following. As they have it who look into the nature and the virtues of plants, the laurel has amongst its excellent and noteworthy properties these three: first that as is plain to see it never loses its verdure nor its foliage; the second is that this tree is never found to have been struck by lightning, which is not recorded to be the case with any other; the third that it is very sweet smelling, even as we all perceive; which three properties they who of old devised this honour held to consort with the virtuous deeds of poets and of victorious commanders. And first, the perpetual verdure of these leaves (they said) sets forth that the fame of the deeds of those who have been crowned and shall hereafter be crowned by them is destined ever to abide in life; and further they held that the deeds of such had so great might that neither the flame of envy nor the thunderbolt of length of time which consumes all things should ever have power to blast them, and beyond this they declared that their deeds should never by lapse of time become less pleasing and winning to whoso should hear them or read them, but should be ever acceptable and of good odour. Wherefore a crown of such leaves was rightly deemed more fitting than another to the men whose doings (in so far as we can perceive) were conformable thereto. Wherefore it was not without cause that our Dante longed most ardently for such honour, or rather such testimony of so great virtue, as is this crowning, to such as make themselves worthy of having their temples so adorned. But it is time to return to the point whence we departed when we entered on this matter.

[From "Commentary on Hell"]   Benvenuto da Imola°

PROEM

"He is himself a flooding sea, completely filling the needs of those who are coming abundantly and copiously" (Averroes, Commentator of Aristotle's *Poetics*).

Since, according to the opinion of the Philosopher in *Metaphysics* XII, "it is better to know a few things about noble matters than many things about ignoble ones," I shall therefore praise the most noble poet, who illustrated the poems of others; indeed, I say he surpassed them. Briefly I gather three things out of the words of the cited theme which foretell and extol the illustrious glory of this most famous man. The first of these is an admirable depth, second, desirable usefulness, third, ineffable abundance. The first is touched upon the aforementioned authority [Averroes's Commentary of Aristotle's *Poetics*] where it is said: "he is himself a flooding sea." Second, where it is added: "completely filling the needs of those who come." Third, where it is further added: "abundantly and copiously." About the first it must be briefly noted that in the most famous poem of our author an immense and inexhaustible profundity is revealed, so that Dante may say about himself, "I have penetrated the depth of the abyss, and in the waves of the sea I have walked" (Eccl. XXIV). For he is a very skilled poet, who perceptively contemplated the immensity of all the heavens and the lands and the depths of the underworld. He described each of these historically, allegorically, tropologically and anagogically, so that concerning his work of so much wisdom and eloquence, with justice I might fully cite what Hugh of St. Victor said in his *Didascalicon:* "Here the little child is sweetly nursed, here the adult is educated, here the teachers of the trivium, here the instructors of the quadrivium, here the professors of law, here the investigators of astronomy, here, in a word, every seeker of knowledge profits." This moreover will become clear to

---

° From Benvenuto da Imola, *Comentum Inferni* (Florence: Lacaita, 1887), 7–10; 523–27. Translated for this volume by Diane Vacca.

each one who examines his powers in a poetical fashion. For as Aristotle affirms in his *Poetics:* "Every poem or poetic speech is either praise or vituperation; for every action and every habit concerns nothing but virtue and vice." Whence the commentator Averroes observes regarding that very passage: "Souls noble and virtuous by nature first invented the art of poetry in order to praise and exalt beautiful and noble deeds: in fact, souls lacking in nobility followed them in composing poetry to vituperate and denounce shameful and disgraceful deeds." And he adds: "It is ever so necessary for him whose purpose it is to execrate evil men and their evil deeds to approve and praise good and virtuous deeds." No other poet, however, has known how to praise or vituperate more excellently or efficaciously than Dante, the most perfect poet, since he indeed praised virtue and virtuous people, and he vituperated vices and depraved people. Concerning this, what is said in Proverbs XII may be justly cited: "From his words each man will be rewarded." And no less apt is what Ovid says in praise of Vergil, the first of poets: "The poet sang of all things in his divine poem." So much for the first.

The second quality specified in the aforementioned authority is a desirable usefulness, a usefulness that I say is multifold: usefulness of invention, usefulness of instruction, usefulness of correction. The greatest utility of invention is made clear by the Philosopher in his *Poetics,* where he says that "two causes of the origin of poetry appear to be rooted in human nature: the first, which exists in man from birth, is the ability to see the similarity of one thing to another and the habit of representing one thing by another, since man among other animals is most greatly pleased by similarity and imitation. Indeed, the second cause is pleasure, which man by nature derives from rhythm and melody." And thus the Philosopher concludes: "Therefore the soul's delight in imitation, rhythmic and melodic, is the reason for the invention of the poetic art." This most perfect poet used imitation so aptly that his poem, which is marvelously figurative throughout, is altogether clear to the reader.

Usefulness of meaning is described by Horace in his *Art of Poetry:*

> Poets aim either to benefit or to amuse,
> Or to say at the same time pleasing and useful things
>   about life:
> He has gained every vote who joins profit to pleasure.

This most distinguished poet, moreover, interwove pleasure and profit so artfully that you could not find one without the other in his work. Usefulness of correction is self-evident, since indeed we read that the Lord ordered the sons of Israel to rob the Egyptians of their gold and silver, morally advising us by this that whether we find the gold of wisdom or the silver of eloquence among the poets, we turn their instruction that leads to salvation to our advantage. Dante, this most Christian poet, strove to apply his poetry to theology, which of itself nevertheless has a great affinity to the latter: for truly it can be said that theology is a kind of poetry about God. For, as the Philosopher affirms, poets were the first to speculate theologically about God. I can therefore say not unreasonably about Dante that which Averroes says about Aristotle: "Nature created him the originator and teacher of this art." So much for the second.

The third and last quality is an ineffable abundance. For truly poetry is counted among the liberal arts because it surpasses all of them and embraces them all together; it excels by rising above all of them. Whence Petrarch, the latest poet, states in a certain letter which he wrote to me: "It is a great thing," he says, "to be among great things, but sometimes greater to be drawn out, just as the leader is drawn from the number of great citizens." Thus we know that theology, philosophy, and medicine are not to be counted among the liberal arts. Accordingly, this most noble of the sciences is deemed worthy above all others to be suitable to noble minds. For the most illustrious leaders devoted themselves to it, such as Julius Caesar, Caesar Augustus, Titus Vespasianus, Hadrian, and African Scipio; the most knowledgeable teachers: Augustine, Jerome, Ambrose; the most celebrated philosophers: Plato, Aristotle, and Solon, the proposer of laws. Thus Claudian, the Florentine poet says appropriately:

> For virtue delights in joining itself to the Muses as
> witnesses:
> Whoever loves poetry treats of worthy things in his
> poem.

In conclusion about the most noble poet, I shall therefore cite Ecclesiasticus 39: He will himself as it were pour forth the waters with the eloquence of his own wisdom. True wisdom, I say, about which Augustine speaks near the beginning of Book VIII of the *City of God*: "An analogy must be made with the philosophers, whose name, if translated into Latin, means the love of wisdom. Furthermore, if wisdom is God, as divine truth and scripture made clear, the true philosopher is a lover of God."

From Canto XV of Inferno

Francis, firstborn son of Accursio, was also a very famous jurist, who was afflicted with a disease of worse and more burning fever than his father. The author says: "et Francesco d'Accorso anco" (and Francesco D'Accorso too) (*Inf.* XV.110) that is, also, whom the author represents spotted with this horrendous ignominy, because he kept badly his own most beautiful law, which he taught others, which says: "When a man marries as a woman, let the laws be armed." And note here, reader, that once I saw men who knew great literature complaining that Dante had surely spoken excessively improperly by naming such men here. And certainly, when I first read this, I was very indignant; but afterwards I learned through experience that the very wise poet had done very well in this case. For in 1375, while I was in Bologna, and I was reading that very book, I found some worms born from the ashes of sodomites, poisoning that whole endeavor. Not able to bear any longer such a great stench, whose smoke was already darkening the stars, not without grave danger to me, I revealed the affair to Peter the cardinal of Bourges. He was then legate to Bologna, a man of great virtue and knowledge. Detesting such an abominable crime, he ordered an inquiry against the principals. Some of them were captured, and many, terrified, fled in different directions. And if a certain traitorous priest to whom the affair was entrusted had not prevented it, because he was afflicted by a disease like theirs, many would have been handed over to the flames of fire. If they escaped these flames alive, dead they do not evade them here, unless by chance good repentance extinguished them with the water of tears and remorse. From this, moreover, I incurred deadly hate and the enmity of many; but divine justice has up to now benignly protected me against those enemies of nature.

"E vedervi" (And you could also have seen) (*Inf.* XV, 110). Here ser Brunetto names another cleric who was a prelate. As to his identity, I want you to know with a broad smile that this spirit was a Florentine citizen, born into the Mozzi family, Bishop of Florence, who was called Andrew. This one, indeed a simple and foolish man, often used to preach in public to the people, saying many ridiculous things. Among other things, he used to say that the providence of God was like a wall, which, standing over the beam sees whatever is going on under him in the house, and no one sees him. He also used to say that the grace of God was just like the excrement of goats, which falling from on high dashes down scattered in various places. Similarly, he used to say that the divine power was immense. Wishing to demonstrate by giving a clear example, he would hold a turnip seed in his hand and say: "You see well how small and tiny is this little seed." Then he would extract a very large turnip from under his cape, saying: "Behold how marvelous is the power of God who from a tiny seed makes such a great fruit." And so this great brute, so bestial by nature, was afflicted by this vice of bestiality against nature. Now understand the text, which is very perplexing, in this way: Brunetto says to Dante: "et potei," that is, you were able "vedervi," that is, to see there in that crowd of animals which, running rapidly, had already mostly disappeared from their sight. On that account he says thusly: "colui," meaning the Bishop Andrew; and he says: "che fu trasmutato d'Arno in Bacchiglione" (he who was transferred from Arno to Bacchiglione) (*Inf.* XV, 113), as if he were saying the one was a Bishop of Florence was made the Vicentine bishop; for the River Arno flows through Florence, and the Bachigliono through Vicenza. And here notice that the author not without reason describes him in such a way by this transfer; for you should know that once this Bishop Andrew, when he preached to his distinguished people, said in the end: "O ladies and gentlemen, may Monna Thessa, my kinswoman who is going to Rome, be recommended to you; for in truth if she was for a little while rather inconstant and pleasing, now she is well corrected; therefore she is going for an indulgence." Know this, that Sir Thomas of Mozzi, his brother, a great jurist, not willing to bear his absurdities any longer, and because the infamy of his vice was growing, prudently took pains so that he would be made Vicentine bishop by Pope Nicholas Orsini. Thus he says: "che dal servo de' servi" (by the servant of servants) (*Inf.* XV, 112), that is, by the Roman pope, who signs himself "servant of the servants of God," which title Gregory I, distinguished teacher, first devised. And he says that afterward he died there, whence he says very obscurely: "dove," that is, in Vicenza, where "lasciò li mal protesi nervi" (where he left his sinfully distended muscles) (*Inf.* XV, 114), that is, badly extended. Some explain this as meaning that the limbs of one who is dying are stretched out because of pain, and thus it seems he wished to say that there he died badly, just as he had lived badly. Others say that he was a prodigal, and thus had his limbs wrongly extended. But I believe for sure that the author speaks more subtly here, meaning the genital member. For these members are extended in natural lust lawfully and appropriately in the proper circumstances; but in unnatural lust, wrongly, evilly and nefariously. Thus he means that this one who lived badly, died badly in infamy and his own turpitude, and he says: "S'avessi avuto di tal tigna brama" (Had you hankered for such scarf) (*Inf.* XV, 111), that is, if you had had the desire of knowing such infamous and blameworthy things about such a priest of pigs.

"Di più" (I would say more) (*Inf.* XV, 115). Here at the end, Brunetto concludes, excusing himself if does not name any more people, whence he says: "di più direi," that is, I would tell about many more other clerics and literati of my company, "ma il venire e 'l sermone non può esser più lungo" (but my going and my speech must not be longer) (*Inf.* XV, 115), because smoke is the most certain sign of fire. And by smoke he understands a new stench of lust of another group of people coming. Thus he says: "là," that is, from far off; for a new crowd was coming that had transgressed more gravely and was tortured more harshly. Thus he says: "gente vien con le quali esser non deggio" (People are coming with whom I must not be) (*Inf.* XV, 118), because they belong to a group different from mine. And in parting ser Brunetto recommends to the author a work of him. To understand this, you must know that ser Brunetto wrote this vernacular book in the French language of prose. He divided it into three books. The first deals with events in the old and new testaments: about the ages of the world, about the kingdoms of peoples, about the prophets, about the apostles, the endowment of the church, the multiple translations of the Roman Empire to the Greeks, Gauls, Germans, about the location and difference of the provinces; about natural things: the elements, fish, birds, serpents, beasts. In the second book he treats of the *Ethics* of Aristotle, that is, about moral virtues and vices. In the third about rhetoric of Cicero, that is, about artistic eloquence and the manners of persuasion: also about the ways of ruling and governing cities and lands. The first part he calls common coin; the second, precious stones; the third, purest gold. He wrote another little book, which is called the *Tesoretto* or little treasure, in verse in the Italian vernacular. In it he treats of the customs of men, of the accidents and inconstancy of Fortune, of the human condition. Thus he says: "siati raccomandato il mio Tesoro" (Let my Treasure be commended to you) (*Inf.* XV, 119): by which should be understood the first treasure, greater on account of its superiority, which is called "treasure" for that reason, for it is as it were an accumulation and collection of many things in one abundant mass; whence in the proem of this book he compares it to a honeycomb of honey collected from the various flowers of many authors.

"Poi" (Then). Here the author closes the chapter and this matter, showing the swift departure of ser Brunetto by a humorous and brilliant comparison, saying: ser Brunetto "poi si rivolse," that is, after he said these words, he turned himself in the direction toward which his comrades were first running at top speed; then he says: "e parve di coloro," that is, of those runners "che corrono a Verona il drappo verde" (and seemed like one of those who run for the green cloth—the field at Verona) (*Inf.* XV, 121). Concerning this you should know about a custom in the city of Verona that every year on the first Sunday of Lent men eagerly race on foot toward a green banner, and for that reason the runners seen there are the fastest. Dante, moreover, had seen this event when he had been at Verona and took note of it for his own purpose: for just as the runners for the cloth of Verona race very swiftly, with the hope of reward and encouraged by the clamor and the exhortations of the spectators, in the same way these sinners on the sand run swiftly with the fear of punishment, goaded by the burning of the flames; and he adds to indicate his greater speed that Brunetto seemed first, not last, of those runners.

[From "Letters on Familiar Matters (XXI.15)"]

Francesco Petrarca*

. . . But since you have brought up a matter that I would not voluntarily have chosen, let me seize the opportunity to refute to you, and to others through you, a widespread misconception of my estimation of that poet (Dante). As Quintilian said of himself and of Seneca, the common conception is not only false, it is insidious and at bottom malevolent. For those who had me say that I hate and despise the man; their aim is to rouse against me the hatred of the masses, with whom the man is extremely popular. This is a new form of mischief, a remarkable device in the arsenal of injury. In this pass let the truth answer for me.

In the first place, there is certainly no reason for me to hate a man I have seen only once, in my early boyhood at that. He was a contemporary of my grandfather and my father, being younger than the first and older than the second, and he was expelled with my father from their native city on the same day. At such a time those who share afflictions often form fast friendships, as was especially the case with them, who not only suffered a like fate but who were very similar in their character and studious tastes. The difference was that my father undertook a new career out of regard for his family, while the man in question fought against exile and persisted the more vigorously on his course, neglecting all else in his desire for fame alone. I cannot admire and praise too highly our subject, who would not let himself be diverted from the course he had once chosen, either by mistreatment on the part of his fellow citizens, or by exile, poverty, the shafts of his rivals, love for his wife, or paternal affection, while so many superior and fastidious minds are swerved from their purpose by a mere breath. This happens most commonly to poets, intent upon words and thought and the structure of their work, who require quiet and silence more than other men. Thus you will understand how my "hatred" for the man, alleged by I know not whom, is both detestable and absurd, since as you see I have no reason for hatred, but many reasons for love, for instance our common fatherland, our family friendship, his genius, and his literary achievement, the best of its kind, which must make him immune to criticism.

There was a second ground for the calumnies cast against me. The argument runs that from my early youth, when one most ardently longs for such things, I delighted in collecting books of all sorts, but never possessed a copy of his works. While, they say, I passionately

---

* From *Letters from Petrarch*, trans. Morris Bishop (Bloomington and London: Indiana University Press, 1966), 177–180.

hunted other books, with little hope of success, I was strangely indifferent to this one book, which was new and easily procurable. I admit the fact, but I deny the inference that they would draw about my attitude. I was then working in the same vein and trying my wits in the vulgar tongue. I thought nothing could be more splendid, and I had not yet learned to look higher. But I was afraid that if I should immerse myself in his words, or in those of any other man, I might unwillingly or unconsciously become an imitator. (At that age one is so malleable, so prone to admire everything!) Such was my youthful arrogance that I shuddered at the thought; such was my self-confidence—or my self-exaltation—that I thought that my own endowments would suffice to create my own style in this field without any mortal aid. Others must judge whether or not I was justified. One thing I want to make clear: if anything in my Italian writings resembles or even exactly reproduces something written by him or by anyone else, it is not due to theft or deliberate imitation, two pitfalls I have sedulously avoided, especially in my vernacular works. Any possible resemblances have been caused by chance, or, as Cicero opined, by similarity of mind, which led us unwittingly on the same course. Believe that this is so, if you are to believe any words of mine; nothing is more true. If shame and modesty were not sufficient deterrents from plagiarism, my youthful vanity was powerful enough.

But today I am far from such concerns. Since I have abandoned those productions and have lost my earlier fears, I now welcome wholeheartedly all other writers and this man above all. Then I was offering myself to be judged by others; now I make my own silent judgments of others. My judgments vary a good deal about the rest of the poets, but to him I readily grant the palm of achievement in the vulgar tongue.

So they lie who accuse me of carping at his fame. Perhaps I appreciate better than most of his foolish, excessive extollers what are the beauties, beyond their comprehension, that delight their ears without penetrating to their spirits, owing to their limited intelligences. They belong to that class of whom Cicero says in his *Rhetoric* that "when they read good speeches or poems, they approve the orators and poets, but they do not understand why they are moved to approval, since they cannot know from what their pleasure derives, or what their pleasure is, or how it is constructed." And if that could occur with regard to Demosthenes, Cicero, Homer, and Virgil among cultivated men, even in the schools, what may not happen in the case of our subject among fools in taverns and marketplaces?

As for me, I admire the man, I love him, I do not underrate him. And I can honestly say that if he had lived to our times he would have found few closer friends than myself—that is, if his conduct matched his genius. And on the contrary he would have been superlatively disliked by those same stupid eulogizers, equally ignorant of what they applaud and what they condemn, who mispronounce, lacerate, and massacre his lines, doing him the greatest injury a poet can suffer. I might even venture to plunge into the fray and avenge this mockery of his work, if I were not so occupied with my own concerns. In the circumstances, I can merely express my reprehension and disgust that the noble face of his poetry is befouled and beslabbered by their ugly utterance.

[From "The Divine Origin of Poetry"]

Cristoforo Landino*

If we reflect as to what is a poet, as to how ancient is the origin of poetry, how divine, profound, and various is a poet's doctrine, we shall certainly come to know that which philosophers have long realized: no writers can ever be found to equal the poets in either eloquence or wisdom. It was exactly this realization to induce Aristotle, a man of great ingenuity and doctrine, unique after Plato, to believe that in the early centuries the poets were theologians. So great was the esteem in which he held poets that he wrote two books on the poetic faculty and came to recognize that poetry is not one of those arts the ancients called liberal.

. . . Poetry is something much more divine than the liberal disciplines, for it embraces all of them. Bound by numbers, circumscribed by meter, adorned with various lights and flowers, poetry adorns with wondrous figments and translates into other realities whatever men have ever made, known, or imagined. By portending that it narrates something more inferior or abject or that it sings a fable merely to give delight to the ears of those who live leisurely, it actually writes sublime things extracted from the very fountain of divinity. The listener, recognizing his error, not only comes to know the greatest things, of which he was unaware because they were hidden under a divine veil, but also takes a marvelous pleasure for such a figment.

That the origin of poetry is more excellent than the origin of the human arts is made manifest by the fact that poetry originates from a divine fury, as Plato shows in his *Ion*. Men learn, as Plato argues, all of the arts after a long training if they are without divine inspiration. But the true poets, such as Orpheus, Homer, Hesiod, and

---

* From Cristoforo Landino, introduction to *Dante con l'Esposizione di Cristoforo Landino* (Venice, 1564). Translated for this volume by John S. Smurthwaite.

Pindar, put some hints of all the arts in their works, and this is a sign that they understand them. Another sign of the divine inspiration of the poets is evident from the fact that they sing many extraordinary things when they are possessed, but once the inspiration ceases, they themselves can scarcely understand their own utterances, as if God through their mouths, not they uttered them. Further, it is clear that those who are better poets are neither men who are prudent nor those who have been trained since their earliest years. Rather, they are those, as Plato says, who are driven by divine madness. Such a distinguished philosopher adds that at times the Muses breathe this divine spirit into men who are not inventions of philosophers but the gifts of God. . . . Finally, poets alone, against the custom of other writers, invoke divine help. They do so because they understand that the poem is not human but divine and that it proceeds from divine inspiration.

This same belief induced Aristotle to call the poets theologians. If we investigate the nature of both the poet and the prophet we shall find no small resemblance between them. The name by which the Latins call the poet, *vates*, from *vi mentis* (force of mind), that is from *vehementia* (vehemence), designates both poet and prophet. The Greeks say "poet"—from the verb *piin*, which means something halfway between "to create"—into being, and "to make," which is the verb of every human art, by which men shape matter into a form. So that, although the poet's figment is not completely nothing, still it departs from mere making and much approximates creation.

Creation is God's poem and He is the highest poet, who disposes creation, that is, the visible and invisible world, which is His work, according to number, measure, and weight. Or, as the Prophet says, "God creates everything according to number, measure and weight." So, the poets by the number of metrical feet, by the measure of short and long syllables, and the weight of sentences and affections, construct their poem. . . .

ON THE ANCIENT ORIGIN OF POETS

. . . For no other reason, if not the sweetness of his verse, could Orpheus stop the rivers, move stones, tame beasts, contain the recklessness and fury of those many, who, trusting in the strength of their bodies, brought down all others. Still others, who were either of wicked mind or stupid and senseless, he could lead to a rational and civil life. Equally Amphion, by the sweet sound of his cither, forced the stones to gather together and to make up the walls of Thebes. The story demonstrates nothing else but that Amphion brought men who were vagabonds and scattered through the woods and caves, to live together in a compact. By the sweetness of verse, he mollified their harshness and composed them according to laws and customs of civil life. . . . But it is difficult to decide who among the Greeks was the inventor of verses. This musical artifice was adumbrated in Syria and Egypt much earlier than in Greece. Among the Hebrews, a people we deem most ancient, David wrote the psalms in verse. . . .

We shall seek to investigate rather, the mind of our citizen, Dante, whose poem is unique in its invention, most artful in its structure, supreme in its elocution and oratory. And he yokes together both color and form, which multiplies the delight of the listeners. Consider, for instance, the following verses:

> Non fronda verde, ma di color fosco;
> non rami schietti, ma nodosi e 'nvolti;
> non pomi v'eran, ma stecchi con tosco.
> *(Inf.* XIII, 4–6)

No green leaves, but of dusky hue; no smooth boughs, but gnarled and warped; no fruits were there, but thorns with poison.

Much depends, in these lines on the repetition, on correction and addition. Each of these rhetorical colors is pleasing to the ear. Nonetheless, since the verses are placed together, such a harmony comes out of it as one gets from well-proportioned and yet different chords of a zither. There is no comparison for this sort of similitude. Its comparisons cannot be expressed by any other comparison. They are proper, more frequent than in any other poem, most efficacious in expressing the mind of the writer, and most convenient to the dramatic place. For the poet does not quarry his comparisons from the same place for both *Inferno* and *Purgatorio,* but in each canticle he finds what is adequate to it. Further he often provides comparisons which either explain or dramatize a natural cause or teach the audience the doctrine of the natural cause. See, for instance, when he says:

> E come a lume acuto si disonna
> per lo spirto visivo che ricorre
> allo splendore che va di gonna in gonna,
> *(Par.* XXVI, 70–72)

And as sleep is broken by a piercing light when the visual spirit runs to meet the brightness that passes through film after film.

Nor does it seem that I should leave out one of the most artificial ones in which various ornaments are included. Let us hear the verses:

> Quante 'l villan ch'al poggio si riposa,
> nel tempo che colui che 'l mondo schiara
> la faccia sua a noi tien meno ascosa,
> come la mosca cede a la zanzara,
> vede lucciole giù per la vallea,
> forse colà dov'e vendemmia e ara:

di tante fiamme tutta risplendea. . . .
(Inf. XXVI, 25–31)

As many as the fireflies which the peasant, resting on the hill—in
the season when he that lights the world least hides his face from
us, and at the hour when the fly yields to the mosquito—sees down
along the valley, there perhaps where he gathers the grapes and
tills: with so many flames was the eighth ditch all agleam. . . .

This is certainly a marvelous comparison, which besides its function,
which is to explain the place he is describing, gives the highest
pleasure to the audience, which seeks mental relaxation in the midst
of the narration of sad things. In addition to this, the poet adorns
the place with a double description of time, which the Greeks call
chronography, because he describes both the summer of the year and
the night in the revolution of the heavens. And to the chronography
he joins a second rhetorical color the Greeks call *periphrasis* and the
Latins *circumlocution.* This occurs when through many words it is
said what could have been expressed through one word. The poet
could have said "in the summer," but he deploys many words to say
this: "when the sun least hides his face from us." But he did not say
"the sun." He said, instead, "he that lights the world." At the same
time he denoted the night through another circumlocution: "at the
hour when the fly yields to the mosquito." He even combines this
rhetorical color with a *denomination,* for he puts "mosquito," which
flies by night, for the night itself.

The poet's descriptions are such that he never leaves anything
obscure or confused in the mind. On the contrary, they represent to
the eyes a form as pictures do so that the internal senses see what
the external senses never do.

There is no other journey better known to us than the descent
to Hell, the laborious ascent of the mountain of Purgatorio, and the
flight to Heaven: the poet guides his readers through fearsome places
not without fear, and he is marvelous in his power to move the
affections and passions of the mind. He accommodates the particular
descriptions to time and place and at times he proceeds at a leisurely
pace, at times at a fast and concise one as in this tercet:

Ali hanno late, e colli e visi umani
piè con artigli, e pennuto 'l gran ventre;
(Inf. XIII, 13–14)

They have broad wings, and human necks and faces, feet with claws,
and their great bellies are feathered.

. . . I leave out the other rhetorical colors through which at times
with great gravity, when the subject matter requires it, at times with

ease, the poet establishes distinctions in the various episodes, adorns and illustrates his poem.

With such eloquence he does not describe the errors of Ulysses or the Trojan battles; the coming of Aeneas to Italy, the Roman Empire, the tears of Venus, the hatred of Juno, the wounds of Mars, which are the subject matter of Homer's and Vergil's labors. Rather (and what genius, immortal God, what depth of intellect) he embraces heaven, earth, and the Tartarus. . . .

And what theologians could express to us mortals with more order and more manifest demonstrations what the immortal spirits contemplate within the luminous core of nature. What physicist ever wrote with more pellucid reasons the movements in the natural world. What course of the stars, what conjunctions, what revolution of the heavens was left out by Dante? What transformation from one element to another, what alteration in the air—hail, rain, winds, thunderbolts? Which composition of mines below the ground have the physicists demonstrated and this poet failed to catch a glimpse of? With Dante we have true cognition of all. . . .

THE POET AND THE PHILOSOPHER

What shall we say of that philosophy which Socrates brought from heaven to earth, and with greatest utility he brought into the Republic, into the individual households, and, finally, into the human breast? In no philosopher, however, are more explicit or more manifest either the arguments that lead us to the highest good and to true happiness or the rules and precepts by which we share in the good life.

With how much passion and acrimony, however, does Dante condemn injustices, perfidy, incontinence, cruelty, pusillanimity, and all other vices? With how much praise and how many rewards does he invite us to virtue and persuade us to observe justice, use temperance, keep a free and constant heart, and never avoid any danger for one's own country, one's parents, and one's friends?

To have true worship of God, piety toward the elders, burning charity toward all: truly, Dante's poem reaches its conclusion on nothing else than the praise of virtue. What can be affirmed of Dante is what the Greeks affirm of Homer: that he is like the ocean: just as all rivers originate from the ocean and to the ocean return, so all the sciences are gleaned from him and in him.

Add to this his knowledge of history and his diligent investigation of antiquity, not just ours, but also the Greek and Hebrew antiquity. . . . We, therefore, by invoking divine assistance, will set sail on such a wide sea, and, as far as we can, we will play the role of faithful interpreter. We shall open up not only the literal sense but the allegorical, tropological, and anagogic senses. These three senses we call allegorical. . . .

[From "On Canto I of Paradise"]

Benedetto Varchi°

PROEM

All of this globe and this great machine, embracing and containing in itself all things—both those that can be sensed and those that are intelligible—is sometimes called the world or ornament and sometimes called the universe. And, noble academicians and all other esteemed listeners, it was divided into two principal parts by both philosophers and astrologers: the celestial or divine and the terrestrial or worldly. The celestial and divine part, called by many the superior or, in fact, ethereal region, begins with the moon's sky as its lowest point and includes everything else above it, and this region is neither creatable nor corruptible. It is because of this that, according to the peripatetics, it always was and always will be. The earthly and terrestrial part, which many consider the inferior or elementary region, beginning with the first and primary element, i.e., fire, is that region immediately below the moon and includes everything below it, air, water, and earth. And this is creatable and corruptible, changing every day and degenerating, as everyone can clearly see. The species, as many as they are varied which are found in this conjunction of heaven and earth, even if they are not infinite (since nothing is infinite according to the philosophers) but neither can they all be accounted for. For no one could ever account for all the species of all animals, those that fly or those that walk on the earth or those that swim in the sea, the latter being thought to be ten times as numerous as all the others. And it is true but also marvelous that among so many different species there is none which is exactly like another and that all are either more noble or less perfect than others. And because of this the Philosopher said, in the eighth book of *Knowledge*, that the species are like numbers, that one cannot find two that are alike, two that contain exactly what the other contains: thus it is impossible to find two identical species, of the same perfection and being one as noble

° From Benedetto Varchi, *Lezioni sul Dante*, ed. Giuseppe Aiazzi and Lelio Arbib (Florence: Societa Editrice del Varchi, 1841), 1:189–220. Translated for this volume by María Rosa Menocal.

as the other. And for this same reason the Philosopher also said, in the fifth book of the same book of *Knowledge* (in the 19th section) that the number six, for example, and likewise all other numbers, is only six times one, not two times three or three times two. And so that we may understand both these concepts better, we have to know that just as all numbers are indivisible and exist only as one, such that one can never find two numbers equally distant from the ultimate unity, source and beginning of all numbers, thus all species consist of only one point and are indivisible such that one can never find two species that are equally distant from the first and true unity, that is God, glorious and sublime source and beginning of all entities. And each species is more noble and more perfect the less remote from the closer it is to its noblest and most perfect type, as will be explained later in greater detail, but suffice it to say for the time being that in general in the universe those things that are noblest and most perfect are those that are least removed from the first and highest heaven, that which is the noblest and most perfect of all. Thus, the orbit of Saturn is more perfect than that of Jupiter, and Jupiter's nobler than Mars, and so forth; thus, fire is nobler and more perfect than air and air more so than water, such that earth, being the last among the elements and furthest from the heavens is the most ignoble and most imperfect of all. And thus, since the heavens, being invariable and immutable, are perfectly beautiful, all good, perfectly ordered and harmonized, but the earth being variable and with a thousand conflicting features is all foul, wicked, disorganized, and discordant. In the heavens there is always peace, always life, always sweetness and happiness, and finally, all goods without evil, while on earth there is always war, always bitterness and death, bitterness and sadness, in sum all evils without anything that could be called good. The life of those up above is always full of joy, laughter, pleasure, and ineffable contentment while ours here below is never free of unspeakable pain, cries, evils, and torments. They are rich, they are happy, they are blessed; we are poor, miserable, unhappy. They are completely just and wise and holy, while we are completely unjust, stupid, and (profane), to sum it up in a word, they are gods and we are men. But, not to delay any longer in this preface, which is perhaps unnecessary (although not without reason), I note that each of us, noble and ingenious listeners, may have already understood, because of what I have said above, how much, besides being great and high and magnificent that beginning is serious, wise, and marvelous. It is no less worthy of paradise than it is of the poet, and as of now, granting your generous and human indulgence, we will call it, with a happy augur, God, great and highest. But first it is only right that I turn humbly to Dante, my teacher and master, who, no doubt, from the highest heaven, forgotten or completely

absolved in love all old grievances, now looks down with happiness
and piety, to this place where so many citizens who have studied
him are gathered together to honor him. And it is appropriate to
turn to him and ask his help and his blessing in such a great enterprise
and say to him, with no less truth and affection in my position those
same words he himself said to Virgil in his:

> O de li altri poeti onore e lume,
> Vagliami 'l lungo studio e 'l grande amore
> Che m'ha fatto cercar lo tuo volume
> (*Inf.* I, 82–84)

(O glory and light of other poets, may the long study and the great
love that have made me search your volume avail me.)

Dear listeners, the subject of this canticle is so lofty and Dante's
doctrine so profound that if, before coming to his text I had wanted
to state all the things that would be necessary, or at least useful (for
such a topic), many such lessons, let alone this one alone, would not
suffice; and thus those who may think I have already said too much
would realize how wrong they are. Thus, we will leave aside so many
other things, including and especially how Dante reached the heavens
in his fiction as well as how long it took him to climb those heavens
and circle them one by one with Beatrice's guidance, all matters that
are no less difficult than beautiful, no less useful than marvelous but
on which Alessandro Vellutello has already spoken with considerable
diligence and knowledge, and in any case we will discuss some of
these particulars as is necessary. Instead, I will talk to you about
what we have here that is theological and philosophical no less than
it is poetry so that we may, briefly and with clarity, so that we may
take profit and pleasure from the doctrines and eloquence of such a
man or, rather, prodigy.

In any author one chooses to analyze, one may, in fact one
should, consider two things principally: the things that are said and
the words with which they are said. As far as the words themselves
are concerned, even if they are by their very nature less worthy and
of less value than the things themselves, nevertheless in orators and
especially in poets they count for so much (they are so much) that
they in fact matter more than the things said themselves. It is thus
that Eloquence takes its name (and position), not from invention or
rediscovery or from its disposition or order, but rather from the third
division of rhetoric, i.e., from good and well-decorated speech, i.e.,
from what the Latins called elocution; and who isn't aware that the
same things said with different words don't seem to be the same
things at all? And those same words placed in one order have infinitely
greater power and greater value than placed in a different order, so
much so that he who carefully thinks about it realizes that the great

difference between good writers and those who are not good is in words, or more accurately, in the ordering and disposition of words, rather than in the things said. I would say then, in order to clarify how one is to consider words, that all things are made up of matter and form, as are all natural things, or of things that resemble and act like matter and form; and just so is speech structured, which the ancients called discourse *(parlatura)*, having its matter and its form: the material is the words, and grammarians deal with them, dividing them into eight different kinds, each of which in turn has two modes: thus, specifically, each word is considered by whether it is declinable, what gender it is, what number, what case, what mood or verbal tense, and other such categorizations; and words are also considered in relation to each other and this is called syntax *(construzione)*. And even if a grammarian considers the meaning of words, he does not do so in isolation but rather *per accidens*, that is, in order to place them in a real and more noble context, such as the philosophers'. The forms of speech and of those words are their meaning; and this meaning is what is considered by the logician, not, like the grammarian, whether they fit together well or not but rather whether they are true or false, i.e., whether they speak truth or falsehood. And these are two means, that of the logician and that of the grammarian, that consider speech per se. Then the rhetorician, whose object of study is also speech, does not consider it either as the grammarian or the logician but rather as an orator, i.e., from the point of view of whether it is ornate and beautiful. Finally, the poet adds to all of these things number and some ornaments and figures, i.e., poetic language, because the poet is more a friend of sweetness than is the orator and he wants not only to teach but also to move and delight, to induce marvel. Thus, in these four modes can one deal with words, and we will consider them in all four whenever it seems to us necessary or useful to do so.

As far as things are concerned, all things necessary fall under the auspices of Philosophy, as we saw in its primary divisions, where things must be either speculative or practical. If they fall into the category of the practical or manual then those are dealt with by specific practical artifices; if they are in the active category they are dealt with by the moral or political philosopher, and these include laws. If (on the other hand) the things are speculative, or if they are divine, then they are the provenance of the metaphysician or supernatural or divine philosopher; and these may be mathematical, and will be dealt with by mathematicians who may be, depending on the different matter involved, an arithmetician or a musicologist or a geometrician or an astrologer, and also in this category fall the cosmographers, and others like them; or they may be natural, and these belong to the physicist, also called the natural philosopher, and medicine is a subcategory of this larger one. And thus we have seen how all things belong to one category or another of philosophy and what analyses must be applied: and to these things must be added Christian theology, which is absolutely necessary in order to be able to understand Christian authors, and most of all Dante, and supremely so this last canticle, where he is all theologian, although no less so philosopher if and when philosophy is in agreement with theology. And it is necessary to know all of these things, at least in part, if one wishes to understand Dante in the other two canticles and especially in this one; and even if this mode of interpretation was not used by the ancients, as far as I know, or by the moderns, I find it very useful. Wishing to be useful, I will make every effort to follow it rather than confiding in my own ingenuity or doctrine but relying instead on the help of He who is the first beginning and the last end of all things. And I will do so if for no other reason than to see if I can, with my hard work and efforts, awake someone else, who, with this same order (but with a different mode of expression and perception, aside from knowledge of the sciences) might shed some light on some of the passages of so many authors who for so many years have lain in the shadows, nearly completely buried.

This third and last canticle is divided up differently by different people, but as we approach the first canto, which is divided into three principal parts, we note that our intent will be to analyze each tercet individually, using that ordering we have set out. And in doing so we leave aside many general things that will be set out specifically at the appropriate moment. We are thus able to be briefer, not having to repeat the same things, and also clearer and easier, trying to avoid annoyance and confusion. And thus, once again invoking God's name and help, we begin.

> La gloria di Colui, che tutto muove,
> Per l'universo penetra, e risplende
> In una parte più, e meno altrove.
> *(Par.* I, 1–3)

(The Glory of the All-Mover penetrates through the universe and reglows in one part more, and in another less.)

In this tercet, which could never be praised sufficiently for either its words or for the magnificence of its concept, the poet means simply to say that the Motor, i.e., God, gives being and life to everything in the world, but this is not equal in all things but rather different in each thing, and thus the meaning is that every thing, whatever and wherever it may be, has its essence from God and depends on God both for being and for continued life; thus without Him, there would have been no life and, later, no ability to conserve life. It is, of course, true that some things are more noble in their existence than others, and it is because of this that all species are different from one another and unequal, i.e., they are more or less perfect. As far as the words go, we will first deal with them as the Grammarians would: *La gloria,* that is, according to some, the work that is glorious and worthy of praise; *Di colui:* of him; *Che:* that; *Muove tutto;* moves all things, and thus this is God; *Penetra:* enters completely and thus penetrates; *e risplende,* and reglows, that is, manifestly appears; *per l'universo,* throughout the world; *piu in una parte,* as in the heavens; *e meno altrove,* that is in another part, as in the world, even though here one has to understand in all things, as we have said. *La gloria,* glory, is none other than the general expectation of common good, i.e., it is to be universally praised by all good men, and wherever there is glory there is fame, but not, however, for its opposite, but rather glory is always for things that are praiseworthy, whereas fame may be either good or bad (although the latter is better called infamy). Here we note form instead of substance; there is glory instead of glorious works, although I would like to analyze more: glory, that is goodness or power or love or Divine providence, or whatever word might be found more adequate than these. *Per l'universo* is a Tuscanism, and good Latin authors would never use it as a substantive, and it means the aggregate of the heavens and the earth together, in sum, all things. Petrarch used it in his *canzone* "Spirito gentil" (Noble spirit) (Song 53) when he says in the third stanza: "Se l'universo pria non si dissolve" (If the universe does not first dissolve).

As far as rhetoric is concerned, anyone who wants to understand the great artistry of Dante and the great difference that exists between philosophers and orators, on the one hand, and poets, on the other, need only look at the hundredth text of the first book of the Heavens of Aristotle, from which Dante undoubtedly dug out this concept. Because what is stated by Aristotle philosophically, in simple terms and without any adornment or affection ("The being and existence of all things depend on eternity, for some more clearly, for others darkly"), is said by Dante poetically, with as much adornment as someone not far from the Muses can know. He used great and magnificent words, both proper and metaphoric, such as *gloria, universo, penetra e risplende;* he uses an expression such as *colui che tutto muove* instead of simply saying God, thus naming him according to so worthy an operation as movement. He said *penetra* to indicate great power and virtue such as that which penetrates everywhere, even to the lowest place. He said *risplende* to show that not only does he penetrate within but also lights up from outside and is thus visible to all who wish to see. He said *e meno altrove,* where he might ordinarily have said "in another place," using the adverb instead of the noun, as is often done in order to vary words. And finally it seems to be that in these three verses he expressed all that which Virgil, his master, so divinely expressed in the sixth book of the *Aeneid:* . . .

He makes his listeners attentive to the greatness of this beginning just as later he will make them docile and benevolent, which is, rightly speaking the purpose of a proem such as this; it is thus that the proposition serve poets and thus the invocation instead of the proem. And this will suffice as the explanation of Dante's words.

As far as the meaning is concerned, we must be aware that this proposition, that all things derive their being and their existence from God, although each one differently, is a part of natural philosophy. Thus, although theologians may adhere to the same principle, they are different in their manner since they concede creation, i.e., a generation, from absolute nothing, while this is denied by the Peripatetics. Thus Aristotle says that all philosophers agree in this basic proposition, that from nothing one creates nothing. Again, they are in disagreement because our theologians maintain, as our faith requires, that creation and thus things have a beginning, something again completely denied by the Peripatetics. Again, they are in disagreement because the theologians, in whom we Christians must believe, want that God should have created and maintained all things, and not so the philosophers. For them, all things from the moon down are generated and maintained directly by the heavens and by their own minds and intelligences, and mediated by God, that is, via the heavens, which is their instrument, and the movement and their worth are the instruments of the heavens. And thus this proposition, understood as we have stated it, is not theological but philosophical. And so that we may understand more clearly not only that all things have their being from God but also that they differ from each other, we must know that all things that exist are thus called entities or substances, and their order may be set out in a number of different ways. For the time being we will note that between these two extremes, i.e., between the first form which is God who is first above all things in existence, and the first substance, in which all things exist potentially and which is as imperfect and incomplete as God is perfect and noble, between these two extremes are contained all substances or entities in seven categories. The first and most noble, within which are found the Angels, is called Intelligence by the Philosophers. In the second are human beings because they have a rational soul. In the third are animals because they have sensitive souls. In the fourth are plants because they have a vegetable soul. In the fifth are inanimate but perfect minerals, such as metals and stones. In the sixth are imperfect *misti*, such as snow and sleet, arrows, the winds, and others like these. In the seventh and last are the four elements.

[From "On the Defense of the
Comedy of Dante"]
Iacopo Mazzoni*

From this we are able to conclude that it is not denied to the poet
to treat things pertinent to the sciences and the speculative intellect,
but he treats them in a credible manner, making idols and poetic
images, as Dante, with most marvelous and noble artifice, has certainly
done in representing all intellectual nature and the intelligible world
itself with idols and images most beautifully to all eyes.

I recall that Plato in the *Phaedrus,* exalting his own invention,
wrote just to this point: "But of that place that is beyond the heavens,
I do not know that any of the poets has ever treated or is likely to
treat it in a manner worthy of the way it is." And so on. But if he
had seen Dante's third canticle, he would without any doubt have
recognized his own invention as inferior and given the palm to Dante,
and consequently to poets for knowing how to make idols and images
appropriate to giving to the popular understanding the quality of the
supercelestial world. Concerning this I have written at length in the
fifth book where I also show with what tact Dante has at times
introduced either a philosopher or a theologian to discuss matters
pertinent to the contemplative sciences in an understandable fashion,
never deviating from the credible. The second conclusion is that,
since the poet has the credible as his subject, he ought therefore to
oppose credible things to the true and the false, the possible and
the impossible, by which I mean that he ought to give more importance to the credible than to any of the others I have enumerated.

Therefore, if it should happen that two things should appear
before the poet, one of them false but credible and the other true
but incredible or at least not very credible, then the poet must leave
the true and follow the credible. And if anyone wants an example,
let him read what I have written in the seventh-third chapter of the
third book, where it is shown that Ariosto has described the mouths
of the Ganges River according to credibility, departing totally from
the truth. And if the Ganges were such that its mouths faced the
south, as Ariosto has said, then it would also be necessary . . . to
say that Taprobana is New Zealand and not Sumatra. And yet Ariosto,
following the credible and leaving the true, has said that Sumatra is
Taprobana. This is discussed in the thirtieth chapter of the third
book.

The third and last conclusion, which is almost a corollary of the

* From Iacopo Mazzoni, *On The Defense of the Comedy of Dante. Introduction and
Summary,* trans. Robert L. Montgomery (Tallahassee: Florida State University Press,
1983), 78–80.

previous two, is that poetry, in order to give more importance to the credible than to the true, must be strictly categorized under the rational faculty named by the ancients "sophistic." And for a complete understanding of this truth, which (unless I am mistaken) has until now remained mysterious, it must be understood that the poetic art may be taken in two modes, that is, either according as it is concerned with the laws of the poetic idol, or according as it is concerned with fashioning or forming the poetic idol.

The first mode ought to be called "poetics" and the second "poetry." In the first mode is the ruling art, which uses the idol and is part of the civil faculty, as we will show a little further on. In the second mode is the art that forms and fabricates the idol and is a species of the rational faculty. As I have said, it ought to be included under sophistic, since it does not care about the true. I am aware that I may have offended the sensibilities of poets by fastening upon an art considered until now virtually divine and the title of sophistic, which has come to be thought repellent and scandalous. Yet to console them a bit I wish to dwell a bit upon the art of the sophists to show where it has or does not have positive or negative meanings. And for an easier understanding of what we have to say, I will set down here the words of Philostratus at the beginning of his *Lives of the Sophists*, which will be seen to contain a summary knowledge of the sophistic art very different from that commonly understood. Here then are the words of Philostratus:

> Ancient sophistic must be called philosophical rhetoric, since it argues the same things treated by philosophers. Those who bring forward questions and doubts about each little item, have neglected to understand the ancient sophists about whom they speak with such assurance. Even so, their introduction says, "I understand this," "I know this," "It is just a portion that I have considered." Or, "Nothing is permanent for men." Either this mode of beginning adds luster to an oration or it makes plainer what is going to be treated. It was part of human prophecy, which the Egyptians and the Chaldeans studied, and before them the Indians prophesied by means of the stars. It . . . belonged to the oracles, as the Pythian oracle said,
>
> "I know the number of grains of sand and how great the seas are."
>
> And this:
>
> "Of wood were the walls which Jove gave to Tritonia [Athens]."
> Also, both Orestes and Alcmeon killing their mothers and many other things similarly fashioned in the subjects that the ancient sophists practiced, and, drawing them out at length, they ornamented them everywhere with conceits, referring to the gods, heroes, justice, strength, and sometimes going even higher, they treated the creation of the world itself.

[From *Della Ragion Poetica* (Book II)]

Gianvincenzo Gravina*

To Madame Colbert, Princess of Carpegna,

> Poetry was introduced through mysterious speech, in which the sources of all wisdom and especially divine wisdom were hidden. Within the fable one could be led to the cognition of the healthiest and most secure thinkers. This was not handed down by the written word, but by the live voice and the tradition of the master to disciple. Thus, from its origins, poetry is the science of human and divine things converted into creative and harmonious images.

I. FROM DANTE'S DIVINE POEM

We recognize that this poetic image reaches the highest peak of expression in Dante's Divine *Comedy*. It also reached the greatest vivacity, because it is more widely and deeply conceived than any other poem in our language: with locution being the image of intelligence from which fabling draws its force and heat. And Dante adds to that such a great understanding and expression so that he could deduce his science from the knowledge of divine things, in which the natural and the human and the civil are reflected as in a terse crystal. Since every event, whether it be natural or civil, proceeds from God and in God is reduced, in the same way understanding of things appears imprinted and delineated in the science of divinity. Therefore, all of the wise men before Pythagoras and all the other Pythagoreans and philosophers up until Democritus, had always linked physics with theology and never did set foot into the obscure and thick woods of the natural motives and corporeal things, without bringing with them as an escort a light kindled by the contemplation of the incorporeal and the infinite substance.

Such were the first ancient poets, cited by us above: Orpheus, Linus, Musaeus, and Homer, who handed down to posterity divine and natural knowledge by way of allegory and fables, accompanied by harmony. In this way the sage, who in the early times was a poet alone, brought together theology, physics, and music, both that which is external to the sound and the song. From this it happened that mental exercise was understood as music, and bodily exercise became known as gymnastics.

* From Gianvincenzo Gravina, *Della Ragion Poetica Libri due* in *Scritti Critici e Teorici*, ed. Amedeo Quondam (Bari: Laterza, 1973), 273–78, 299–304. Translated for this volume by Mary Ann McDonald Carolan.

Democritus was the first who openly separated physics from theology and explained the natural effects from only the motion, representation, and site of the body, without mixing in the action of the vivified and divine nature. By this it was believed that he wished to exclude it from the being, when he did not exclude it even from his consideration of the purely corporeal effects, separating divine science from the natural science, which had always gone together. Before prose was introduced into doctrine, one confided in poetry, which was the speech of the wise men for a very long time.

Dante wished to transport those mysteries from distant times and places to our language, and he also wished to consecrate his poetry with religion and revealed heavenly theology, which is more worthy of the natural theology of the philosophers and the first poets. From this he takes the substance of his poetry-making, but he could not take the number and meter, which was one with the Latin language, yet so lost and changed in the rhyme of the vulgate with the rough usage of leonine verses.

II. ABOUT THE RHYME

One would like to attribute the filthy invention to those verses of one author or another, depicted by a Leonius, a Benedictine monk, or a Theodolus, a priest at the time of the Emperor Zeno, exactly as if one would like to attribute a contagion generated by the corruption of the universal air to one or another infected body.

We are accustomed to find double barbarity in literature: one in nature, the other in artifice. The barbarity of nature is in each one and at the beginning, or in the infancy of the arts. Because it is born of involuntary ignorance, it becomes domesticated and amended by the culture, to which the simple and innocent ignorance of nature easily bends. The barbarousness of artifice succeeds in doctrines when they tend toward the extreme and head toward corruption, and because this artifice is not born of a lack of news, but from perverted judgment, which wishes to dominate nature with the growth of arts and pomp. For this reason barbarity came to rebel against reason, being transported by voluntary and presumptuous ignorance. Because of the lack of hope of improving, it exceeds just measure and produces monsters, since the beauty of art lies near the boundary of nature. If art passes beyond this boundary on account of ornamentation and wit, instead of growing it destroys the whole and perfect form: like excessive food, which instead of nurturing it consumes, and like all things, when they exceed the prescribed lines.

Both the natural ignorance of barbaric nations and the already corrupted judgment of the Latin nations converge at the destruction of the ancient meter and at the production of the rhyme. They participate in the ignorance of nature, since the exchange of the Goths and the Vandals impaired the ear and disturbed pronunciation, such that the sense of quantity became extinct, which the ancients expressed in speech and discerned in their hearing. And therefore with the delicate distinction of verse from prose by feet having been generally lost in common usage, the usage of gross, violent, and nauseating distinction of similar endings was introduced.

There was also the barbarity of artifice. From the second century of our Redemption the declamatory school of rhetoricians had so honed ideas and so adorned style (as one sees even in the best of them, who were Seneca, Pliny, and Quintilian) that the invention, like the texture and the number, becomes affected and nauseating through pleasantries, juxtapositions, and similarity of sound. These ornamentations managed to be pleasant and agreeable to the ancients because they were used sparingly and almost prompted more by nature than by art.

Following that example of nature, Homer, who is the source of all beauty, displayed the first discreet use of similar endings, which was imitated by the poets and orators following him, Greeks as well as Latins, who were very great dissimulators of the artifice. After that, with judgment corrupted by the ear and the ear corrupted by judgment, the usage of similar endings became quite diffuse. The people became immediately accustomed to this usage, such that ever since the fourth century of our era, prose has been filled with it. In the prose, juxtapositions, parity of clauses, and similitude of denouement grew more by the use of the ecclesiastical writers than by any other group. This was particularly evident in the sermons given to the people, in which they sought to flatter the common ear, which was hungry for embellishment in order sweetly to bend the soul of the listener to the austerity of the Christian morality. The Holy Fathers make prudence appear well through the variety of their style, which in the disputes and the treatises addressed to serious and educated people is fine and virile, but in the harangues or sermons directed at the plebeians, it is more florid and pompous than usual.

And because in the Latin language similitude of the terminations in verses was already present, it is no marvel that this was received in the new vulgar tongue as a principle distinguishing verse from prose. The vulgar verse was not distinguished by feet, like the Latin, but only by the number of syllables, as evidenced by the great number of Latin meters, such as the hendecasyllable, the sapphic, the asclepiadian, and iambic, as Lodovico Castelvetro, the Varro of the Italian language, observes. Where there was space for a more expressive distinction, that is, that of the similar termination and sound, rhythm was called rhyme by the voice: because this rhyme followed in the place of the ancient rhythm or poetic harmony, it was identified by the barbarians more in the rhyme than in the accent or number of syllables. Yet the artifice of the rhyme is too far from nature because it reveals itself completely outside nature. On the contrary, the Greek and Latin verse is very close to nature because the measure of feet is hidden and relays to the ears only that harmony that results from it. But yet, Dante, wishing to compose in this new language, abandoned the rhyme; he would not have been reputed by the crude, rough ears of those times as author and composer of verse, which along with the rhyme was particularly distinct. Nevertheless, he wanted with all his power to conceal affectation and artifice from the similar endings, mixing in the middle of two rhymes one new one and interrupting the other rhymes with the new one to escape surfeit in the way he made the first tercets.

III. About the Vulgar and Popular Language of Italy

We shall now discuss the language in which Dante wrote, and we will draw as well as we are able the clearest and sincerest light of truth from the long and arduous controversies, which began in those most happy times, yet never again reopened in Italy, of the century of Leo X with the new glory of the Italian nation and speech, in which the most valiant and renowned men woke up from the torpor. As a matter of fact they still live in the eternal books of our authors, divided among themselves partly by the uncertainty of the material, partly by affection for the particular country, for the native Tuscan soil, for the common glory of Italy. In this context the major champions for Florentine language are Bembo, although he is a foreigner, followed by Varchi and almost all the rest of the Florentine formation; for the Tuscans, Dolce and Tolomei, with the rest of the Tuscans; for the rest of Italy in general, Trissino and Muzio, and as it appears to me, Castelvetro, and as everyone has noted, Castiglione.

Language is the university of words. Words are signs of things and concepts that can be expressed either by the sound of the mouth, called pronunciation, or by the motion of the hands, eyes, and face, which is called geste and action. Now one language can be better than another by its very nature: partly on account of the multitude of words and the similarity or proximity of the signified things, like those harsh-sounding words that express harsh things and those soft-sounding words that express pleasant things; partly for the harmony that is generated in the language from the pleasing mixture of vowels and consonants and from the thunder, or the raising or lowering of the voice, which we call accent, as well as from the duration of the long or short syllable, which have come to be called quantity and measure. The pleasure in the ear grows from the convergence of these elements, and to the ear belongs the judgment of the exterior perfection of speech. Other than the value that a language garners from nature, it can also get much value from artifice when it is applied to science, the arts, and doctrine and when it is disposed in oratorical and poetic harmony, combining with such use new numbers, new voices, and new proportions, with new colors, locutions, and representations, by which it becomes more flexible, more majestic, more varied, and more sonorous. . . .

XIII. About Dante's Morality and Theology

But it is time now to enter into the moral and theological feeling of this poem. If I wished to exhibit that feeling part by part, Dante alone would consume my entire work. Thus, we will turn solely to a general description. This poem, as everyone knows, is divided into three canticles, that of *Inferno, Purgatory,* and *Paradise,* which are the three spiritual states after death, corresponding to the three states of mortal life, which the poet also wished to represent under the three spiritual states, which in this poem serve as truth and image, that is, the signified and the signifier. Dante wished that the moral science of the three temporal states were still signified by the theological doctrines of the three spiritual states. According to its class and proportion, the penalty or prize that man is dealt after death from God's justice is also dealt him in some part during his lifetime from his own vice and virtue. From this similar teaching comes philosophy for the temporal life, and it also gives theology for spiritual life. Dante, after having entered into Hell and having known the penalties of all the vice, passes to Purgatory and observes the remedy of these very same vices; then, already purged and clean, he rests in the eternal beatitude and is in paradise. With that mysterious course he wished also to strip the voyage of every soul in this moral life, where, at birth, each one enters Hell, that is, in the shadows of vice of the original sin of all of us, which then is washed clean at baptism. Yet there are stains of concupiscence that remain after baptism. These remain propagate and distend themselves into civic life; they absorb us and beckon us to enter into a whirlwind of lust, ambition, avarice, and all the other vices by which our world is transformed into a temporal hell.

Seeing that in Hell every vice has an established punishment, so too in the world each vice brings by its own nature its own torture: since misery and travail of the mind are indivisible companions of each passion, which is followed by misery like the body is followed by its shadows and assisted by misery even in the middle of riches and victories and triumphs and acquisitions of provinces and entire kingdoms. The deformed aspects of those punishments conceived by Dante in his *Inferno* inspire dread and fear. Moved by this fear, the mind can prepare for flight from vice and pass to the state of purgation and amendment that the poet represents in *Purgatory*, where we can find the remedy of the new virtues opposed to the ancient wrongful actions and the hope of tranquility that enters into the soul when vice leaves and relinquishes its place to virtue. Whereas the punishments represented by Dante in *Inferno* tend to cause us to fear, those represented in *Purgatory* give us the remedy to evil, since with the opposite operation from vice we can happily acquire the suit of virtue. Tranquility follows the suit of virtue when it is joined with the cognition of God, represented by Dante in *Paradise*. Since as we are rising to the contemplation of the divine infinity, we strip from our mind the senses that tie us to vice and travails, and by removing the divine infinity from our senses we exclude it from particular and finite ideas, which, because they do not come into being except through our imagination, are the occasion for all errors and the roots of passions, to which greater troubles than pleasures are linked.

Now the mind frees itself from these developments, since while pilgrimaging in the body it lives in the infinite, perceiving the effects that derive from reasons other than the apparent ones, and leaves the mind to wait for that which it cannot reach and to fear that which it cannot attain and that from which we cannot flee. Therefore for its own good, it only learns from the divine order of things that which it is capable of possessing, which cannot be changed by our passions and forces. In that way, the errant and uncertain movement of the will is arrested by the intellect, happy and satisfied by the divine and infinite idea. In relation to this idea, all created things, and the judgment it has imprinted on us, are like the shadows that disappear in the sunlight, and with their departure they liberate the mind from desire and travail; in such a way that everything turns to that good, which the mind brings to itself not through dubious and fallacious external help but by its own ideas and its own faculty. And because each power of man has for its own object a good different and distinct from that of other powers, like we see in the senses that one takes pleasure in—one of which is sight, and the others are hearing and smell and taste. Therefore the mind, which is the source of life in that it shares and animates the functions of the body, also has as its object the same pleasures. But it employs its own faculty, that of intelligence, without involving the body. The mind has an object of good that is separate and distinct, that which is hidden in knowledge, which is characteristic only of and unique to thought, which is a continuous act and in no way separable from the soul.

Since the being of man is constituted by the mind, which is the dominant and enlivened part of man, so therefore the most appropriate object of his good and that most suitable to his nature is knowledge and science. Man can enjoy that good more if he liberates himself from those particular and limited ideas of the finite and narrow capacity of the corporeal senses and roams freely through universality, enlarging the knowledge of the true being, that is, the knowledge of divine and infinite nature. In Plato's philosophy such a separation from the senses and passage from the particular and corporeal ideas toward the incorporeal and universal was called the meditation on death: because while contemplating the soul withdraws from reality and while it still lives, it imitates the act of death. Therefore Dante also wanted *Paradiso* to signify the beatified life that the wise man enjoys, when through contemplation he detaches himself from the senses. One does not attain such enjoyment of natural beatitudes without having amended the mind from the realm of reason, represented under *Purgatory*, where Virgil also travels; for reason cannot exercise its forces against vice without first experiencing the fear of *Inferno*, under which the horrendous, and to us, painful, nature of vice becomes figured.

All the rest of the moral doctrine is exhibited by the poet bit by bit in the entire plot of his poem, where by means of representation and description each act of passion, as well as of reason, is applied to one character and then to another. The variety of characters gives a more lively idea of vice and virtue and more reason to escape those vices and to follow that virtue which produced the philosophers' definitions and rules. The poets are equal to the philosophers in the abundance of their opinions suitable to convince the intellect, but poets are superior in their efficacy to inspire imagination and change the course of operations by their expression, numbers, and valid representations. With a morality as Christian as it is philosophical, Dante also introduces the revealed theology, exposing in its place the mysteries. Yet he does not leave the texture to be infused, like the internal spirit, with a general feeling that the revelation theology of the Christians and the natural philosophy are equally suited. That feeling, because it results more from the harmony of the poem than from an express and certain place in the poem, will therefore be reduced to light by us from inside those depths, to serve as defense against those who, while not penetrating the high advice of the poet, believe that he confused Christian theology with the Gentile philosophy, going against all reason and dignity. Therefore, according to the Apostle who teaches us, the point and the center of all the rules is charity, that is, the complex and the knot of all virtues, which are the soul of the rules and of the law, just as the soul of the lyre is sound, of watches the motion, of day the light, where the poet Ariosto had to say of the sinful Christian: "Christian d'acqua e non d'altro ti fenno" (Christian by water and nothing else).

For that reason the observance of rules by sheer custom, like clothes, which is vulgarly called fashion, and the profession of which, directed not so much toward God but toward the human advantage, seems according to the same Apostle, a bell or a tambourine. These instruments issue forth a vain sound of words and the pure appearance of works devoid of internal virtue, in the same way as the operations of the Hebrews were reduced to pure ceremony.

On the contrary, wherever one finds a rule of virtue or an example, there Dante perceived the image and the dawn of Christian law. There the Holy Fathers proved the antiquity of this to the Gentiles, because they ran with horror from our law, as from novelty. Therefore the same Fathers demonstrated that the new revelation of mysteries had already been compiled quite a long time before the Hebrew prophecies and in the sibylline books, even though some crass simile of rules and Christian virtue also appeared in the teachings of the philosophers and the operations of the ancient wise men. For this reason Dante considered himself free from every blame in having placed Catone Uticense outside *Inferno* and in having intermingled examples of the Scriptures with secular stories and fables among the sculptures of the virtues in *Purgatory*. In the fables, however false the signifier, true no less is the sense of the signified, which is the moral doctrine and the seed of virtue contained within the fable. And he valued belonging to true piety, of which insofar as the honest and virtuous for all is sparse, and also insofar as the good of true or false narrations teaches. He used the secular stories as well as the fables only as representations of those virtues that cooperate with the law. The particular seeds, then, as with theology as well as moral and natural philosophy, are in particular sentences disseminated in all of this poem and linked to the rhetorical and poetical colors that can never be invented by art and can be learned and reduced to usage better through examples of imitating this poem that by the vain science of common rules. In the same way that the ancient Greeks extracted wisdom and eloquence solely from Homer, so Dante wanted to lend the same kind of utility with his poem. From inside it he offered to the disciples as much light as it was needed in order to understand well and reason better than one learns from the vulgar schools, where with public expense and private foolishness one learns only how not to recognize the true and the natural and to fortify ignorance with presumption. And just as Homer provided all the forms of speech, such that in him Aristotle discovers both tragedy and comedy, so Dante also describes the form of all styles, tragic in the lofty sense, comic and satirical in the mediocre and ridiculous, and lyric in praise and elegiac in sorrow, by explaining all the characters of the souls and their passions.

The Discovery of
the True Dante
Giambattista Vico°

Dante Alighieri's *Commedia* should be read from a triple perspective: as a history of the barbarous times of Italy, as a source of beautiful Tuscan sayings, and as an example of sublime poetry.

As far as the first one is concerned, it is ordered and set out by nature in this way: poets sing of true stories at the time when, within a certain uniformity in the course taken by their common spirit, nations begin to refine their own barbarousness—which is naturally open and truthful because it lacks reflection that, applied to evil, is the only mother of falsehood. So in the *New Science around the Nature of Nations*, we have professed Homer to be the first historian of gentility; this is confirmed in the *Annotations* that we wrote to that work, in which we have found Homer to be entirely different from what the world has hitherto believed him to be. And certainly the first historian of the Romans known to us was Ennius, who sang of the Carthaginian wars. In the same manner, Dante was the first Italian historian, or one among the first. What he mixed as a poet in his *Commedia* is the narration of the dead who reside, according to the merits of each, in hell, in purgatory, or in paradise. And here, as a poet, he must "sic veris falsa remiscet" in order to be like Homer or Ennius—conforming, however, to our Christian religion, which teaches us that the rewards and the punishments of our good as well as of our evil actions are eternal rather than temporal. Thus, the allegories of this poem are no more than those reflections that the reader of history must make by himself so as to profit from the examples of others.

Second, Dante should be read as a pure and vast source of beautiful Tuscan sayings. In this area he has not yet obtained a profitable commentary, and this is why it is commonly said that Dante has gathered the sayings of all the dialects of Italy. This false opinion can only be due to one thing: during the sixteenth century (cinquecento), learned men began to cultivate the Tuscan tongue, which was spoken in Florence in the fourteenth century—the golden century of this language. They noticed in Dante a great number of sayings that were not to be found in other Tuscan writers; since they realized by chance that some of them were still alive in the tongues of other Italian peoples, they believed that Dante had gathered them and brought them together in his *Commedia*. The same fate befell Homer: almost all of the peoples of Greece claimed him as their citizen, for

° From Giambattista Vico, "Discoverta del vero Dante ovvero nuovi principi di critica dantesca," in *Scritti vari*, ed. Fausto Nicolini (Bari: Laterza, 1940), 79–82. Translated for this volume by Cristina M. Mazzoni.

each people recognized in his poems its own native and living sayings. But such an opinion is false for two very serious reasons. First of all, in those times Florence must have had the majority of the sayings shared by all the other cities of Italy; otherwise the Italian tongue would not have been the same as the Florentine tongue. The second reason is that, in those unhappy centuries, there were no writers in the vulgar tongue in the other cities of Italy, as in fact none has come down to us. Therefore, Dante's own life would not have sufficed to learn the vulgar tongues from so many peoples so as to have available, during the composition of his *Commedia*, all those sayings that he needed in order to explain himself. Hence it would be necessary for the Academics of the Crusca to send throughout Italy a catalog of such words and sayings, especially among the lower orders of the city, who preserve the ancient customs and languages better than the noblemen and the men of the courts, and then among the peasants, who actually preserve even better than the lower orders of the cities such customs and languages. Thus, the Academics would be informed about how many and which ones of these are used and in what way, and they would thus gain a true understanding.

Third, Dante should be read in order to contemplate a rare example of a sublime poet. For this is the nature of sublime poetry: it does not let itself be learned by any artifice. Homer is the most sublime poet among all those who came after him, nor did he have a Longinus before him who could have given him some precepts of poetic sublimity. And even the principal sources shown by Longinus can only be enjoyed by those on whom it was bestowed and fated by the Heavens. The most sacred and the most profound of these are only two: first, a loftiness of the spirit, which cares only for glory and immortality and despises and disdains all that is admired by avaricious, ambitious, loose, and delicate men of effeminate habits; second, a spirit infused with great public virtues, above all, magnanimity and justice. The Spartans, for example, were forbidden by the law to be literate. However, without any artifice and thanks to the sublime education of their children imposed on them by Lycurgus, every day they used commonly such great and sublime expressions that the most famous heroic and tragic poets would do well to use similar ones in their own poems. But the greatest value of Dante's sublimity lies in the birth of his great mind during the times of the dying barbarousness of Italy. Because human minds are like plots of land: after being uncultivated for long centuries they are finally put to cultivation, and if at first they yield marvelously perfect, large, and copious fruit, they are soon tired of being more and more cultivated, and they yield few, tasteless, and small fruit. This is the reason that, at the end of the barbarous times, there came Dante for sublime poetry, Petrarch for delicate poetry, and Boccaccio for exquisite and graceful prose. All three are incomparable examples, which must in all cases be followed but which can in no way be attained. But in our most cultured times, some beautiful works of the mind are being crafted, in which others may erect themselves in the hope not only of attaining them but of actually surpassing them.

The anonymous author, I believe, took all this into consideration when he wrote his *Annotations to Dante's "Commedia."* In these, through a rare mixture of clarity and brevity, he makes probable the story of the things, events, and people mentioned by the poet, and he explains his feelings with reasonableness. It thus becomes possible to understand the beauty as well as the gracefulness of his sayings, their ornament as well as their loftiness. (This, in fact, is the most efficient way of attaining the language of good writers: to enter into the spirit of what they felt and of what they intended to say. And it is in this way that, in the cinquecento, so many very famous writers succeeded, both in prose and in verse, even before the celebration of the Calepini and of many other dictionaries.) The author of the *Annotations* omits every moral and any other erudite allegory, nor does he pontificate about poetic art; rather, he makes an effort so that youth may read him with that pleasure savored by human minds— a pleasure thanks to which, without the danger or being disgusted, they shortly learn much from long commentaries, to which commentators usually reduce with uneasiness all that they comment. Therefore I consider them most useful especially during these times, in which we want to know the essence of things with clarity and ease.

The Subject of the
Divine Comedy   Francesco De Sanctis[*]

Early critics did not and could not understand Dante. The *Divine Comedy* stood too far above their rules, too far outside them. Accustomed to judge a work by its conformity to established models, they did not know what place to assign to a poetry so original; believing that form consisted in style and language—which are simply its material means—they found its form still crude and coarse. This explains their preference for Petrarch as it does the manner in which the *Divine Comedy*, after long being unintelligently admired, fell into virtual oblivion. It was still quoted, still admired, as if by tacit

[*] From *De Sanctis on Dante*, ed. and trans. Joseph Rossi and Alfred Galpin (Madison: University of Wisconsin Press, 1957), 3–32.

agreement. *Sit divus, ne sit vivus.* They kept on calling it divine, but quit reading it.

The first modern critics, as romanticists, were biased and opinionated; this period of exaggeration is now past. Rising from controversy to a sense of higher unity, they have replaced the traditional, passive respect for the ancients with an enlightened admiration for them; they have restored the authority of the rules, which had become blind dogmatism, by relating them again to their generating principles; and they have opposed the imitations of the ancients while demanding in art at once the freshness and the truth of modern life. By withdrawing criticism from the petty disputes to which it had stooped, they have raised it to the contemplation of art in its essence and made it a science. They now proclaim the truth and independence of art and the freedom of form: in the name of truth, they proscribe all the literary and factitious elements that have crept into art; in the name of independence, they eliminate all those religious, political, and moral aims which mislead conventional criticism; in the name of freedom of form, they have learned how to appreciate and assign to its due place every true greatness, Homer's as well as Dante's, Shakespeare's as well as Racine's.

But these critics are not entirely free of the defect noted in the older school: they, too, often judge *a priori;* they set up certain general rules and measure everything by that standard. We already have a metaphysics of the beautiful which goes under the name of esthetics. From it critics have extracted and put into circulation a score or so of formulae which, detached from their generating principle and repeated on every occasion, are gradually losing all serious meaning, no longer understood by those who utter them and irritating to those who hear them. You can no longer discuss a work without having dinned into your ears such terms as dignity, order, decorum, elegance, purity; or finite and infinite, real and ideal, social literature, historical or philosophical literature, poet, painter, sculptor, musician, Idea and Truth, the Good, the Beautiful.

General rules are mere abstractions when viewed apart from a given subject matter to which alone they apply. They are applicable to the creations of art as they are to individuals in real life or to any category of the mind, but in each case they are subject to specific conditions and limitations which make each individual case what it is and not something else. Therefore, the essence of a subject is not what it shares with all other literary or artistic subjects, but what is peculiarly and incommunicably its own. A subject is not a *tabula rasa,* a thing on which you can imprint any shape you please. It is matter conditioned and determined, already virtually containing within itself its own poetics, that is to say its organic laws, its conception, its parts, its form, its style. It is a little world concealing in its bosom great treasures visible only to the poetic eye. A mediocre talent either fails to see anything at all, or sees only fragments of its riches, and by adding to it something extraneous, spoils it and does it violence. But the real poet yields lovingly to his subject, is carried away by it, buries himself in it, so to speak, and becomes its very soul, forgetting everything in his own nature that is not in harmony with it. You must fall in love with it, live in it, turn yourself into it; and then you shall see it, as if animated by your gaze, gradually moving and unfolding in accordance with its nature and revealing all its riches.

We shall try, therefore, freeing our mind of all preconceptions, to contemplate the Dantean world, to question it patiently, to call it back, insofar as we are able, to a second life. For the positive task of the critic is to relive, in his own way and with different means, the creative experience of the poet.

In Dante's time, epic narratives grouped around a few traditional characters—a king, a hero, paladins—were the fashion outside of Italy. Only later did the Italians take them in hand, and then only to make light of them while immortalizing them with a perfection of form unknown to the other nations.

As Italy lacked a Cid, an Arthur, a Charlemagne, so it lacked traditions of chivalry and feudalism. From this some critics, like Wegele, have too hastily concluded that it lacked national traditions, but there is a vast difference between the premises and the conclusions.

The traditions of chivalry derive from the early history of those whom the Italians at that time called "barbarians." The history of Italy, during a part of the Middle Ages, was the history of these, her conquerors. Later came an age of liberty and culture: the people waged war on the castles, the cities organized themselves into commonwealths, refusing to bow even to the Emperor. Now, this people that won its freedom was not the Goth, the Saracen, the Norman, or the Lombard; it was the conquered people, the Italian people, which had maintained a sense of national identity throughout all those invasions. It is a sense of national identity throughout all those invasions. It is a noteworthy fact that the Gauls became Franks; the Britons, Anglo-Saxons; the Spaniards were profoundly transformed by the Arabs; but the Italians remained Italians. And when, after a long and silent serfdom, they became their own masters; when, with the spread of a certain culture throughout the country, they were able to formulate their ideas; then they did not seek their traditions in the times when their homeland was under conqueror's heel, but leaping over the Middle Ages which they considered an age of oppressions, darkness and barbarism, they went straight to the history of Rome as to their own.

The *Reali di Francia*, for instance, widely read and distributed throughout Italy, inspired no literature. We awoke to find ourselves still Romans. So long an interval of time and such portentous events, were not strong enough to cut us off from the past which was ours. We were transformed but unaware of the change, believing ourselves to be still the same Roman people, masters of the world. With Roman pride we still called all foreigners "barbarians." No address was made to the Emperor without some mention of the grandeur and glory of Rome. Cola da Rienzo harangued like an ancient tribune. The historian never began his story without lingering a while on those pristine days. The Florentine boasted of his Roman origin. Even old wives told tales, not of Charlemagne or Arthur, but "De' Troiani e di Fiesole e di Roma" (Of the Trojans, of Fiesole, and of Rome.— *Paradise*, XV, 126).

These traditions had an important political significance in Dante's time; the Ghibelline party was founded on them, and Dante availed himself of them to support his own system in the *Monarchia*. He wished to continue the story of the Roman Eagle, to revive and perpetuate our past. At the base of those traditions was the *Aeneid* of Virgil, which combines the story of the origins of Rome with a glorification of the Empire. To it was added Roman history, mixed with the errors, customs, and opinions of Dante's time.

But while the poets of other countries could fashion epic tales out of traditions not basically inconsistent with their own times, our Poet was separated from our traditions by differences in religion and ways of life. Traditions, after all, do not consist in mere facts; they have their inner life in religion, customs, institutions, and doctrines which now for the most part were so dead that no poet could revive them. Hence those traditions could inspire nothing of essential value to literature; they contributed only accessory elements which contrasted, often grotesquely, with the living present.

Apart and aside from these memories was the fact of contemporary life, with the Christian ideal at its center. But while, with other peoples, this ideal could fuse with their national traditions, could descend to earth and mingle with their passions, with their vital interests, in Italy it remained as it was bound to remain, outside our national past. Thus we did not develop a type of poetry like the poem of chivalry, in which tradition and religion were molded into poetic unity. We had two purely religious types, the *Vision* and the *Legend*, dealing with the supernatural or marvelous. The first presented it in terms of the afterlife; the other in terms of miracles performed on earth. The two types often merged, the Vision penetrating the Legend and increasing the element of the marvelous in it. Cavalca's *Lives*, Passavanti's stories, the *Little Flowers of St. Francis*, offer many instances of this fusion, besides the long list of visions given us by Labitte, Ozanam, and Kopisch.

The emotion that dominated in these visions was generally the one best calculated to impress rude imaginations, terror. The Devil had the leading role, and the authors vied in ferocity in inventing the punishments of Hell and of Purgatory.

From the pulpit and the written page the visions soon passed into the market place; they were transformed into dramas and performed in public. The Devil, the damned and the penitent souls must have made as vivid an effect on the spectators as had the terrible Eumenides of the ancients. There was in all this a tragic concept, the damnation of the soul, presented in specific actions, in part narrated, in part acted out, as at the beginning of Greek drama. Now Dante took this subject, of which earlier writers had only glimpsed a fragment here and there; he took it, grasped it in all its breadth, and put at its base the concept of the soul's redemption. Thus the tragedy was transformed into a *comedy*, which later generations called "divine."

This subject is the final page of the human story; to use the language of poetics, it is the denouement of the earthly drama. The curtain has fallen; the gate of the future is closed; the action is over; the movement of freedom is followed by immutable necessity, by an eternal present. What essentially is all this? It is the death of liberty, the annihilation of history.

It is a perfect world, the last word of God, the final creation made in His image, in which matter is completely subdued by spirit. There is no accident, no mystery, opposition, or contradiction. Everything is determined, everything is set according to a pre-established and visible logic, according to the moral ideal. The antimony of real and ideal vanishes, the two terms have become identical. Hence art cannot reduce to its own terms this alien world sprung from pure thought and aware of its origin. Thought persists about form and no effort of the poet can make poetry rise from this prosaic substratum. Poetry, daughter of Heaven, should descend to earth and become incarnate; here she leaves the earth, soars above the human, above history, becomes a disembodied spirit, as immobile as a mathematical symbol, becomes science.

Our poet does not grasp this world in its immediacy, but must construct it himself from theological and philosophical concepts, according to Aristotle and Saint Thomas. He must be the philosopher and architect of his world before he can be its poet.

Here Nature is not the mysterious handiwork of God, the veiled Isis. Here you no longer have the fleeting phenomenon which, in the little it reveals, allows a glimpse into the unknown beyond, unattained and forever unattainable, the greatest charm of poetry.

Here appearance and substance are one: you are in the realm of Truth. The veil is transparent; the chaste secrets of Nature, the shadings of color, of light and dark, the false and half appearances, the contrasts, the individual features—all this is destroyed. On earth, Nature stands aloof from the varying interplay of human passions. This discord art at times attempts to overcome by calling with passionate illusion on Nature to share our joys and sorrows, or at other times accepts as the expression of a higher dissonance, of the indifference of Fate to human misery.

> . . . Roma antica ruina;
> Tu sì placida sei?

> . . . ancient Rome declines; so unmoved art thou?
> (Leopardi, "Bruto minore," 11. 82–83)

Here discord no longer exists. Nature becomes here the state which the poet sets for his play, a perfect image of the idea, an emblem of thought. The enigma vanishes, taking with it a whole world of poetry.

As accident is destroyed in nature, free will is likewise destroyed in man. In this world of immutability there can be no action, for it would be an absurdity. Clashes, intrigues, vicissitudes, catastrophes, all that which is the usual subject of poetry, no longer have any meaning. Consequently, there can no longer be an action gradually unfolding in the midst of opposing forces, arousing interest and suspense, as in the *Iliad*, the *Orlando*, and in similar poems and romances which are read so eagerly, in a single breath, as it were. You have instead separate scenes, each complete in itself; no sooner does one character awaken your interest than he suddenly disappears before your eyes, making way for another. Not only has all action ceased: every tie that binds men on earth is dissolved. There is no place here for fatherland, family, riches, dignities, titles, customs, fashions—every element in society which, however artificial and conventional, plays so great a role in poetry. Man stands here naked— Philip the Fair without his purple [*Paradise*, XIX, 120], and Nicholas III without his tiara [*Inferno*, XIX, 31]. What then is left to man? A general feeling of joy and sorrow, without succession, without gradation, without contrast, without echo, a sort of interjection. You have an eternal repetition. Here man fades into nature and nature into science.

Such is the subject. An epic is impossible because there is no action. Drama is destroyed at its roots because there is no liberty. The soul is as if stricken with paralysis and endures eternally in the state in which the affliction struck it. There is no clash of characters or passions; here man is dead—man as endowed with freedom, will, power, action. The lyric is reduced to a single string that repeats its solitary refrain, resembling rather the vagueness of music than the clarity of speech. What remains is existence in its changeless external traits, a mere object of description; even man is merely described, the poem remains in essence descriptive and didactic.

We have, then, two subjects: one, purely religious, thrusts poetry outside humanity, the other, historico-political, rests on traditions radically inconsistent with modern life. Hence, we have two poetic conceptions, each incomplete: one turns its back on life, the other blurs it by introducing discordant elements.

It is useless to dispute as to which of these two subjects came first to Dante's mind: namely, whether his passionately held political opinions led him to find the other world a fitting medium for their manifestation, as some believe, or whether the other world, as I am inclined to think, was first and seriously conceived for its own sake.

Be that as it may, Dante fused these two subjects, making of himself not merely the spectator but the protagonist of his world. A living man, he pierces the realm of shadows, brings to it all his passions as a man and a citizen, makes even the tranquil vaults of heaven shake to the echoes of human agitation: thus drama returns, and time is reborn amid the eternal. The Poet is like a bridge thrown between heaven and earth. At the sight and words of a living man, the souls are reborn for an instant, feel anew old passions, see again their fatherland, their friends. From the womb of the infinite springs again the finite. History reappears, and with it, characters and passions. Stirring amid the fixed woof of the future, Italy, indeed all Europe of the fourteenth century, lives and moves with its pope and emperor, its kings and its peoples, with its customs, errors, passions. It is the drama of that century staged in the next world and written by a poet who is himself one of the actors.

By means of this happy conception poetry embraces all life, heaven and earth, time and eternity, the human and the divine, the most abstract concepts and the most concrete reality. The doctrinal and mystical aspect of the next world is partially softened, and a poetry founded upon the supernatural becomes profoundly human and earthly, taking a distinctive imprint from the author and his time.

Earthly nature appears in the midst of the supernatural in the form of contrast, comparison, reminiscence; we see again our valleys, rivers, mountains, our cities and fields. The earth, transported to the other world, communicates to it something immediate and tangible, gives it a homelike atmosphere, and at the same time becomes there somehow more solemn, more ideally beautiful.

Accident and time, history and society reappear with all their inner and outer life—religious, moral, political, and intellectual; hence there takes shape in the bosom of the other world the epic, the natural heroic poem. It is the poem of humanity and also the poem of Italy. Dante can represent Italian traditions without being obliged, like other poets, to do violence either to antiquity or to modern life. In the afterlife social or national differences have vanished, all men are made equal by a common destiny. There is similarity of soul, not of appearance, title, or fatherland: Alexander can well stand next to Ezzelino [*Inferno*, XII, 107, 110], and Brutus can abide with Judas [*Inferno*, XXXIV, 62, 66].

Contemporary history can be paraded against this background of ancient traditions. The Pope, the Emperor, the King of Naples, the Cerchi, the Donati, the wraths and ambitions, the discords and customs of the time—such is the picture to which the Virgilian tradition can now serve as a magnificent framework.

Man is no longer motionless, and becomes flesh again. He is concerned about his memory on earth; he grieves or rejoices over the tidings he hears; he threatens, grows angry or revengeful; he preaches, admonishes, satirizes, and eulogizes. Passions, characters, earthly interests are reborn in all their manifold variety.

The Poet can portray himself to us in his most intimate and personal traits, in his loves, his hatreds, his private life. While striving toward a universal goal he can seek personal aims also, without thereby altering the unity of his world. He becomes the center of his own creation, its lyrical cry, its passionate echo.

Thus an infinite variety springs to life in a subject that by its nature is narrow and monotonous; there is now a place in it for everything in life, even the most transitory of its aspects.

This bold conception, which few of Dante's interpreters have shown themselves capable of comprehending, has been called a mixture, and qualified as strange and barbaric. Unable to perceive the link that binds the two worlds, and wishing to uphold the unity of the poem, critics have regarded one world as the principal, the other as accessory. Vellutello, Landino, Schlegel, Quinet, Ozanam, and, in part, even Hegel and Schelling, consider principally the mystical and supernatural side of the subject; others, instead, view the next world as a means, an occasion, almost as a weapon which the poet has forged in order to belabor his enemies with it. This latter group would restrict the immensity and the poetic wealth of Dante's conception to a narrow, prosaically conceived political scope, carrying the exaggeration so far as to see the other world as an allegorical veil of the present. To the former group, the earthly element is an intrusion, due to the passions of the poet, so that the poem, as one of them states, results in a strange mixture of the sacred and the profane. Schlegel waxes indignant at the poet's ghibellinism; Edgar Quinet is shocked to see that the singer's earthly passions trouble even the calm of Paradise; and did not Lamartine call this poetry a

"Florentine gazette"? For the others, who look principally to the historical and political aspect, like Marchetti, Troya, Foscolo, Rossetti, Aroux, the seriousness with which the Poet represents the next world, too genuine for an allegory, is very embarrassing. Thus the two schools sacrifice one world to the other. Dante intended to put into his poem both heaven and earth; they see only heaven, or only earth.

What is this poetry? It is human life viewed from the other world.

Life has inexhaustible wealth and, depending on your point of view, it reveals to you new sensations, new emotions, new aspects. If the horizon changes, the view changes with it; the same things appear to you with a different face; you seem to have acquired a sixth sense which reveals a new world and brings it before your eyes with all the freshness and wonder of first impressions.

Dante has added this new sense to poetry by changing its point of view. Ordinary poetry has its abode on this earth; the celestial beings descend to earth, mingle with men, become actors. Dante, by transporting earth to heaven, has reversed the basis. The other world transforms bodies into shades; the emotions, the grandeur and pomp of the earth, become shadows; history is transfigured and spiritualized. The most commonplace persons, the most unimpressive things, acquire a meaning and become poetry when envisaged from the other world. Ciacco and Taide, with the seal of eternity on their brows, attain ideal proportions and arouse feelings they would not excite on earth. Contemporary history resists poetic treatment because it portrays a reality without shadows, with fixed outline, refractory to the imagination; but when placed in the other world its reality quivers before you, becomes transfigured; the best known characters acquire a different aspect as they stand before you on the pedestal of the infinite. Farinata, appearing as a contemporary of Capaneus, is viewed in a perspective of two thousand years. The marvelous comes forth by itself, without any need of being sought for, by virtue of the situation alone. You have new attitudes, new sensations, and new ways of expressing them.

What is this poetry? It is the earth seen from the other world. You may add: it is the other world seen from the earth.

In vain will you tell the Poet: "You are entering a temple; divest yourself of your passions, purify yourself, turn your back on mundane interests." He will say the same himself, and repeatedly; but he will do nothing of the sort. The earth pursues him even within the sanctuary; in the very presence of God he curls his lips to sarcasm and hurls a last imprecation upon Florence:

> . . . al divino dall'umano,
> All 'etterno dal tempo era venuto,

E di Fiorenza in popol giusto e sano.

> *(Par.* XXXI, 37–39)

. . . (I, who) to the divine from the human, to the
eternal from the temporal, had come, and from Florence
to a people just and sane.

"Human" and "divine," "temporal" and "eternal"! Heed him
not, they are abstractions of his mind. The human persists alongside
the divine, and the temporal beside the eternal.

Like a traveler who observes faraway lands with his mind still
possessed by his fatherland, through the memory of which he views
all that he encounters, even so Dante sees the other world through
the earth and through his own passions. Thus life is integrated, the
other world emerges from its abstraction, heaven and earth mingle,
and a poetry conceived in the heights of the most abstruse mysticism
descends into the most intimate and vivid reality. Here is the greatness
and the verity of the conception in this omnipresence of the two
worlds reacting upon one another, explaining and tempering one
another. One world constantly follows, crosses, penetrates, alternates
with the other; everything is replete with this unity. The Poet breaks
the earth into fragments from which he reconstructs his two worlds,
so that the reader, looking at the whole, can well say, "I have a new
world before me"; but considering a detail here or there, is forced
to think of Florence or of Rome. You stand in "a place mute of
light" and stormy, and there suddenly looms before you the seashore
where the Po descends,

> Per aver pace co' sequaci sui.
> *(Inf.* V, 99)

To have peace, with its followers.

Francesca, enraptured in memories of the "happy time," strolls
in memory through her beloved garden; then, coming to the kiss,
the thought of Hell flashes through her mind and that kiss becomes
motionless, is prolonged through all eternity:

> Questi, *che mai da me non fia diviso,*
> La bocca mi bacio tutto tremante.
> *(Inf.* V, 135–36)

> The one, *who never shall be divided from me,*
> kissed my mouth all trembling.

How heart-rending is this parenthetical remark, which seems to
be made so casually! The two worlds meet at the instant of sin and
are fused together.

Farinata, at the news of his party's fall from power, remains absorbed; his mind is concentrated on Florence when, to express the immensity of his grief, he is reminded of his fiery bed:

Ciò mi tormenta più che questo letto.
(*Inf.* X, 78)

It torments me more than this bed.

In the very heart of the past, as he relives it, the present returns as a term of comparison—and what a comparison! Nothing can equal the grandeur of Farinata as the Poet, without any effort, simply by virtue of the situation, puts Hell under his feet. Poets, when they wish to represent beauty and strength on earth, are wont to borrow colors from heavenly things, in which they place the true abode of everything ideal. Here the metaphor is reality, the figure is the letter; one world is the paragon, the image, the light of the other.

If this subject is not left in its doctrinal generality, in its abstract spiritualism, that is because the seer is Dante. Other writers of visions either related them Homerically, remaining outside them, or like Passavanti they intervened to intrude moral observations; they were, for the most part, clerics and ascetics, detached from the world, inexperienced in life, alien to mundane passions and interests. Dante threw himself completely into the subject; and *Dante* means all the life of that epoch, in its various forms, summed up in a poetic soul. By becoming an essential element of his subject, Dante modified it profoundly to the advantage of his poetry.

In order, then, to complete the study of the subject, we must study Dante, an inseparable part of that subject; Dante not only as the Homer, but also as the Achilles of his world; not only the poet, but also the man.

CHARACTER OF DANTE AND HIS UTOPIA

I call that man a poet who feels a whole world of forms and images stirring confusedly within him; forms fluctuating at first without precise determination, rays of light not yet refracted, not yet graded in the brilliant colors of the iris, scattered sounds not yet combined into a harmony. Everyone, especially in his youth, is something of a poet; everyone has sometimes felt within him the knight-errant, has dreamed his Fairies, his golden palaces, has had, in Goethe's words, some lady to protect, some villain to chastise. For most of us this state is transitory; reality snatches us only too soon from golden dreams and puts our nose to the grindstone. The world of imagination endures only in the soul of the poet, over which it takes possession, straining within, eager to break forth. Now, there is a solemn moment in everyone's life when he discovers his real self. We need an outside stimulus to receive this divine revelation, to be able at last to say, "*That* is what I was born for!" The life of Dante began the moment his eyes met those of Beatrice; and when he saw her a second time, when in the heat of emotion he recalled the powerful impression she had made on his still boyish spirit, then art was revealed to him and he knew he was a poet.

It is principally through love that the poet can realize and allay the vague world of images that storms within him, because other ideals that deeply stir the soul, like glory, liberty, fatherland, cannot be represented unless they are given a human likeness. In love a soul discovers itself in another soul; in love alone, what elsewhere is a figure becomes a reality. Read the *Vita Nuova*, the first intimately personal narrative in modern times, read Dante's lyrics! You will find *canzoni* and sonnets inspired by some real event which, like a flint, strikes sparks from his soul; some event insignificant and commonplace in itself, but affecting most powerfully the lover's heart. A greeting, a chance encounter, a glance suffice to arouse in him ecstasies, visions, raptures, frenzies of ineffable emotion. Nor is this surprising: because his feeling is infinite and invisible, the lover can find his own reality only in the beloved, whose least trifle—a glove, a flower, a smile— will cause all his heartstrings to respond.

Beatrice died, and after lamenting her loss for a time, and com- memorating it in song, Dante turned to practical affairs and politics. Peaceful studies and young love were succeeded by family cares and political passions; Dante the artist became Dante the citizen. In this field a man usually discovers his own character, acquires full con- sciousness of his personality and strikes to impose it upon others. One man's personality may be weakened in the struggle against obstacles, another's strengthened. In this power of resistance lies mainly what we term a great character. But there are different sorts of greatness. There are men of action, born to rule, who know how to stoop and blandish in order to draw others to their side more easily; who, keeping their goal constantly in view, are nevertheless able to assume countless deceptive appearances, and though misun- derstood by the multitude who call them fickle, are conscious in their own hearts of having always been true to themselves. Dante did not possess this kind of greatness. He was not a born party leader, and he resembled Cato rather than Caesar. Men with this disposition are born unlucky, always admired but never heeded.

Giusti son due, ma non vi sono intei!

(*Inf.* VI, 73)

There are two just men, but they are not heeded there!

Inflexible and severe, he was a man of passion and conviction. He could neither comprehend nor tolerate the vices and errors of his contemporaries; nor could he turn them to his own advantage, nor throw himself into the struggle of selfish interests, hypocrisy, and violence, in order to draw good out of evil, as those who wish to rule are forced to do. As a Prior he found himself compelled to banish his best friend, in a hopeless attempt to pacify the contending parties; he allowed himself and his party to be overpowered by the craft and violence of the Blacks, and he gave them time to perfect their sinister schemes by accepting an insidious and ineffectual embassy. As an ambassador to Boniface he succeeded only in getting himself lulled and beguiled, and saw himself deprived of country and goods, and Florence of freedom, almost before he knew what was happening—a sequence of events that later became a source of unending wrath to the poet. As an exile he cannot long retain in his party the position befitting his mind and character, and he could neither impose his own views nor conform them to those of theirs. Almost inevitably he developed a distaste for mankind, became as harsh to friends as to foes, and eventually stood alone, a party for himself.

Some have found grounds for praise in this attitude, imagining Lord knows what hidden and magnanimous intentions; but Dante was alone not by choice but by a necessity of his nature. He who wishes to live among men must accept them as they are, and he who wishes to rule them must understand them. Dante was too scornful of all baseness, too intolerant; the present escapes the grasp of such solitary characters, but the future is theirs.

Withdrawing from action, taking refuge in study, Dante returned to the composition of his only true action, the *Divine Comedy*, whose effects transcend the narrow circle of contemporary aims and interests and whose only bounds are those of humanity and the world. There he brought together in one volume, together with the destiny of mankind, his own sorrows, his hates, his vengeance, his hopes. And I say "hates" and "vengeance" advisedly, for Dante hated and was hated, was offended and took revenge.

I cannot compare, without a feeling of sadness, the young lyric poet with the mature author of the *Comedy*. In his lyrics you see a man to whom the world is still strange and new, on which everything smiles; his universe is all in the eyes of a woman, his virgin soul has no place for any feeling but love, his verses have not a word of hate or of rancor. And how changed is he now! His horizon has widened, he has seen many cities, many people; courts, councils, peoples, characters, passions, customs, all reality lies spread out before him like an open book. Heretofore he has contrived sonnets and ballads; experienced in life, he can now compose a poem. But the world in which he moves causes a profound disquiet in his spirit. "What seekest thou?" a friar asks him: and the tired old man replies, "Peace!"—a peace he was to find only in death.

The seeds of all the passions lie dormant in a man's heart, until some spark kindles them to flame and they burst out with a violence that surprises even himself. In Dante, civic strife roused passions of great violence, hitherto unknown to him and exacerbated by misfortune. Happy the days when the artist could yield serenely to contemplation, without the profane cry of mundane interests to disturb him! Happy the Greek artist! There are times when the poet's pen is a sharp sword. Dante's poetry is a battle engaged against his enemies, his world a stage on which he plays a part, singing and fighting at the same time, at once Homer and Achilles.

But the new man did not obliterate the old, and under that wrath is hidden a great treasure of love, a great tenderness under that violence. Biographers present only one side of Dante's character. Most of them show him disdainful and vindictive, while the others, rushing to his defense, try to show how every word he wrote conforms to historical truth and justice. When I read his life as written by Cesare Balbo, a writer so amiable in his severity and so dignified in his temperance, I see gradually emerging from those pages a figure of Dante all love and sweetness like a dove.

The real Dante is neither one of these simplified portraits—or rather he is both of them together. A passionate and impulsive man, of straightforward nature, he yielded completely to the fleeting impression of the moment, as terrible in his wrath as he was compassionate in his tenderness. Those who see a logical connection among the varied outbursts of eloquence or sermonizing that have flowed from his pen, waste their time and their effort. One who would write a true life of Dante must first abandon the field of polemics where in combating one extreme we are driven into another position no less untenable; one who will draw his portrait full-face, not in profile, will present him in his entirety, just as he is, with all his sorrowful alternations of love and hatred, wrath and despair, as energetic in love as in hate, conceiving both Hell and Paradise, Francesca and Filippo Argenti, Farinata and Cavalcanti; now calling his fellow citizens "bestie fiesolane" [Fiesolan beasts—*Inferno*, XV, 73], then exclaiming pitifully, "Popule mi, quid feci tibi?" [O, my people, what wrong did I do thee?]

We are inclined to idealize men and to imagine them cast all in one piece. He who commits a crime is immediately called a tiger. But nature is varied in her ways, and often delights in contrasts harmonized by imperceptible gradations. Achilles bestially outrages the corpse of Hector, and in the presence of Hector's old father is moved to tears. Dante is so compassionate that he swoons at the story of Francesca and Paolo, and so ferocious that' he can conceive and describe with frightful precision the skull of one man crushed under the teeth of another.

In civilized times we learn to control gestures and words, to preserve at all times an air of kindliness in our countenance, so that a so-called well-bred person is more likely to commit a vile deed than an incivility. Dante is closer to nature, and reveals himself bluntly.

He is essentially a poetic character. His dominant trait is a power that breaks forth freely and impetuously. Misfortune, rather than humbling him, fortifies him and raises him still higher. Compelled to eat the bread of others, to beg for patronage, to endure the banter of servants, no one has ever felt more clearly his own superiority over his contemporaries nor raises himself higher above them. The famous letter in which he refuses to return to his home with loss of honor not only reveals a spirit never inclined to cowardice, but in almost every line shows the mark of this noble pride. "It is not this the way of my return to my fatherland; . . . but if another may be found that does not injure the good name and the honor of Dante, I shall accept it gladly. And if one cannot enter Florence in some such manner, then I shall never enter Florence."

This is the language of a great soul but a proud one; there is a man conscious of his own greatness, "I, Dante Alighieri!" From the height of his pedestal he looks down with scorn on the plebs, on all that is plebeian, more ready to forgive a crime than an act of cowardice. A serious and ideal nature is best apprehended in terms of its opposites; the opposite of Dante is the plebeian. You almost have the impression that he felt he belonged to a race superior not just in blood and intellect, but in spirit. Yet there is nothing of merely passive dignity in this attitude, for his is not a coldly stoical nature: his inner fire blazes forth violently. He has the virtue of indignation, the eloquence of wrath. All the faculties of his soul break forth with passionate impetuosity. And when from his state of wretchedness he rises to his full height above the powerful who trample him, and inflicts upon them everlasting wounds, we can understand Virgil's enthusiasm [*Inferno*, VIII, 45]. To be sure, he has his moments of discouragement and surrender, but in him the most piercing emotion of grief gives way almost at once to energetic resistance. With all his misfortunes, there is not a page of his work dominated by that sentiment of moral prostration, that gloom and debility that are so common among moderns. One might even say that his grief turns to wrath in the very effort of expression, so prompt is the reaction of his energetic nature. Now, this supreme scorn for all that is base, this way of building his own pedestal, of crowning his own brow, this inner grief so proudly restrained—so that while his heart bleeds his countenance threatens—stamp his austere figure with a moral grandeur truly colossal, reminiscent of his Farinata.

In his youthful years everything sings of Beatrice; later, when he enters public life, Florence becomes the center toward which all his thoughts converge. Finally, when he takes up with more ardent zeal the study of theology and of philosophy, his horizon widens, he emerges from the narrow circle of Florence rising toward a unity not merely Italian but human: he becomes cosmopolitan. He looks beyond his contemporaries, thinks of posterity; fame is not enough, he wants glory. To be sure, as we grow old we are inclined to generalize, and what in us was personal feeling becomes maxim and sentence. But in Dante the personal element survives in a higher form. Underneath his "humanity" there is still Florence which can still arouse longing in the exile's heart, as you can tell by his very imprecations; and underneath the Beatrice of his mind you can still sense the Beatrice of his heart. Do not believe him when he professes to have no concern except for posterity, to be a fearless friend of truth. There is too much bile in his truth, too much passion in his justice. The thought of posterity is inseparable from his longing for vengeance, his hatred for his enemies, his partisanship, his hope of repatriation, from all the vital issues of his time. His passions obsess him at times amid his most abstruse speculations, and Florence, his party, his enemies mingle with his syllogisms.

And yet, even when he is patently in the wrong, even when he gives way to wrath, to accusations and unrestrained vituperation, you cannot, I shall not say scorn him—Dante is always above scorn—but you cannot feel irritated with him. You realize that his passion is always sincere, that those impulses spring straight from the heart, that he works and speaks with the most profound conviction. If he affirms that he speaks the truth, he believes he speaks the truth; if he accuses, he has faith in the accusation; and if he exaggerates, he is unaware of it.

He is the type of the proscript that has continued to our own time. With such warmth of spirit, such power of passion, he is out of active life just when he most feels the need of it. He is banished, the world goes on without him and against him, but Dante is not resigned to the situation. Plotting with a "compagnia malvagia e scempia" [an evil and senseless company—*Paradiso*, XVII, 62] soon disgusts him, and the only activity of this great man consists of a few futile epistles occasionally addressed to peoples and princes, of a few treaties and settlements negotiated in behalf of his protector. His passion, intensified by inaction, explodes with all the greater violence and bitterness in his writings. Now he bursts out thunderously like a storm long held in check; now he seeks refuge in the realm of fancy and plunges into the most abstruse mysticism. He becomes taciturn, melancholy, restless, impatient. Remote from active life, seeing the realm of the real and the possible ever escape his eager grasp, he builds a world of imagination in which he arranges people and things in accordance with his desire. Such are the dreams of exiles, which most of them carry with them to their graves; but Dante's dream was immortal.

What was this Dream? That is to say, what was Dante's concept of the universe? Our dreams and our aspirations are outgrowths of our opinions and of our knowledge.

Dante was very learned; his mind embraced almost all knowledge. Learning at that time was so rare, so difficult to acquire, that it was in itself sufficient to establish one's fame as a great man. And Dante was celebrated more for the abundance and variety of his erudition, than for the greatness of his mind; while few are capable of appreciating greatness of mind, anyone can pass judgment on the material fact of learning.

He mastered the whole intellectual world of his time: theology, philosophy, history, mythology, jurisprudence, astronomy, physics, mathematics, rhetoric, poetics. And when to all this you add his travels and embassies, which gave him the opportunity to know such a variety of people and things, you can affirm without exaggeration that he surpassed his contemporaries in experience and learning. Nor was his information superficial, for there is no idea that he cannot express with clarity and mastery.

Science was still a new world imperfectly explored. Antiquity was barely rising on the horizon, and men's minds were more intent on gathering than on discerning; it was the age of admiration. Men bowed to the ground before great names, and accepted eagerly any opinion to which they could attribute a noble ancestry. A mass of ideas, drawn from various sources, had thus been gradually accumulated; no one cared how consistently for no one looked at it too critically. Most people were satisfied with provisional synthesis of facts which, examined separately, would often appear incompatible or contradictory. But serious thinkers were not easily satisfied; casting a penetrating glance on this jumble-heap, they strove in some cases to harmonize philosophy and dogma, in others to point out the conflict between them.

Dante was pre-eminently a dogmatic spirit. The science of the time seemed to him the last word, and he endeavored rather to master than to examine it. He knew everything, but he left on nothing the imprint of his own thought: consequently he cannot properly be called a philosopher, a physicist, a mathematician, or the like. He accepted with perfect credulity the most absurd statements of fact and a large share of the errors and prejudices of his time. With what naive reverence he quotes Cicero and Boethius, Livy and Orosius, placing them on the same level! His mind submitted to the authority of the *Ethics* as to the Bible, to Aristotle as to St. Thomas; he believed implicitly that the great philosophers of antiquity agreed with the teaching of religion, and that they were wrong not because they saw wrongly, but because they did not see everything. I cannot see where Kannegiesser, Witte, and Wegele have discovered that Dante, having lost his faith through excessive love of philosophy and fallen into the vacuum of skepticism, wished to express in his allegorical journey his recovery, his return to faith. This is judging other times by the ideas of our own. Dante's theology does not conflict with his philosophy but completes it; Beatrice is not in contrast with Virgil but above him; Dante and Faust are centuries apart.

Dante, then, expounds things supernatural in accordance with Revelation, and for the rest puts together pagan and Christian writers. A citation is an argument. Of course I do not mean to suggest that he is always satisfied with quotations; he too wishes to demonstrate, but his philosophizing is no better than his philosophy, he has the usual shortcomings of his time. He demonstrates everything, even the commonplace; he gives equal importance to all questions; he lumps together all kinds of arguments, and beside some of real value you will find others altogether childish; he is often unable to see the heart of the question, to view it from above, to sift the incidental from the essential; he gets lost in minutiae and subtleties, and drowns you in distinctions.

Philosophy was not a vocation for Dante, not a lifetime goal toward which he directed all the forces of his spirit. It was a postulate, a point of departure. He accepted philosophy as it was taught in the schools, and acquired a complete and exact knowledge of it. Upon this groundwork he labored to erect a political system. He was therefore not a man of pure speculation; finding himself involved at an early age in public affairs, he turned his thoughts to politics.

It is remarkable that the famous contention between pope and emperor did not give rise to two different schools of philosophy. There was not a Guelf philosophy and a Ghibelline philosophy. Both parties accepted the same basic principles. There were indeed some individual exceptions, Ghibellines who pushed on daringly beyond Catholicism, but even for them the dissent lay in a certain number of more or less unimportant details, the system as a whole never being questioned by anyone. No new theology and philosophy were created.

The struggle was therefore not between two philosophies. The two parties accepted the same foundation, but each raises on it a different structure.

They accepted the distinction between mind and matter, and the pre-eminence of mind—the foundation of Christian philosophy. And, as a corollary, they accepted the principle of the two powers in society, the spiritual and the temporal, the Pope and the Emperor.

Thus far Guelfs and Ghibellines, Boniface VIII and Dante, were in agreement, but the systems they built upon that common base were different.

If it is true that the spirit is superior to the flesh, Boniface argued that it must be equally true that the pope is above the Emperor. "The spiritual power, says Boniface, has therefore the right to institute the temporal power, and to call it to judgment when it is not good. . . . And he who resists, resists the very order of God, unless he fancies, as do the manicheans, two principles; which we condemn as error and heresy. . . . Therefore every man must submit to the Roman Pontiff, and we declare . . . that this submission is necessary to the salvation of the soul."

Dante accepted all the premises, and in order to deny the consequence he maintained that spirit and matter were endowed each with its own life, without interference with the other; and from this he inferred in independence of the two powers, the spiritual and the temporal. Having started on this path, Dante went all the way, and built to suit himself. The people are corrupt and wish to usurp power, society is wicked and contentious: the only remedy is the Emperor. Dante attributes to him all the privileges of the Pope and makes him, like the Pope, directly responsible to God. Both are organs of God on earth, "two suns" [*Purgatory*, XVI, 106] who guide humanity, one in the ways of God, the other in the ways of the world, one to heavenly and the other to earthly happiness; both are equal, except for the reverence the Emperor owes the Pope—the only concession Dante makes to the superiority of the spirit. Rome by divine right should be the capital of the Empire and therefore of the world. The franchise of the communes and the independence of the nations were to remain inviolate. The Emperor would be all-powerful, but in his very omnipotence he would find his check. Through him justice and peace would triumph on earth. Such was Dante's utopia.

It was no simple return to the past, as Wegele claims. In it we find elements of the past and of the future, progress and regression. What belongs to the past need not be indicated here. But in it we see the germ of the liberation of the laity, and the pathway to larger social units. You glimpse the nation succeeding the commune, and humanity succeeding the nation. It is a dream which has in part become history.

It was basically the dream of the Ghibellines. Dante's merit lies in having expanded it into a system, in being its philosopher, in rising to the concept of humanity. The foundation is weak, but the edifice is beautiful by the vastness of its design and the harmony of its parts.

In any age two opposite extremes can be found, represented by parties or individuals. Seek Dante at these extreme points and you will not find him. Nevertheless, partisans insist on dragging Dante over to their side, each advancing plausible arguments. Some see in him a good Catholic, some a heretic, some a visionary, some a conservative. As they view his character from a biased position, so they see his opinions. Theirs is a Dante divested of part of himself and placed at an extreme position.

Dante reflected the feelings of the masses. As in the masses past and future stir confusedly together, so in Dante two men are mingled together, the man of the past and the man of the future. Catholic in intent, he was neither a Catholic in every respect nor was he in every respect a heretic. Inseparable from his Catholicism is the bitter way he wages against the corruption of the papacy, as are certain bold opinions already revealing a kind of vague disquiet, confused aspirations which were to penetrate the human consciousness in later ages. But basically the problem for him, as for the masses, was not religious but political. If he boiled with indignation, if he threatened, scolded, and cursed, it was because he faced, not a hostile religion, but a hostile politics. Yet even in politics he kept his ideas within a golden mean, letting Ghibelline ideals predominate but without rejecting the main tenets of the Guelfs. If indeed he wished the papacy reformed, he respected its independence; if he wanted the communes to submit to the emperor, he also insisted that their liberties be respected; if he wanted nations unified, he wanted their autonomy upheld. To be sure, the realization of his system would have destroyed all those things, but nevertheless Dante did want to keep them. The Guelfs, of course, did well to follow logic rather than Dante.

His system did not remain a pure and serene speculation like Plato's *Republic*, but took total possession of his whole being. It was not merely his conviction, it was his faith; and faith is more than mere belief, it is will, love, and labor; it is more than mere thought, it is also sentiment and action: Dante was a man of faith.

He had faith in God, in virtue, in father land, love, glory, in the destiny of mankind. His faith was so vital that misfortunes and disappointments could not enfeeble it; to the last he held hopes of imminent redemption, and he died with all his youthful illusions and passions intact. Who can say at what moment Dante felt old: was it when his pen dropped from his weary fingers?

Faith is love; and it is not only wisdom, but love of wisdom. It is not only Sophia but also *filosofia* [philosophy]. And philosophy was Dante's beloved, his second Beatrice, the "amor che nella mente *gli* ragiona" [the love that discourses in his mind].

Philosophy is "amoroso uso di sapienza, figliuola di Dio, regina del mondo" [loving use of wisdom, daughter of God, queen of the world]; when God set the spheres in motion, she was present:

Costei penso chi mosse l'universo.
                    (Second Song of *Convivio*, 1, 72)

Of her was he thinking who set the universe in motion.

Philosophy, then, was for Dante the science of things human and divine, the science of the world, the universal content in which he found defined all the objects of his faith—God, virtue, humanity, love, and so on. It was not only speculation on the sweetest truths, but also the foundation of his life, and he conformed his conduct to its teachings. "Absi a viro Philosophiae domestico temeraria terreni cordis humilitas. . . . Absit a viro praedicante justitiam, . . . Nonne dulcissimas veritates potero speculari ubique sub coelo?" [Far be it from a friend of philosophy this abasement befitting a heart of clay. . . . Far be it from a preacher of justice. . . . Can I not speculate on the sweetest truths anywhere beneath the sky?] This "friend of philosophy," as he with rightful pride termed himself, did not believe in her only in the abstract, but devoted his whole life to her, was impassioned by her, enraptured in that mystical exaltation called enthusiasm.

One who sees with what fervor Dante plunges into the most profound speculations, might say, "There is something mystical about this man, something ascetic"; and this is true. But this ascetic does not stay locked in his cell, a solitary contemplator. He belongs to the church militant, he is a soldier in the service of truth. He envisages a philosophic world, and endeavors to make the world of reality conform to that image. He strives for that goal with his pen when he cannot do so with his deeds; he writes letters, treatises, poems, always with that image before him. But he finds the world too far removed from his vision, and the contrast between idea and reality perturbs and embitters him; in every page he writes, you sense not the tranquil philosopher but the warrior, made more savage by the resistance encountered.

Is his passion always the result of unalloyed enthusiasm? I shall not try to make a saint out of our hero: the heavenly spark in him is mixed with clay.

Enthusiasm is the poetry of passion; take away enthusiasm and passion becomes an animal instinct. In our passions there enter elements, often unknown to us, of pride, personal interests, enmities, antipathies, prejudices; these are purified and ennobled by enthusiasm.

You may tell me, "You are angry with such a person because he insulted you"; I need not blush with shame if I can reply, "True, *homo sum,* I am only human; but I am also indignant because he is wicked, because he is an enemy of my fatherland!" That is a reply which Dante could always give. At times he speaks out because he yearns to return to his fatherland, because he longs for revenge, because he hates those who injured him. But even in the mire you always find the divine spark, you always find a saintly soul who stands before an ideal world in which he believes and with which he is in love. His outbursts are partly born of that faith, and his hatred born of that love.

Dante is one of the most poetical and most complete images of the Middle Ages. His fiery soul mirrors human existence in all its range, from the most intellectual elements to the most concrete. This man, going to the next world, takes the whole earth along with him.

Character and Virtue
of Dante's Poetry
Benedetto Croce°

What is it then, this soul, the ethos and pathos of the *Commedia,* and its "tonality"? It is, we can say in a few and simple words, a feeling of the world based on a firm faith and a sure judgment and animated by a strong will. What this reality is, Dante knows, and no perplexity prevents or divides and weakens his knowledge. Of this knowledge what's mysterious is only that which one has to submit to reverently, and which is intrinsic to the conception itself, namely, the mystery of creation, providence, and divine will, which unveils itself only with the vision of God, in the beatitude of Heaven. It seemed to Dante sometimes that maybe even this mystery would fade away from him, especially in those moments in which he experienced or imagined mystical raptures; except that this mystical knowledge in his poetry was translated and had to be translated in a negative way, as a tale of one's own experience of ineffable things. At the same time, he knows how the different human affections should be judged and how to behave toward them, and which actions to approve and to fulfill and which to blame and repress, in order to orient life toward a dignified and true purpose. His will doesn't hesitate and sway between conflicting ideals, and it is not tortured by wishes that pull it in different directions. The disagreements and the contrasts

° From Benedetto Croce, *La Poesia di Dante* (Bari: Laterza, 1921), 161–69. Translated for this volume by Fiorella Magrini.

that we can discover in his concepts and in his attitudes are in the depth of things themselves; they will take place in subsequent history, but in himself they remain in embryo, undeveloped and not belonging to his conscience, a compact and unitary conscience: firm faith and constant habit, certainty of thought and action. However, in this strong intellectual and moral frame, as we have said, the sentiment of the world is restless; it's the most varied and complex sentiment of a spirit that has observed and experimented and meditated on everything and that is fully expert of human vices and virtues, expert not just in a summary and generic way, a second-hand expert, but it has experienced those feelings within himself in everyday life and in the lively sympathizing and imagining. The intellectual and ethical frame contains and dominates this turbulent matter which is entirely subjugated by it, but in the same way as one subjugates and enchains a powerful adversary that, even under the ruler's foot, even in the chains which hold him tight, stretches his strong muscles and assumes grandiose features. The various other definitions that can be found here and there among critics and interpreters about the character of Dantean poetry, bear in mind and try to catch and determine no more than the spiritual attitude that has been defined so far. How can one not see at all what is so real and actual and evident? Truth always asserts itself or nevertheless shines with many flashes. However, those formulas try hard in the intent but do not succeed, either because they use inadequate concepts, or they resort to metaphors, or they get lost in abstractions and catalogs of abstractions. It is usually observed, for example, that Dante depicts not the becoming but that which has become, not the present but the past; and what else is meant by this abstruse distinction, or what else is implied by the observations that have brought it up, if not exactly that, in Dante, all the affections are contained within and depend on a general thought and on a constant will that does not take into account only the particular? But this energetic representation of a force that surpasses or dominates another force is also, as any other poem, a representation of a becoming and not of that which has become, of a motion and not of a stasis. It is usually said that Dante is extremely objective; but no poem is ever objective, and Dante, as we all know, is exceedingly subjective, always himself, always Dantean; so that evidently objectivity is, in this case, a vague metaphor to designate the absence of perturbation and of disagreement in his conception of the world, his clear thinking and his firm will and, therefore, his representing with definite outlines. It is usually observed that it is a Dantean characteristic to abolish all lapses of time and diversity of customs and to place men and happenings of any time on the same plane: this means that he measured worldly things of each period and of each kind with a unique and firm measurement, with a definite model of truth and good, and projected and fleeting on the eternal screen. The characteristics of Dantean form, the intensity, the precision, the concision, and others are enumerated; it is certain that whoever is able to dominate through the strength of will the strong passions, he expresses something vigorous and intense, and, since he fixes his attention on them and knows them, he is precise, and since he does not get lost in their peculiarities, he is concise; but to take into account only these enumerations of characteristics would mean to limit oneself to the extrinsic. We usually refer to Dante as the "poet-sculptor" and not as the "poet-painter"; certainly if the act of sculpting and chiseling represents a virile, vigorous, strong, resolute gesture unlike painting at one's leisure with the stroke of a "very light brush" (as Leonardo spoke of his work), Dante will be a sculptor and not a painter; the images that one likes to use are not questioned, even though they might not have any logical and critical meaning as the famous parallel between Dante and Michelangelo is meaningless. There is a passage in the *Ottimo Commento:* "I, writer, heard Dante say that no rhyme ever tried to say anything more than what it meant to say, but that he ever so often in his rhymes, made his words express much more than anyone else could with the same words." *Verba sequentur,* and, if they don't follow immediately they are dragged by force, as Montaigne added. Even when it is said that the character and the unity of Dantean poetry stay completely within the metric on which the poem is sung, enchained in tercet, tight, disciplined, vehement but calm, one says the truth and doesn't; besides, this is true in such attempts to get to the essence of art in abstractively conceived forms, attempts that are now in fashion in the criticism of figurative arts. Doubtless, Dante of the *Commedia* is born only with the tercet and only in it, and by it he lives the drama of his soul; the tercet couldn't have been (as it has sometimes been conjectured) chosen intellectually and voluntarily only because it symbolizes the Trinity, because even if he had thought of this allegory, his thought, this time, had to superimpose or form an alliance with the needs of his soul, with the spontaneous expression of his fantasy, with which the tercet is one and all. But which tercet? Not certainly the tercet generally referred to, but the Dantean tercet, mixed with the linguistic, syntactic, and stylistic material proper of Dante, measured with the inflection and the accent that he gives to it, different from the tercet used by other poets; by this obvious consideration it is clear that the tercet is mentioned in this case not as a determinant by itself of that particular poetry but because it recalls all the ethos and the pathos of the *Commedia,* its intonation or tonality, the Dantean soul.

That this spirit is an austere one, a universally accepted concept regarding Dante, is implied by the characteristic mentioned above, because he who restrains and dominates the passions is austere, and, as such, he contains a great experience of pain. However, when the imagination portrays Dante with his face perpetually contracted in disdain or when the critics speak, as they have spoken, of his "black mood," of his "misanthropy," of his "pessimism," it might be the case for an exhortation not to exaggerate, and it is useful to try to touch up and to soften (as we have tried to do during our exposition) some of the strokes of that tradition and conventional portrait. No matter how Dante appears to his contemporaries and passed into the legend, and even allowing that his face was "thoughtful and melancholic," as is written by Boccaccio, it is certain, since the poem proves it to us, that he had in his soul such a richness and variety of interests to take him from the present to the past, from the immediacy of everyday life and suffering to the enjoyment of his scholastic and erudite memories, and a richness and variety of affections which from the most violent or sublime turned into the sweet and tender ones extending even to the jestfulness and playfulness. He was a poet: with his eyes of a refugee through the regions of Italy, he did not look at the political and moral things only politically and amorally, but he also spaced in every sort of sights enjoying them, and he turned to the beautiful things admiring them and he bent down with sympathy to the humble ones. Besides being a poet, he was specifically an artist: he always studied the arts, and he theorized upon them, and he glorified of the "beautiful style," and he had great joy from the word, from the appropriate, suitable, sensuous word, that is, the thought itself which generates its own living body with a divine quiver of creation. His soul was thus animated by the most varied sentiments and, above all, by much more gladness than we generally think; although even those sentiments and that gladness were set in his austere appearance and were tempered and tuned to it.

The controversy, debated both abroad and in Italy, on the "modernity" and the "nonmodernity" of his spirit often focuses on Dante's ethos and pathos and on the intellectual conception and the practical tendencies that condition him. This is the same as asking ourselves if Dante can or cannot be our master and the guide of spiritual life, of political and moral ideals, and of everything else. The truth is that all the great people are masters of life, but nobody can be such by himself, because each of them represents a moment in history, and the real master is all of history, and not only what we keep on recreating but also, and above all, the one that we create in each moment. The *Commedia* is an eternal poem, but, on the other hand, it is limited by its topic to the historical moment in which it was created and of which we have already briefly outlined the particular physiognomy. The consideration of this historical creation is enough to discriminate what is in Dante, that was not before, and what is not in him, and could not be, because it came out afterward, and to take away from his portrait some shadows and colors that have been badly added.

The Middle Ages are no longer part of Dante—the crude Middle Ages, both those of the ferocious mystical practice and those of the bold and cheerful battling; in fact, probably no other great poem is, like Dante's, without passion for war as war—the commotions that go along with the military battle, the risk, the effort, the triumph, the adventure. The medieval epic poem and the Carolingian cycle hardly rumble from a distance in a tercet used as analogy. The mystical practice is replaced by the firm faith, reinforced by thought and doctrine, while the war fervor is replaced by the civilian ardor. The latter and not any longer the former belonged to his age, to his contemporary Italy, or, in any way, belonged to his conscience and were object of his continuous and intense concern, of his human passion. Although I have several times shown my distrust and disgust toward the ethnic characterizations of the poets, nevertheless I will say that if the name *Germanic,* which was given to Dante (and not only by the Germans, and indeed not by the Germans in the first place), symbolizes sometimes the mystic and ascetic impetus and sometimes the war impetus, Dante was not "Germanic," and he should be called *Italian* or *Latin* or by a similar name. In the very beautiful evocation by Giovanni Berchet, in the "Fantasie," about the meeting between the Italians and the Germans in Costanza for peace negotiation, Dante would not be among the "blond people" and among the barons who, with their iron hats and with their busts closed in the iron links, "emerge as signal of an old age," but he would be among those wrapped up in long and simple capes, "conspicuous only by their wise dark looks."

On the other hand we must abstain from making too close a comparison between Dante and Shakespeare. Shakespeare is the first poet of his same grandeur that we encounter after him in the history of European poetry. In fact, since Shakespeare represents and is another age of the human spirit, in which the Dantean conception of the world had been upset, the clearness that illuminated, as well as the need for mystery, was obscured by a new shadow of mystery, and the perplexity of the mind and of the soul, that Dante did not know or he had soon won, had become the dominant note.[1] Concerning the romantics who came afterward, what shall we say? Their infinite is not his, their dreaming is not his dreaming, their style is not his "beautiful style," their "sentiment of the nature" (that Iacopo Grimm for these reasons denied to Dante) is not his, and, generally, their sentiment of life was the opposite from his; whoever reads and declaims Dante romantically disfigures and is unfaithful to him. Even here, if "Germanic" no longer symbolizes "romantic," Dante can neither be called a Germanic of the Middle Ages nor of the nineteenth century. If he had known the heroes of romanticism—the Werthers, the Obermanns, the Renees, and their pale descendants—he would probably have placed them in the "black slime" among the "indolents." He had to know something about this sad mood that, exactly in the romantic period, became enriched, complicated, spread, and obtained admiration and apotheosis, but it is nevertheless common to every age. Maybe, he himself, as a young man, had suffered from that illness for some time, and, like the romantic heroes, under the effect of melancholy, sadness, and indolence, he let himself go to dissolute living. This can be implied if such is the meaning of the sonnet that his friend Cavalcanti addressed to him, rebuking him about the "dissolute life" he "was leading," his "degraded soul," and the "bored spirit" that had taken possession of him. Anyway, he soon came out of this bewilderment, and he placed it among his other experiences as he placed among his experiences those furious love passions, which his biographers talk about, and he created from them the episode of Francesca. In the *Commedia* there is not any sort of sentimentalism but only joy, pain, and courage of living, controlled by moral fear, supported and animated by heavenly hope.

This is, briefly, the image of Dante, the authentic image, the one that is drawn from his own work. We must never forget—and in conclusion it is useful to repeat—that the image, which serves to differentiate Dante from the other poets and to help the intelligence and the comprehension of his work, does not retain any characteristic, anything straight, and, so to speak, prosaic. This is the case only if it is not placed and resolved in the amplitude of poetry, of that poetry that does not limit itself in anything or in any group of particular things, but always spaces in the cosmos. That is why we are raptured by Dante's rhythms and words, even by the smallest and fleeting ones, which come before us circumfused with that charm as, for example, referring to mythology, he calls the sunrise "the concubine of the ancient Titon" that comes "out of her sweet friend's arms," or when he calls the snow "white sister," and others. This, and it is the main point, does not imply other characteristics than the universal character of the poetry. With regard to this, Dante is not Dante any longer, in his definite individuality, but he is that wonderful and moved voice that passes on the human soul in the perpetually recurring creation of the world. Every difference, at this point, vanishes, and only that eternal and sublime refrain resounds, the voice that has the same fundamental tone in all the great poets and artists, always new, always old, always welcome by us with renewed trepidation and joy: poetry without adjectives. Those who speak with that divine or rather profoundly human accent used to be called Geniuses, and Dante was a Genius.

Note

1. Cf. my Shakespeare essay in *Ariosto, Shakespeare e Corneille* (Bari: Laterza, 1920).

The Structure of the *Comedy*   Erich Auerbach°

The structure of the great poem is made up of three merging inter-woven systems which are conceived of as corresponding in the divine order. There is a physical, an ethical, and a historico-political system; each of them, in turn, involves a synthesis of different traditions.

The physical system consists in the Ptolemaic order of the universe, as adapted to Christian dogma by Christian Aristotelianism; as a whole and in most of its details, that order was already formulated in the writings of the high scholastic philosophers and in the didactic works inspired by them, so that Dante was able to derive its basic traits from his sources—Aristotle, Alfraganus, Albertus Magnus, Thomas Aquinas, Brunetto Latini. The globe of the earth is at the center of the cosmos; round it revolve nine concentric celestial spheres, while a tenth, all-embracing sphere, the Empyrean, the seat of God, is conceived to be at perfect rest. Only half the earth, the northern hemisphere, is inhabited; the eastern and western limits of the "oi-koumenei" [in Greek characters], or inhabited world, are the Ganges and the Pillars of Hercules; its center is Jerusalem. In the interior of the earth, or rather of the northern hemisphere, like a funnel narrowing down toward the center of the earth, lies Hell; in its deepest part, at the very center of the earth, is the eternal abode of Lucifer, who in his fall immediately after the Creation, bored deeply into the earth, pushing aside an enormous portion of its interior and driving it upward; that portion of the earth is the great mountain which alone rises above the ocean which covers the whole southern hemisphere. It is the mountain of Purgatory, abode of souls headed for Paradise but still in need of purification. On the summit of the mountain, the point where the earth comes closest to the lowest celestial spheres, lies the Earthly Paradise, where the first man and woman lived before the fall from grace. The celestial spheres, which

° From Erich Auerbach, *Dante, Poet of the Secular World*, trans. Ralph Manheim (Chicago: University of Chicago Press, 1961), 101–33.

are the true Paradise, are ordered according to the heavenly bodies situated in them; first the spheres of the seven planets of ancient astronomy in the order: Moon, Mercury, Venus, Sun, Mars, Jupiter, Saturn; then the sphere of the fixed stars; the ninth is the invisible crystalline heaven, and the last is the Empyrean. The motion of the celestial spheres is concentric and circular; a burning desire to be united with God imparts a circular motion of the highest velocity to the ninth sphere, that closest to the motionless Empyrean where He dwells; the ninth sphere in turn, through the hierarchy of Intelligences, or Angels, communicates its motion to the lower spheres within it.

> Within the heaven of the divine peace [the empyrean] a body whirls [the *Primum mobile*, or ninth heaven], in whose virtue lies the being of all that it contains [the entire cosmos]. The next heaven, which has so many things to show [the heaven of the fixed stars with its many luminaries], distributes this being among various essences, different from yet contained in it. The other spheres [the planetary heavens] by various differentiations bestow to their own ends the distinctions which they have within themselves, together with the seeds. These organs of the world move, as you now see, from step to step, receiving from above and acting on what is below. . . . The movement and virtue of the holy spheres must be inspired by the blessed movers [the intelligences, or angels], like the hammer's art by the smith; and heaven, which so many lights make fair [the heaven of the fixed stars], takes the stamp from the profound mind that turns it and makes of that stamp a seal. And as the soul within your dust is diffused through differing members shaped to different functions, so the Intelligence [i.e., God] unfolds its goodness multiplied through the stars, itself revolving upon its unity. Different virtues make different alloys with the precious bodies that they quicken [the starry heaven], to which they are bound like life in you. Because of the happy nature from which it derives, the virtue shines, mingled, through the body like joy through a living eye. From this comes what seems different between one light and another, not from density or rarity. This is the formal principle. (*Par.* II, 112f).

From this passage we learn the following points:

1. The Being and the entire motion of the universe stem from the *primum mobile* or prime motion (hence from God's love as well as from the love of God). All Creation is an unfolding and reflection of divine Being—*non e se non splendor di quella idea che partorisce amando il nostro sire (Par.* XIII, 53) (it is nothing but the reglow of that Idea which our Sire, in loving, begets); its motion and all its activity have their eternal source in Him. The lines translated above are drawn from a passage about the nature of the Moon and that is why they speak only of the celestial spheres. Actually the same is

true of all Creation, both of that part which is created directly by God (intelligences, celestial spheres, *Prima materia,* and the human soul) and of that part which is produced indirectly through His organs (elements, plants, animals) (*Par.* VII, 124ff). Everywhere it is "la divina bonta che 'l mondo imprenta" (the divine goodness which stamps the world; *Par.* VII, 109), and the motion it produces is Love: "Ne creator ne creatura mai . . . fu sanza amore, o natural o d'animo" (Neither creator nor creature . . . was ever without love, either natural or rational; *Purg.* XVII, 91ff).

2. The universe is a multiplication of the first motion; the Intelligences, or Angels, communicate it to the lower degrees of Creation and impart to all created things the energy and motion peculiar to them, but in spite of all that the unity of divine Being is never relinquished: the Trinity, as Dante quotes St. Thomas as saying (*Par.* XIII, 58ff):

> per sua bontate il suo raggiare aduna
>   quasi specchiato, in nove sussistenze,
>   etternalmente rimanendosi una.
> Quindi discende a l'ultime potenze
>   giù d'atto in atto, tanto divenendo,
>   che più non fa che brevi contingenze;
> e queste contingenze esser intendo
>   le cose generate. . . .

[of its goodness focuses its own raying, as though reflected, in nine existences, eternally abiding one. Thence it descends to the remotest potencies, down, from act to act, becoming such as makes now mere brief contingencies; by which contingencies I understand the generated things . . .].

Thus the source of the multiplicity of Creation is the unfolding and reflection of divine goodness through the *nove sussistenze,* or nine existences, that is, the Angels, who are the movers of the heavenly spheres and of their luminaries. Here the relation between astrological conceptions and the divine order of the world is made perfectly clear. In the first canto of the *Paradiso* Dante expresses his surprise that he, as a material body, should have been able to rise up to heaven, and Beatrice replies: "Le cose tutte quante hanno ordine tra loro . . . : All things whatsoever observe a mutual order; and this is the form that makes the universe like God. In it the exalted creatures [those endowed with intelligence] trace the impress of the Eternal Worth, which is the goal for which the norm now spoken of was made. In the order of which I speak all things incline, by various lots, nearer or less near to their source; for which reason they move to different ports across the great sea of being, each one with instinct given it to bear it on. This bears the fire toward the moon; this is the mover in the hearts of things that die; this draws the earth . . . together and unites it. This bow shoots not only the creatures that lack intelligence but those that have both intellect and love. The Providence that ordains all this, with its light makes ever still the heaven in which that one whirls which has the greatest speed; and there now, as to the site ordained, the power of that bowstring bears us . . ." (*Par.* I, 103f; Cf. Aquinas, *Summa Theologica*, I, 59, i *ad resp.*; Dante, *De Monarchia*, I, 3).

This instinct is the work of celestial spheres, "ovra de le rote magne, che drizzan ciascun seme ad alcun fine" (operation of the mighty spheres that direct each seed to some end, *Purg.* XXX, 109f); the whole of earthly Creation is subject to them with the exception of man; for although man as a body, and hence also the sensitive powers of the soul, are subject to inclination by the influence of the stars, he possesses in the rational part of his soul the power to guide and limit that influence; that power is his free will. "The heavenly bodies," says St. Thomas, "cannot be the direct cause of the free-will's operations. Nevertheless, they can be a disposive cause of an inclination to those operations, in so far as they make an impression on the human body, and consequently on the sensitive powers which are acts of bodily organs having an inclination for human acts." And similarly in another passage: "The heavenly bodies are not the cause of our willing and choosing. For the will is in the intellectual part of the soul . . . the heavenly bodies cannot make a direct impression on our intellect. . . ." The *pars intellective* of the soul is man's *vis ultima*, or ultimate essence, what makes him a man, and he must employ it for good or evil. Without it he could no more do evil than a plant or an animal: for "lo naturale [amore] è sempre sanza errore." The natural is always without error.

These remarks on the special position of man bring us to the second of the systems underlying the *Comedy*, the ethical system. Man alone possesses freedom of choice, a power compounded of intellect and will, which, though closely connected with the natural disposition and hence always individual, reaches out beyond it; it is that power which enables him during his lifetime on earth, to love in the right or wrong way and so decide his own fate. In the ethical system he builds up on the basis of that conception, Dante follows the *Nicomachean Ethics* as elaborated in St. Thomas. Brunetto Latini had set forth the ethical doctrines of Aristotle and St. Thomas in his *Tresor*, particularly in the sixth and seventh books. His exposition shows many points of contact with Dante, and the words "m'inseg-navate come l'uom s'etterna" (*Inf.* XV, 85) (you taught me how man makes himself eternal) make it clear that Dante regarded Brunetto as the foremost authority on those ideas.

Man's ethical nature is grounded in his natural inclination or disposition. As such that is always good, for it is love, more specifically the love of some good. The highest good and the source of the good is God. The *anima rationalis,* or reason, can choose the immediate love of His as the main goal of earthly life, and attain the highest earthly excellence through the virtues of the *vita contemplativa.* But reason, which is intimately bound up with the individual disposition, can also choose a mediated love of God and turn to His creatures, that is, to the particular earthly goods. That choice leads inevitably to an active life, which however may take very different forms; it is good as long as the intermediate, "secondary" goods are loved with due moderation, and then it leads to the virtues of the *vita activa.* Natural love, however, can be corrupted by immoderation or faulty choice in immoderate or misguided love.

In the Other World which Dante explores in his poem, men are already judged; the balance sheet of their lives is drawn and they are put in the place that is theirs forever; the physical character of each station accords with the ethical worth of its inhabitants. Some souls are damned; others, in Purgatory, savor the anticipation of a beatitude soon to come; still others possess it already. Within each of the three realms, the souls are arranged in groups corresponding to their earthly acts or dispositions. And within those groups each man who appears as an individual is represented in the attitude and dignity befitting his own particular life and character. Each of the three systems of classification—the three realms, their internal group- ings, and within each group the individual character—has in itself an ethical significance, and sometimes the individual character de- termining Dante's—and our own—sympathies. That is of course par- ticularly true in connection with the *Inferno;* even aside from the virtuous pagans, including Virgil, who dwell in Limbo, the *Inferno* is rich in significant figures whose extraordinary virtues are not annulled by the vice for which they have been damned; though perverted, the original drive toward the good is still so strong in them that they preserve all their humanity in our eyes and some of them stand foremost in our sympathies. Though Dante never says so explicitly, it seems to me unquestionable that the preservation of individual attitudes indicative of such dignity or the contrary should be looked upon as part of the eternal judgment.

The principle of grouping is different in each of the three realms, as is only natural when we consider the different purpose pursued. In Hell, the realm of eternal punishment, there can be no classification by virtues, and in Paradise there are no sins or vices; in Purgatory there are both. There, since the purpose is purification, the basis of classification must be the evil impulses in need of expiation, but it cannot coincide with the classification of sins in Hell, for punishment is meted out for acts accomplished and not effectively repented, while purification applies to corrupt inclinations after individual acts have been confessed and repented. Sin, as we have seen, has its source in immoderate and misguided loves, which are classified according to the vicious dispositions they create in the soul. Immoderate love is broken down into a "too much" and a "too little." The too much involves the passion for earthly goods, hence lust, gluttony, and avarice; the too little is sloth. As to misguided love, it is directed toward evil. In the Thomist conception, however, evil is purely negative, since Creation as the diffusion of divine goodness can never in itself be evil; consequently misguided love can consist only in a desire to pervert the good, to turn away from its goodness, and since no one can hate himself, it is directed toward one's neighbor; it is a love of one's neighbor's evil and a "wishing of evil to one's neighbor"; its subdivisions are *superbia*, or pride, *invidia*, or envy, and *ira*, or anger. That is the classification of the *Purgatorio*, where the souls which have repented and confessed their sins are purified, and the stations ascend from the gravest to the most venial sins: the order is *superbia, hinvidia, ira, accidia, avarizia, gola, lussuria*, that is, pride, envy, anger, sloth, covetousness, gluttony, lust. When, on the other hand, we consider the sins punished in Hell, the evil deeds that have not been forgiven by God's grace, a new consideration enters in, the consent of the will, for without it no act can be carried out. Here, accordingly, the disposition of the will is the basis of judgment and classification. If after mature and careful reflection the will consents to an evil deed, we have a deed of pure wickedness *(malizia)*; if reflection is clouded by an excess of desire, we have an act of passion *(incontinenza)*. Thus Hell is divided into two sections according to the severity of the punishment; those who have sinned through passion are punished less severely than those who have sinned through wickedness, and here the descent is from the less to the more severe. That fundamental difference in the ethical order of the two realms—the fact that in the one evil deeds are punished, while in the other perverted dispositions are purified—explains why pride and envy have no groups in Hell, for they are dispositions with which no definite acts can be correlated. And it also explains why in Purgatory anger is represented as love of evil and assigned to the second, more grievous category, while in Hell it takes two forms: sudden anger, viewed as a sin of passion and assigned to the less severe section; and premeditated, vengeful anger, assigned to the lower circles of *malizia*. *Accidia*, or sloth, has no place in Hell proper, for it does not result in any action—it is the cowards of Limbo who correspond to the "accidiosi," or slothful ones, of the fourth circle of Purgatory. In Paradise, finally, the souls are ordered according to their good, unperverted dispositions, their just and measured love: each class is situated in the sphere of the heavenly body whose influence for good their *anima rationalis* has preserved pure and in just measure, or which, if perverted, they have purified in Purgatory; each soul is assigned to the sphere of the heavenly body that has exerted the dominant influence upon him.

The general classification of evil deeds in Hell is derived from the Aristotelian ethics; but in Limbo, in the first and sixth circles, and in many particulars elsewhere, other sources and conceptions are utilized. In devising punishments and inventing diabolical spirits, Dante's poetic fantasy works with a vast store of traditional mythology, whose sources and significance have repeatedly been investigated but never with wholly satisfactory results. The crater of Hell is divided into nine circles; the sins become more heinous and the punishments more terrible in descending order. The first circle harbors virtuous pagans and unbaptized children, both of which categories are barred from Paradise only because they are not Christians; it is not given them to see God, but that is their only punishment. The figures of antiquity move with a solemn dignity recalling ancient conceptions of the after-life. The second of fifth circles are occupied by those who have sinned from *incontinenza;* first those given to earthly passion—lust and gluttony—then those guilty of spiritual immoderation—avarice and anger. The fifth and last circle of the section is Styx, the river of Hell; Virgil and Dante cross it to enter the walled city of *malizia,* the true *civitas diaboli,* or city of the Devil. Here again the uppermost circle (the sixth) contains a category for which Aristotle did not provide, that of the heretics and godless "Epicureans"; then, in the Aristotelian order come the violent (seventh circle) and the deceivers (eighth circle), both groups being subdivided according to the special character of their sin and punishment. There are three classes of violence: against one's fellow man, against oneself, and against God. The deceivers, on the other hand, are subdivided according to concrete offenses: procurers, flatterers, simonists, fortune-tellers, swindlers ("barattieri"), hypocrites, thieves, evil counsellors, trouble-makers, forgers. Removed from the group and relegated to the ninth and lowest circle of Hell are those deceivers who have abused a sacred bond of trust: the traitors. In his three sets of jaws Lucifer, dwelling in the deepest abyss of Hell, grinds up the worst traitors: Judas who betrayed Christ, and Brutus and Cassius who murdered Caesar and betrayed the Imperium.

To Limbo Dante banished the vast multitudes of the cowardly and pusillanimous, "che visser sanza infamia e sanza lodo" (*Inf.* III, 36) (who lived without blame and without praise), and with them those angels who did not take sides in the rebellion of Lucifer. The classification is perfectly natural because sloth begets no specific evil deeds and consequently does not fit in with the system of punishments in Hell, while, on the other hand, it is definitely regarded as a sin by Aristotle and St. Thomas, since without love a man cannot see God. But what strikes and appalls us in reading the *Comedy* is the intensity of Dante's contempt for those who were neither hot nor cold. Their punishment is not so much torment as loathsome molestation: running about noisily in circles they are stung by insects. But their moral suffering is far greater: Compassion and Justice turn scornfully aside from them; not a trace of them remains on earth, Heaven excludes them, and worst of all, they are not even in Hell "ch'alcuna gloria i rei avrebber d'elli" (*Inf.* III, 42) (for the wicked would have some glory over them). In a way they are inferior to the lowest category of sinners, who at least were men, doing good or evil in a human way, while these, the slothful and lukewarm "never lived," for they made no use of man's *ultima vis*, his capacity to act in accordance with the decision of his reason and will. With these words: "questi sciaurati che mai non fur vivi" (*Inf.* III, 64) (these unfortunate who never were alive), Dante accounts for their eternal fate; here as everywhere else the sinners are assigned their eternal abode in accordance with the law of appropriate retribution, of "contrapasso." But the violence of Dante's tone when he speaks of them reveals the very personal bias of a man who was passionate, fearless, and indomitable in his espousal of the good, and for whom active struggle was the natural form of life.

The law of appropriate retribution governs the system of punishments in Hell, giving rise to a very concrete and realistic allegorism which in turn provides suitable and varied backgrounds for the appearance of the various figures. The punishments are chosen with a fantastic and gruesome ingenuity which reveals the richness, the dark pathos, and the almost pedantically precise concreteness of Dante's genius. With all their evocative power and emotional overtones, there is never any vague impressionist suggestion in these landscapes of Hell. The exposition is always orderly and methodical, as in a realistic record, and even where he raises his voice to adjure, even where he arouses sympathy, anger, dread or horror in the reader, he never sacrifices the strictest clarity. The landscapes and punishments of Hell are the basis of the fame that Dante has enjoyed in romantic periods and not entirely without justification they still have a good deal to do with the popular estimate of him. They were also the basis of the revulsion from him of strictly classicist periods. In the last analysis both points of view are misunderstandings. Dante was indeed one of the creators of Romanticism; his work was largely responsible for its fantastic Gothic dream world and for its exaltation of the horrible and grotesque; but he would not have been pleased with his followers. It was an Italian, Giambattista Vico, who, in a century hostile to Dante, gave expression for the first time to that form of admiration which culminated in the Romantic aesthetics. He compares Dante with Homer; both poets, he tells us, lived at a time when their peoples had just emerged from barbarism, and they mirrored the barbaric age in their poems; in bold, generous strokes they related true stories; both were endowed with a vigorous, naive imagination, without a trace of the philosophical, rationalistic subtlety characteristic of civilized periods; Dante took the same naive delight in the terrible punishments of Hell as did Homer in the cruel, bloody battles that are the sublime content of his *Illiad;* neither of them was in any sense a philosopher; their wisdom was the heroic, mythical wisdom of primitive, barbaric peoples. Here we shall not concern ourselves with the element of truth in that judgment from the early eighteenth century; what is astonishing is that Vico, who to be sure had no conception of the culture of the *trecento,* should not have been led to a more accurate view of Dante by comparison with Homer and by the actual text of Dante's work itself, which he had before him. He completely overlooked, or rather he was unwilling to accept, the facts that the *Comedy* was a work of high Scholasticism, of "umana ragione tutta spiegata," of human reason fully explained, and that Dante the barbarian was far superior in "intellectual subtlety," that is in precision and clarity of thought to himself, Vico, who, though with distaste, had plowed his way through Scholastic, Jansenist, and Cartesian logic. Vico failed to see it because he was no more able to read what is clearly set forth in the text than were Dante's romantic admirers who have never wearied of citing the *Inferno* in support of their literary ideals, although even, or one might say most particularly, in the *Inferno* Dante's poetic power actually springs from a clear and precise intelligence, thoroughly disinclined to disorderly, sentimental effusion. In conceiving the punishments of Hell, Dante employs mythical material and elements of popular faith; they are enormously imaginative, but each single one of them is based on strict and precise reflection, on the rank and degree of the sin in question, on a thorough knowledge of rational systems of ethics; and each one, as a concrete realization of the idea of divine order, is calculated to provoke rational thought concerning the nature of this sin, that is, the way in which it deviates from the divine order. The slaves of desire are driven hither and thither by the storm wind; the gluttons cower on the ground in the cold rain; the sinners from anger battle one another in the swamp; the suicides are transformed into bushes torn bloody by a pack of hounds racing through them; the flatterers are stuck in human excrement and the traitors in eternal ice—such examples of Dante's rich imagery are not haphazard products of an irresponsible fantasy seeking to pile up horrors, but the work of a serious, inquiring mind which for each sin has chosen its appropriate punishment and which owes the compelling force and concreteness of its images to its conviction that its choice is just and in conformity with the divine order. The same applies to the mythical monsters which serve both as guardians and as heraldic symbols of the circles of Hell. Nowhere is Dante more "medieval" in the French romantic sense than in those creations; moreover, they are imbued with the spirit of the vulgar-spiritualist iconographers who, in their striving to make hidden historical and moral meanings concretely visible, blended and exaggerated mythological traditions in accordance with a principle that has been lost to us and represented demonic forces as monsters moving in a fantastic half world. Like the monsters and grotesque figures of Gothic sculpture which delighted Victor Hugo and his friends, those inventions of Dante show the survival of an antiquity strangely distorted by mixture with heterogeneous doctrines; but in Dante they have cast off the element of arbitrary fantasy that they may have in other works by artists who have either forgotten the rational meanings or been able to assimilate them only in a confused, incomplete way. For though at first sight Dante's creatures retain the undiminished horror of dark fantastic monsters, closer scrutiny reveals that the poet carefully apportioned and defined their meanings, so that they require no commentary but rather help to elucidate the text. Their meaning is almost always clear, and in one of the few passages of this kind that are not easily explained, Dante says expressly that a specific doctrine is concealed within the strange lines.

As we have seen, the ethical order of the *Purgatorio* is governed by the Thomist-Aristotelian principle that the vices are perversions of love; in it particular offenses are no longer taken into account; the steps before the entrance gate and the words of the angel who opens it symbolize the sacrament of confession, and it is only when the gate has been passed, when the soul, freed from earthly guilt and started on its final *conversio ad deum*, or conversion to God, is no longer accessible to temptation, that purification sets in and with it the healing of the soul's wounds. But before reaching the gate, Virgil and Dante pass through a region of waiting souls, who have not yet been admitted to Purgatory: those who died excommunicated and, whether from negligence or because they died suddenly and violently, repented only in death. Those waiting outside Purgatory also include the souls in the Valley of Princes, who ruled under the imperfect, still unfulfilled world order; at night the serpent of temptation comes to them; to ward it off they implore and obtain the divine aid of the two angels with swords. Here Dante is overcome by a miraculous sleep, during which the mysterious Lucia raises him up to the entrance gate: only now begins the actual path of purification through the seven circles surrounding the mountain. Here the souls are purged of their vices in the order explained above: *superbia, invidia, ira, accidia, avarizia, gola, lussuria*. In this conception the doctrine of *Amore* is fused with that of the seven deadly sins. Purification is effected in accordance with the Aristotelian principle of the golden mean [mesoteis]; the souls strive against their sinful nature until they feel free from all failing; then they are able to continue their journey upward. Though in his choice of penances Dante naturally subjected himself to narrower limits than in devising the punishments of Hell, his images are no less concrete, and here again they are based on the sharpest rationality; and here again the landscape and surroundings are at every stage suited to the particular variety of purification. Surrounded by images, visions, voices, disclosing examples of virtue rewarded or vice punished, the souls are healed by suffering. The suffering that heals them is either, as in most cases, of a nature opposed to the ailment—the haughty are bowed beneath heavy burdens; the envious, transformed into blind beggars, support one another; the slothful race about at breathtaking speed; the gluttons waste away from hunger and thirst within view of food and drink; the lustful live in purifying fire—or else it is similar to the ailment, a concrete symbolization of the vice, and then the activity of the penitent is in painful contradiction to his good will—that is the case with the covetous, who are chained to the ground with their faces down, and with the wrathful who move in a cloud of dark smoke. Though the destinies exhibited in the *Purgatorio* are far less diverse than those of the *Inferno*, that does not in the least impair the continuity of the earthly personality. Each individual who speaks or even appears is not only a penitent belonging to this or that group, but also remains what he was on earth, Oderisi the illuminator, Buonconte the Ghibelline, Hugh Capet the prince, Statius or Arnaut the poet. For as with punishment in Hell, penance here is not something new and additional which submerges the character of the individual, causing him to disappear amid the throng of those charged with the same failing and the same penance, but an actualization of potentialities that were already contained in his earthly character and hence a continuation and intensification of that same character. Hence, despite the uniformity of the penance itself, individuality is preserved in the way the penance is borne and the way in which it is related to the events of the individual life. The individual life is not forgotten, but carried over into the penance, where it remains wholly present with all its particularity, its mental and physical *habitus*, its temperament and its actual striving.

On the summit of the mountain of Purgatory, in the *nobilissimo loco totius terrae* (the noblest place on the whole earth), lies the Earthly Paradise, where Adam and Eve were created and lived until the fall from Grace. Dante linked it with Purgatory on the basis of a tradition which, like the conception of Purgatory itself, originated in the Orient and was widely diffused in the Middle Ages; St. Thomas himself says that the Earthly Paradise was not an abode of the dead, but a place of passage. As the scene of earthly bliss it could only be situated at the summit of completed purification, still a part of the earth but already freed from the natural conditions pertaining on earth and directly subject to the effects of the celestial motion. But at the same time the region, to which Beatrice descends in order to receive Dante, represents the earthly perfection which he forsook when he turned away from her after her death; and consequently, it is only there, after all the degrees of purification have been absolved in Purgatory, that the particular penance and atonement, applying to Dante alone and relating to his fall from perfection, sets in. In his early youth Dante was distinguished by high divine grace, so that he seemed destined to the highest perfection that mortal man can attain; but after Beatrice's death and transfiguration, the light of her countenance was no longer able to keep him on the right way, and he turned away from her. Nowhere does Dante clearly reveal the exact nature of that apostasy; from the place of his confession and penance we can only gather this much, that the vices purged in the circles of Purgatory, though all or a part of them may have contributed to his falling-away, did not constitute the core of his error, which was, on the contrary, something entirely personal, peculiar to the extraordinarily favored poet; the text tells us that after the seeming loss of that highest good, he was seduced by other, lesser earthly goods, but the seduction cannot have been identical with any one of the vices of the *Purgatorio*; rather, it was an extraordinary sin such as can be committed only by one on whom extraordinary grace has been conferred. To serve as the place of atonement for that sin is one of the functions of the Earthly Paradise, which Dante lost by his falling away; another, no less appropriate function is to provide the scene for the great allegory of the world's history, the particulars of which we shall consider in connection with the historico-political system of the *Comedy;* only in the place of the first, uncorrupted earthly order and of man's fall from it could the second order and the second fall from it—and this was Dante's view of the world's history since the coming of Christ—be appropriately represented.

Re-created by his bath in Lethe and Eunoe, Dante, now under the guidance of Beatrice, embarks on the ascent to the heavenly spheres. They are the "paese sincero," the unsullied country, created directly by God, the abode of the redeemed souls. The ethical order of the *Paradiso* presents greater difficulties than those of the *Inferno* and *Purgatorio.* For one thing, the poet himself gives no systematic explanation of it corresponding to those contained in the eleventh canto of the *Inferno* and the seventeenth canto of the *Purgatorio;* another difficulty is that in the *Paradiso* the same souls make two appearances, ordered in two different and seemingly unrelated hierarchies, first in one of the revolving spheres and once again in the rose of the Empyrean. Consequently the *Paradiso* has provided exegetes with an almost unparalleled opportunity to exert their speculative ingenuity; to our mind their speculations have often been too ingenious and sterile for that very reason. Yet they have seldom been entirely unprofitable; even when it seems unsatisfactory as a whole, a penetrating explanation in the spirit of Scholastic theology is bound to deepen our understanding of the poem and its complex doctrinal implications and consequently to increase our sensuous and intellectual enjoyment of the *Comedy*. No lover of Dante can read Filomusi-Guelfi or Busnelli or Ronzoni, to mention only a few of the leading commentators, without benefit; nevertheless it seems to me that neither the theory of the seven gifts of the Holy Ghost, nor the theory of the degree of *Caritas*, important as the latter may be, can provide a truly exhaustive principle by which to explain the organization of the *Paradiso*; as soon as we attempt to apply any of them systematically, we run into difficulties that can only be mastered with the help of undue violence. Nor does it seem likely that Dante would have employed a single theory for the whole *Paradiso* without explicitly expounding it in a central passage. Though it is permissible to regard the entire *Summa theologia* as a source of information about Dante's thinking, it is dangerous to draw on specific dogmas from it in solving particular problems unless Dante himself refers to them, for he never conceals the dogmatic foundations of his work.

The spheres of Heaven through which Dante is raised to the presence of God, are not, like the circles of Hell or the degrees of Purgatory, the actual abode of the souls Dante meets there; they make their appearance in one of the spheres only in order to give Dante a clear idea of their rank in the heavenly hierarchy; their actual dwelling place, their ultimate destiny, is beyond all places, in the congregation of the blessed, that is, in the white rose of the Empyrean. Here again the hierarchy of the blessed is described, but what is said of it—the throne of the Emperor Henry, the division into saints of the Old and of the New Covenant, the partition between them, the blessed children, the two summits Mary and John the Baptist, and those who sit closest to them—does not refer directly to the ethical order of the world, but represents the goal of the history of salvation and thus pertains to the historico-political order. Of course the two orders cannot be looked upon as distinct, they must coincide, and it is evident that the great patricians of the realm, the roots of the rose, occupy the highest place from the standpoint both of historical providence and of ethical dignity; at the summit the identity of the two orders is actualized. But at least in the lower degrees, the ethical hierarchy of the white rose does not seem to be complete, unless we choose to round it out with the names of the Hebrew women and of the saints who occupy the ranks intermediate between the blessed of the old and of the new covenant. This has been attempted by various commentators, and some have tried to establish a thoroughgoing concordance between the hierarchy of the rose and that of the heavenly spheres; but the results are not satisfying. For though Dante sees "more than a thousand tiers" in the white rose, he mentions only seven names on one side of the "partition" and three on the other, and says expressly—as one may gather from the whole presentation—that the series continues downward. The seven ranks represented by Mary-John, Eve-Francis, Beatrice-Rachel-Benedict, Sarah-Augustine, Rebecca, Judith and Ruth necessarily constitute only the highest degrees of the hierarchy, and consequently cannot be brought into a parallel with the order of the heavenly spheres, which symbolizes the entire ethical order of Paradise. The attempts that have been made to overcome or to spirit away this difficulty strike me as too ingenious.

Consequently a complete ethical system of the *Paradiso* can be arrived at only on the basis of the celestial spheres where the blessed appear in order that their rank may be clear to Dante. Common to them all is beatitude through the vision of God, *visio Dei*, in which they all find peace; but from individual to individual the vision varies in degree, as it does with the "other host," the Angels, for it hinges on grace. None can know God fully, not even Mary or the highest ranks of the Angels; only God sees and knows Himself entirely. The degrees of the vision of God are based on grace, for the acquisition of which merit is a necessary but not a sufficient condition; grace is conferred freely and outweighs all merit, but to receive it is meritorious, for it can be received only with the help of good will. Grace engenders the vision; the vision determines the degree of celestial love, the *Caritas patriae*, which in turn is manifested in the degree of light that the soul radiates. This order of rank is extremely subtle and ultimately each individual soul reflects it in its own way. By way of making the picture clear to himself and his readers, Dante has recourse to the astrological traditions of late antiquity. Since it is virtue that prepares the soul to receive grace, since virtue springs from earthly love of God, *Caritas viae*, and since, moreover, the particular direction of this love is determined by natural predisposition, that is, by the influence of the stars, the right love, virtue, being the rational soul's right and moderate use of its natural predispositions, Dante found in the astrological classification of the natural predispositions a hierarchical order of Paradise which was consonant with the doctrine of love and made it possible to preserve diversity of human character in the eternal hierarchy of the kingdom of God.

The lowest, least luminous sphere, that of the moon—according to the astrological tradition cool, moist, variable and readily responding to all influences—is a kind of anteroom of Paradise; the souls that appear there, such as Piccarda and Constanza, occupy their rank not, like those of the other heavens, because of the special nature of their love, but because of a deficiency in their love; ceding to the power of others, they had been unable to fulfill their oath. The second sphere, that of Mercury, may also be interpreted as an anteroom to Paradise; the planet is a symbol of varied activity and artifice and also of the striving for fame and influence; here Dante situates those who performed good actions on earth but were too much concerned with fame and worldly interests. The next four spheres seem to represent the forms of the *Caritas* of active life, the four cardinal virtues: Venus, the planet of lovers, represents temperance; the sun, where the Church Fathers and theologians appear, represents wisdom or prudence; Mars, planet of the warriors and martyrs, symbolizes fortitude; and Jupiter, planet of the princes and of the Eagle justice. In the last planetary sphere, that of Saturn, appear the souls of the contemplative life, who devoted their lives wholly to ascetic contemplation and so achieved the form of earthly existence closest to God. Saturn is the highest rank of the ethical hierarchy in its human aspect, and there begins Dante's preparation for the divine vision of God. From there the divine ladder which Jacob saw in his dream rises up to the sublime heights of Paradise, to the Empyrean. But that is still to come. For the present Beatrice does not smile, for Dante would not yet be able to bear the sight, the heavenly choirs are silent, Dante's question about Providence cannot yet be answered, and his desire to see the soul of St. Benedict in its true, unveiled aspect cannot yet be satisfied; the privative nature of the preparation and also the cry of indignation following Peter Damian's bitter speech against the clergy, suggest something of the planet's dark, problematic character which, as other passages show, was well known to Dante.

With Saturn the ethical order of the world, in so far as it involves concrete portrayal of the ultimate fate of individual souls, is concluded and the ascent begins to the true *civitas Dei* with its two hosts. After a glance back at the earth, Dante enters the heaven of fixed stars in the constellation of Gemini (the constellation of his own hour of birth). Here the triumph of Christ appears as a great sun which illumines the many thousands of stars and gathers them round it; when that symbol of the redemption of the "prima milizia," the first host, the human race, has raised Dante's spirit above itself, he is permitted to behold Beatrice in her true aspect, and the actual presence of his youthful vision is disclosed to him as the truth revealed to man. She guides his eyes back to the host of the blessed; he is permitted to behold the coronation and ascension of Mary, who follows the already exalted Saviour. Then comes the threefold questioning of Dante, or rather, his proclamation of the spiritual fruits of redemption, of the three theological virtues: he replies to Peter concerning faith, to James concerning hope, and to John concerning love. In the crystal heaven he sees the other host of the pure Intelligences, or Angels, learns the time and nature of their creation, the concordance of their hierarchy with the heavenly and earthly order, the infinitely diverse ways in which they reflect God. But that vision too vanishes; once again he ascends: in the flowing light of the Empyrean and in the flowers on its shores he sees a symbol of the action of divine grace; in response to Beatrice's command he bends down to the glittering stream that touches the rim of his eyelids; a new degree of ecstasy comes on him, the vision changes, and in the heavenly rose, in the "convento delle bianche stole," (Par. XXX, 129) among the white-robed concourse, the two hosts appear joined in a glory; Mary's faithful follower, St. Bernard, symbol of supreme ecstasy, intercedes with her to grant Dante the ultimate fulfillment, the vision of God; in rising illumination, impelled by will and necessity in one, his eyes penetrate deep into the light that fulfills his longing and causes his will to fuse with the movement of universal love.

In the Paradiso there are but few redeemed souls who appear as individual figures fraught with memories of earthly existence; and these do not, as in the other two parts of the poem, show themselves in their earlier form, so that Dante can recognize them, but are concealed in the dazzling garment of their beatitude. The higher Dante rises, the more universal and impersonal become the souls that appear; beyond Saturn, there are only the great dignitaries of the Kingdom of Heaven, whose earthly life, which prepared them for their high rank, is generally known and requires no new narrative embodiment. But he did wish to devote special treatment to two of these saints, Francis and Dominic, whose earthly lives were separated by only a century from his own and whose living action still bore a special character for him, standing out distinctly against the general background of the history of salvation. Since there was no room for such matters amid the glory of the Empyrean, where they would have had to appear, he contrives to have their lives related by other characters elsewhere. In the sphere of the sun, the Dominican St. Thomas speaks of St. Francis, while the Franciscan Bonaventure speaks of St. Dominic. Both narratives supply something that is rare in the Comedy, a complete biography, though a sparse one, in which Dante's goal and the saint's ultimate destination are never lost from view. There is no digression into the epic reaches of legend although, particularly in connection with St. Francis, the biographical material of Dante's disposal, with its abundance of enchanting detail, must have offered a great temptation. He sets down, almost as though drawing up a report, only what was most relevant to goal and ultimate fate, and this simple correlation of the saints' action with Dante's goal creates a compelling picture of the two saints, each with his very personal and very different ethos. They do not appear, they are merely spoken of; and it is not very different with the other figures of the planetary spheres, whose concrete reality is veiled in light. Their true, earthly figure is not seen, their only gesture is to shine with greater or lesser brightness; but their words encompass their gestures and preserve the character of the earthly man who lived in them and still lives. Often they speak very briefly but always of the crucial actions and happenings, avoiding all mere anecdote or naturalistic detail; but despite the lofty tone, the words are always very much to the point, explaining the individual's heavenly rank, connecting it with his past existence on earth, and portraying the whole man, transfigured but intact.

In the heaven of fixed stars, the heaven of the *prima milizia*, where redeemed mankind is united in the Triumph of Christ, a fourth figure joins the three examining Apostles; it is Adam, the first man, who closes the circle by relating, at the scene of its completion, the primordial beginnings of the drama. The events that he relates or explains form the starting point of the third, historico-political system of the *Comedy*.

For through Adam's fall mankind lost the original purity and goodness in which it was created and was damned like Lucifer, the fallen Angel. Eve's original sin was not the mere tasting of the forbidden fruit, but a transgressing of limits, a striving to exceed her allotted destiny: earth and heaven obeyed, only a woman who had just been created could not endure to remain within her predestined sphere. Of all created things on earth man was the most perfect: he possessed immortality, freedom, and likeness to God, but the sin of apostasy robbed him of those gifts and flung him down all the lower because he had stood so high. And man disposed of no means of reparation, for no amount of humility could fully compensate for the terrible crime of his fall away from God, the highest good; only God himself in His infinite compassion could forgive him and restore him to his former place. But God is just as well as good; justice is the eternal order of the world, and accordingly it was His pleasure to satisfy the dictates of justice even in the practice of His infinite mercy; through the incarnation of His son, born of a human mother, He engendered a pure man, who in his humility could justly and fully expunge the original sin; the union of divine and human nature in Christ is the mystery which satisfied the requirements of God's justice, for here a man by the humility of his life and Passion atoned for the original sin, but in view of the man Christ's other, divine nature, his act of atonement was an undeserved gift of God's unlimited goodness, in excess of all justice.

With that idea which is known essentially to every Christian, Dante combines another which in this context may strike a modern observer as strange: it is the idea of the special mission of Rome and the Roman Empire in history. From the very beginning Divine Providence elected Rome as the capital of the world. It gave the Roman people the heroism and the spirit of self-sacrifice necessary to conquer this world and possess it in peace; and when the work of conquest and pacification, the sacred mission announced to Aeneas, was accomplished after centuries of bitter battles and sacrifices and the inhabited world lay in the hands of Augustus, the time was fulfilled and the Saviour appeared. For it was decreed that the redeemed world should abide in perfect peace, in supreme earthly perfection down to the last day; that is why Christ rendered unto Caesar the things which were Caesar's and submitted to his judgment; that is why Peter and Paul went to Rome, why Rome became the center of Christianity and the seat of the papacy. Since the very beginning of the Roman legend the two plans of Providence have been intertwined; Aeneas was granted his journey to the underworld with a view to the spiritual and secular triumph of Rome. Rome was the mirror of the divine world order, so much so that Paradise is once referred to as "quella Roma onde Christo e Romano" (*Purg.* XXXII, 102) (that Rome whereof Christ is a Roman). In the earthly Rome, as Christ made clear by his words and deeds, it was decreed that two strictly separate powers should rule in perfect balance, the spiritual power of the Pope, who must possess nothing, for his kingdom is not of this world, and the secular power of the Emperor, who is just, because God appointed him and all things earthly are in his power.

Thus the whole Roman tradition flows into the history of salvation, and the two prophecies seem complementary and almost equal in rank: Virgil's *Tu regere imperio populos* (Thou shalt rule as an empire over the nations) and *Ave Maria.* Before the appearance of Christ, the Roman Eagle, whose deeds Justinian relates in the heaven of Mercury, was the herald, and afterward the executor, of God's plan of salvation; Tiberius the third emperor, considered as the legitimate judge over Christ the man, who the executant avenger of original sin, who satisfied God's wrath; Titus, the conqueror of Jerusalem, was the legitimate executant of vengeance against the Jews; and in the bottommost Hell, in the jaws of Lucifer, Judas has as his companions Brutus and Cassius, Caesar's murderers.

But for a second time the world fell away from the divine will, and once again the sin consisted in a "trapassar del segno," (*Par.* XXVI, 117) a transgression against the earthly world order appointed by God; this sin is symbolically represented by the fate of the mystical chariot in the Earthly Paradise. Christ the griffin has fastened the chariot to the tree from which Adam once plucked the forbidden fruit and which now signifies the earthly world order or the Roman empire. Beneath its branches mankind can rest in peace (Dante's sleep), and in the shadow of the tree the revealed authority of the Christian doctrine finds its natural place. The chariot of the Church resists the assaults of the Eagle (the persecutions of Christians under the first Roman emperors) and of the fox (the early Christian heretical sects); but when the Eagle covers the chariot with its wings—an allegory for the Donation of Constantine—disaster sets in. Satan rises up from the depths, breaks a piece—the spirit of humility—out of the floor of the chariot, the rest of which is filled to the brim with the Eagle's feathers (earthly goods), and the seven deadly sins appear as death's heads on the shaft and in the corners. On the seat of the chariot sits a harlot, the Roman curia, fornicating with a giant; the giant symbolizes unrestrained illegitimate power, probably in particular the French king, and in order to gain complete power over the harlot detaches the chariot from the tree and makes off with it.

The lesson of the allegory is stated clearly and passionately in many passages in the poem dealing with examples of earthly corruption. The world is out of joint, its God-ordained balance is upset, and the root of all the evil is the wealth of the Church which according to the divine order should possess nothing. Greed, the she-wolf—in a broader sense the illegitimate lust for earthly power, the striving to exceed the sphere of power appointed by God—is the worst of vices, the ruination of the world. Ever since the Roman Church with its unrestrained greed usurped even the Imperial power; ever since the Hapsburg Emperors, forgetful of their duty, abandoned Italy and Rome, the head of the world—chaotic immoderation has reigned everywhere, so that everyone stretches out his hand for whatever seems within reach. The passions of men are unleashed, and the result is war and confusion. The Pope battles with Christians for earthly goods; the kings, free from the supreme sovereignty of the Emperor, rule incompetently and aimlessly; in the towns the parties struggle for a power which God has not legitimated, exploiting the cause of the Emperor or Pope for their own disgraceful ends; Church offices have become venal and their holders have taken to living in loathsome and un-Christian ostentation; disregarding their rules, the monastic orders, even the Franciscans and Dominicans, are disintegrating; disorder and corruption vie with one another, and Italy, mistress of nations, has become a brothel, a ship without helmsman in the storm.

Dante's own city of Florence occupied a special position in this world of wickedness, and not only because it was his home. It is true that his unchanged love and yearning, the bitterness of his own experience, lend a special force to his condemnation of its wickedness. But quite apart from his own motives and from his personal ties with it, Florence of all the Italian towns offered the clearest example of what Dante could not but regard as absolute evil. For it was here that the new commercial, middle-class spirit first flowered and achieved self-awareness; it was here that the great metaphysical foundations of the political world were first, in a consistently pragmatic spirit, evaluated and exploited for purely political ends; it was here that every earthly institution, regardless of its transcendent origin and authority, came to be considered, with cold calculation, as a counter in a game of forces—an attitude which became prevalent in every section of the population. And despite many setbacks that way of thinking brought Florence success even in Dante's time; trade flourished, the city increased in population and prosperity, the Florentine bankers achieved a position of European pre-eminence which was soon to be reflected, more and more conspicuously, in the political sphere. A race of worldly, calculating men arose, intent on profit and power, to whom the bonds of the traditional world order meant nothing, even though for business reasons they paid it lip service when possible; and when a new culture arose among them, it was no longer an ecumenical wisdom authorized by God, which permeates and regulates all earthly life, but an aesthetic hedonism utterly devoid of moral obligation. Party strife with all its vicissitudes and turmoil brought the city more profit than harm; for it promoted the free play of forces and with it the process of selection by which an organism preserves its youth and is enabled to adapt itself at every moment to the shifting demands of practical life, to assimilate and master them. That is the idea which is expressed only half consciously in the often cited passage of Machiavelli, where he says that nothing more clearly indicates the innate strength of the city of Florence than the greatness it has achieved despite the terrible party strife that would have been the downfall of any other state. But Machiavelli was too much inclined to regard the city's intestine struggles as a mere obstacle that had been overcome; actually the obstacle was productive, and when he goes on to say that the city would have achieved incomparably greater flowering if it had preserved inner unity from the start, we believe him to be mistaken; Florence, "fior che sempre rinovella," flower forever renewed, grew great by its inner strengths.

Dante wanted none of it. He would never have recognized a political life based on autonomous earthly success; the earthly world lies in the hands of God; only those who draw legitimacy from God are entitled to possess its goods, and then only to the extent provided for by the legitimation. A struggle for earthly goods is a trespass against the divine will; it signifies anti-Christian confusion, and even on the practical plane it can lead only to disaster, to secular and eternal ruin. It never occurred to him as he deplored and condemned the disunity, the struggles and calamities of his time, that they might be preparing the way for a new, immanent but fruitful order of life.

Nowhere does the poet strike a modern observer as so alien and reactionary, so unprophetic and blind to the future. But when we consider with what sacrifices that future, the culture of the new era, was bought, how the schism between inner and outward life became more and more painful, how the political and human unity of life was lost, how the fragmentation and inefficacy of all ideologies became evident to everyone, even in the lowest stations; when, further, we bear in mind that all modern attempts to restore a human community have rested on foundations far shakier than those of Dante's world order—we shall not, to be sure, cherish any futile, absurd desire to revive what is irretrievably lost, but neither shall we be tempted to despise or condemn the meaningful order on which Dante's thinking was based.

As we have seen, the source and at the same time the most glaring sign of political evil was for Dante the temporal expansions of the Holy See. Free from the Imperial power, it became untrue to its mission and drew all Christendom with it into perdition. And yet, though Dante went so far in his attack on the Curia as to liken it to the Babylonian harlot, he did not question its authority. Strange as it may seem, he looked upon even the most depraved of Popes as a *successor Petri*, vicar of Christ on earth, endowed with the power to loose and to bind: "Ye have the Old and the New Testament," says Beatrice, "and the shepherd of the Church to guide you; let this suffice you, unto your salvation." It would never have occurred to Dante to extend his opposition to the Curia to the realm of faith. Dante and others of his day could well be horrified at the thought that a man, whose soul has been relegated to the lowest reaches of Hell, should have been the legitimate vicar of Christ on earth, legitimately wielding the highest power, but they saw nothing impossible or absurd in it.

We know that Dante's political hopes revived once again when the Emperor Henry VII came down from Luxembourg on his Italian campaign, and that Dante supported him by word and perhaps by deed. Henry's failures and death did not discourage him. Henry VII is the one figure in the history of his own time whom Dante expressly situates in the Empyrean: Beatrice shows him the throne destined for the Emperor's soul, the soul "of the lofty Henry who shall come to straighten Italy ere she be ready for it." Italy was not yet ready; but one day the sacred order would be restored on earth. That was Dante's passionate faith, and he professed it in dark, fantastic prophesies, which have never ceased to arouse the interest of posterity and the zeal of the exegete, though in six centuries no one has found an altogether reliable interpretation of them.

There are two main prophecies: the one is uttered by Virgil after Dante shrinks back in horror from the wolf of covetousness; this ever hungry beast, says Virgil, will be the ruin of many until the greyhound, the *Veltro*, comes to slay it, saving unhappy Italy and chasing the she-wolf back into Hell, whence Satan's envy turned her loose upon the earth. In the other passage, it is Beatrice who speaks; the allegory of the chariot, that we have described above, is at an end, the giant has gone off with the harlot enthroned upon the chariot of the Church; Beatrice utters the glad prophecy from the Gospel of St. John (16:16): *Modicum, et non vidibitis me . . .* (A little while, and ye shall not see me . . .); then she prophesies the salvation of the Church: the Eagle will not always be without heirs; already the constellation is near under which the "cinquecento dieci e cinque" (*Purg.* XXXIII, 43) (the five hundred ten and five) sent by God will slay the giant and the harlot.

It seems obvious that those two prophecies, in which Reason and Revelation speak of future things on earth, are related, that the first is contained in the second which completes and clarifies it; and indeed, no one has ever seriously denied the connection between them. It is also quite clear what is meant in both passages by the present evil that the future savior will slay: the she-wolf and the harlot are symbols for the sin of covetousness which has taken hold of the spiritual leader of the world, the papacy, and hence also for the papacy itself. Many passages in the poem make it clear that the papal usurpation of temporal goods is the source of all earthly confusion; the image of the shepherd turned into a wolf by the "maledetto fiore," the accursed flower, that is, Florentine gold, which is leading Christendom to perdition, recurs in many variations. Dante's own lot, the many diatribes in the *Comedy,* particularly St. Peter's vehement words in the heaven of the fixed stars, the whole texture of Dante's political theories—all that makes so clear who it was he regarded as the true obstacle to earthly beatitude, that any other interpretation seems strained. We can also arrive, with some degree of certainty, at a general idea of who the expected savior is. For what is lacking in the world? Imperial sovereignty: the Eagle is without heirs, the German Albrecht forsakes his empire, Henry comes too soon: but Rome, the head of the Christian world, requires two suns to illumine both paths, the earthly and the heavenly; now, however, one has extinguished the other, the sword has merged with the pastoral staff, and the right order has been destroyed by violence; the earth lacks a legitimate ruler, and that is why the "humana famiglia," the human community, is going astray. To me there seems no doubt, and it is the prevailing opinion, that the savior can only be a bearer of the Imperial power; but from the symbols and chronological specifications that Dante adds, I can derive no definite information; only one thing is stated clearly, namely, that Italy above all must be saved, whence it follows that the mission of Rome as sovereign of the world remains as valid for the future as for the past.

But those historico-political symbols are rooted in much deeper layers of ancient mythical faith. For the first, the Virgilian prophecy, is given at the foot of a sunlit mountain, which is the "beginning and ground of all joy," after Dante has tried in vain to climb it by his own strength; the second is uttered on the summit of Purgatorio, in the Earthly Paradise. But the mountain of Purgatory, inaccessible in the ocean of the southern hemisphere, with its seven terraces, with the Garden of Eden and the miraculous tree, is the element of Dante's cosmology which is most deeply rooted in the world-renewal mysticism of the Near East. It points back to the seven terraces of the tower of Babylon, mountain of the gods and symbol of the planetary spheres, to Ezechiel's mountain of God, to the seven gates of the Gnostic journey of the soul, with the seven spheres of purification, each watched over by an archon (after passing the last sphere, that of fire, the soul is privileged to partake of the marriage feast of Christ and Sophia); to Cabalist, Joachimite, and Franciscan myths of world renewal. Dante is borne upward to the first gate by the ambiguous figure of Lucia-Aquila—an anagram—who at the very beginning of the poem has acquainted Virgil with the mission of Beatrice and in whose person the symbol of illuminating grace, *gratia illuminans*, seems to be combined with that of the right world order, the Roman Empire; at the summit of the mountain he is received by Matelda, unquestionably a symbol of pure and active life amid still uncorrupted nature, who leads him to his bath in Lethe and Eunoe, to purifying oblivion and new birth; and here too he beholds the mystical procession with the chariot bearing the transfigured Beatrice. Thus if Dante's journey to the Other World signifies the preparatory way of purification and the rebirth of the individual soul through the immediate *visio Dei*—then the prophecies at the beginning and the end of the journey, concerning the future of the human community, can only refer to the future rebirth of all humankind and to the future Golden Age: the age when not only the heavenly kingdom but the earthly kingdom as well will be perfect and immaculate in accordance with its God-ordained destiny, when the Earthly Paradise will be realized on earth. I cannot make up my mind whether to accept the theory that "Il Veltro" is a composite of the Veronese Cangrande with the Grand Khan of the Tartars—from the land of felt ("veltro") huts and blankets—or the notion (which strikes me as more likely) that the "cinquecento dieci e cinque" is an allusion to the Age of the Phoenix—but one thing that stands out compellingly in the works of the Germans who have formulated such theories— Bassermann, Kampers, and Burdach—is the important part played by the world-renewal myths of the Near East in Dante's work. It is not easy to prove that Dante drew directly on any particular source, and so far no one has succeeded in doing so; however, it does not seem unlikely that certain of his sources were little known at his time, for otherwise his sons and the other commentators of the next generation would surely have had something more definite to say about some of the more puzzling passages. In Dante innumerable myths of rebirth (and the same is true of many other traditions and currents of thought) flow together and take on new force and vitality. And indeed it is only in his work, ordered and embedded in the hierarchically balanced system of his vision, that they have retained the measure and dignity they deserve. As they appear in Dante, they are neither the extravagant outpourings of an irresponsible fantasy nor impatient makeshift utopias.

The hierarchical structure of the historico-political world order is not set forth in the *Comedy* with the same clear continuity as the physical or ethical order; it is difficult, for example, to maintain that each stage in the journey symbolizes a particular stage of social life, and the attempts to demonstrate a concordance of that kind—Fritz Kern in his *Humana Civilitas* has offered a highly instructive and well thought-out attempt of the sort—strike me as exceedingly far-fetched. Nevertheless, when we consider the *Comedy* in that light, our attention is drawn to an image which calls for such an interpretation. It is the antithesis of the two cities: Dis the *civitas diaboli* in the *Inferno*, and in the *Paradiso* and *civitas Dei*. The walled city of Lucifer, whose gates are closed to the wise poet of the Roman world order, so that a divine messenger, perhaps "Il Veltro", must force admittance, is the realm of *malizia* (wickedness) and the aim of wickedness is injustice. And injustice is not only a sin against God, but also an offense against one's neighbor and against the right life on earth; the city of Dis is the abode of social perdition. It is represented, to be sure, as part of the total divine order which includes evil, and in that sense it is well ordered; but it persists in impotent rebellion against the high power of God, for their evil will has deprived its inhabitants of sound insight and hence of freedom; of the freedom, which men possess in their earthly life, to choose the right course. Consequently, they can will only evil, and they consume themselves in the hopeless corruption of hatred and blindness. They cannot perform any fruitful work in common, for the evil will, though common to them all, does not bind but confuses and isolates; the perverted will that dominates each one, is directed against his fellow in perdition. The community is hopelessly enmeshed in war and misery; though powerless to act, Lucifer, its king, is still strong enough to blow the icy petrifying breath of hatred over his country; through the center of it, in the circle where the violent against God suffer the rain of fire, Phlegethon, the river of seething blood, flows in its hard stony bed; it is a part of the river of Hell, formed by the tears of the Old Man of Crete, his back to the East and his eyes turned toward Rome as though peering into a mirror, who symbolizes the gradual decline through the ages of the human race forsaken by grace.

By contrast, the *civitas Dei* in Paradise is a land of justice; here dwell the souls in their proper order, working in common, each delighting in its rank, partaking of a true good, which is inexhaustible in supply and confers ever increasing enjoyment as more redeemed souls have a share in it. In the manifestations of the blessed in the planetary spheres, the diversity of dispositions and vocations forms the natural order within which man becomes a citizen; in the measure of his aptitudes he becomes a member of the human community whose aim is the actualization of the divine order on earth, and it is that human community which in the course of an upright life leads him to sound insight and beatitude; and thus he becomes a citizen of the kingdom of God, the true *Roma aeterna,* occupying the rung of the hierarchy befitting his predisposition.

Between the two cities lies the mountain of Purgatory; it is not only a place of penance, for here also the souls practice living in common and are trained in the exercise of true freedom. In ante-Purgatory, the waiting souls, still unable to rise by their own power, require outward guidance and help; Cato, the righteous fighter for earthly freedom, sternly shows them the way when sensual pleasure threatens to turn them aside, and the angels with the two swords protect the defenseless souls from temptation. Once the souls have passed through the gate of Purgatory proper, an independent will awakens in them, a striving for purification in common; first they atone for the grave vices which endanger the life of the community, then for the less serious sensual disorders which hamper their ethical freedom and hence the social order chiefly when they are carried to excess. The last purification in the fire of the seventh circle confers freedom: in crowning Dante sovereign over himself, Virgil frees him from all authority. Liberated, Dante enters the Earthly Paradise, where man lives in the midst of peaceful nature in a state of innocence, needful of no master; but this is only a place of transition, a *status viatoris,* for even the most perfect earthly life is not the ultimate purpose of the human community, but preparation for the sight of God, which means eternal beatitude.

As we see, this order is perfectly consonant with the two others, for the whole poem, whether considered from a physical, an ethical, or a historico-political point of view, builds up the destiny of man and his soul and sets it before us in a concrete image: God and creation, spirit and nature lie enclosed and ordered in perfect necessity (which however is nothing other than perfect freedom allotted to each thing according to its essence). Nothing is left open but the narrow cleft of earthly human history, the span of man's life on earth, in which the great and dramatic decision must fall; or to look at the other way round, from the standpoint of human life, this life, in all the diversity of its manifestations, is measured by its highest goal, where individuality achieves actual fulfillment and all society finds its predestined and final resting place in the universal order. Thus, even though the *Comedy* describes the state of souls after death, its subject, in the last analysis, remains earthly life with its entire range and content; everything that happens below the earth or in the heavens above relates to the human drama in this world. But since the human world receives the measures by which it is to be molded and judged from the other world, it is neither a realm of dark necessity nor a peaceful land of God; no, the cleft is really open, the span of life is short, uncertain, and decisive for all eternity; it is the magnificent and terrible gift of potential freedom which creates the urgent, restless, human, and Christian-European atmosphere of the irretrievable, fleeting moment that must be taken advantage of; God's grace is infinite, but so also is His justice and one does not negate the other. The hearer or reader enters into the narrative; in the great realm of fulfilled destiny he sees only himself alone unfulfilled, still acting upon the real, decisive stage, illumined from above but still in the dark; he is in danger, the decision is near, and in the images of Dante's pilgrimage that draw before him he sees himself damned, making atonement, or saved, but always himself, not extinguished, but eternal in his very own essence.

Thus in truth the *Comedy* is a picture of earthly life. The human world in all its breadth and depth is gathered into the structure of the hereafter and there it stands: complete, unfalsified, yet encompassed in an eternal order; the confusion of earthly affairs is not concealed or attenuated or immaterialized, but preserved in full evidence and grounded in a plan which embraces it and raises it above all contingency. Doctrine and fantasy, history and myth are woven into an almost inextricable skein; often an almost unconscionable amount of time and effort is required to fathom the content of a single line; but once one has succeeded in surveying the whole, the hundred cantos, with their radiant *terza rima*, their perpetual binding and loosing, reveal the dreamlike lightness and remoteness of a perfection that seems to hover over us like a dance of unearthly figures. Yet the law of that dream is a human reason operating according to a plan and conscious of its destiny, which it is able to govern and order because its courageous good will has been favored by divine grace.

Whether Dante Was a True Prophet

Bruno Nardi*

Was Dante really a prophet? We see right away that, just as Thomas Aquinas denied the gift of prophecy to the "Calabrian abbot Joachim" whom Dante regarded as gifted with prophetic spirit, those who will not grant the quality of true prophet to the Florentine poet are the same ones who have been making the racket for some time now— "Dante is one of us!"—that is, the ones who most of all "ought to give praise." Instead they reproach him his too frequent invectives against the pastors of the church as spoken in anger, "wrongfully blaming and defaming" him, and displaying the comprehensive good-will owing to a man of such moral stature and of such great faith. And as if to distract the reader's attention from what is the *Commedia*'s principal intent and make him forget this fundamental aspect of the Dantean soul, some among us are trying to blunt with subtle and cunning hermeneutic tricks the too pointed arrows shot from such a forceful bow. Others are at pains to stress the poet's supposed fidelity to Thomistic philosophy, even touching on doctrines often and no-toriously combated by Saint Thomas. For these, the Dantean vision is a simple fiction and literary artifice.[1]

Still others do not deny that Dante claimed for himself a mission from on high but think the renewal he announced to be a generous utopia, a poetic illusion belied by events, though not having viewed with a "realistic" eye the true forces at work in the social and political world he lived in, and whose play a Villani, a Dino Compagni, and, of course, the intriguer Lapo Salterelli were far better acquainted with than he. Dante for them is a dreamer, certainly, but not a prophet.

Now it seems to me that if we think with an unprejudiced mind of what the great inspired men and the seers of the Old Testament represented in the historical framework of the religion of Israel, Dante really continued its tradition and language, so as to deserve being considered a prophet as they were. Moreover, by his explicit reference, not only is the poet's ascent to heaven likened to the rapture of Saint Paul, but the apocalyptic vision in Eden is reconnected as well with the New Testament Apocalypse and with the revelation made to Ezekiel; and into this framework Dante inserts the motif of the twice-robbed tree and that of the eagle, which left its plumage to the chariot, whence it transformed itself into a monster. (Cf. *Purgatorio* XXIX, 100–105.) And as the Christian Apocalypse delib-

---

* From Bruno Nardi, *Dante e la cultura medievale* (Bari: Laterza, 1984), 318–26. Translated for this volume by Marilyn Myatt.

113

erately works out and completes the motifs of the revelation made to the son of Buzi, so the Dantean vision develops the vision of him who was enraptured on Patmos and that of Ezekiel.

And then it is to the point to remark that, just as the biblical prophets speak in the name of a direct revelation of God and represent individual inspiration, which, though fed by the religious life of a whole people, asserts itself from without the priestly institution and sometimes in conflict with it, in the same way Dante, layman, made daring by the vision granted him by singular divine grace, did not fear to denounce in the misdirection of the pastors of the church the reason for the world's turning wicked, and to hurl against them his bitter invective.

And just as the Old Testament prophets announced the advent at hand of the Lord's Anointed, which would restore the throne of David, so Dante predicted the restoration of the Roman Empire and the reform of the church, freed from adultery and brought back to its divine mission as guide of men to eternal felicity, through one sent by God whom the poet does not hesitate to call the new Messiah, the Christ, God's Anointed (*Monarchia*, II, 1, 3), and to foretell his apparition with the fervent words of the Baptist: "Behold the lamb of God, that taketh away the sins of the world" (*Epistle* VII, 10).

It is precisely here that Dante, unlike the ancient seers, was no prophet, but if anything a false prophet, since his dream of the restoration of the empire vanished at the very time of its prophesying, through the failure of Henry's venture, and the church long went on trafficking with the kings of the earth, becoming worldlier in the Renaissance than before. It can be answered that, as for the restoration of the throne of David, announced as imminent by the ancient prophets, the same thing happened. Far from seeing the revival of the kingdom of Israel, the Jewish people saw a calamity more terrible than the other befall it, deportation, a long bondage, the destruction of the temple, until every hope of political resurrection seemed to have passed away forever or manifested only in ephemeral attempts given up to failure. But over the ruins of political hopes, in the heaven of human consciousness, the shining star rose that guided the three kings from far countries to Bethlehem.

The same can be said of Dante's prophecy. In it there is an aggravated perception, if you will, but clear, of religious and political decadence and of the causes that produced it; there is the exact intuition of what was lacking for the good government of men, of the confusion of the two powers, one overpowered and obscured by the other, and above all of the harm deriving from the absence of a feared and respected authority to restrain the greed of the parties and the cities. These, while they saw a strong resurgence of economic life through industrious craftsmen, proved incapable of establishing a lasting political order based on justice and civil harmony. Whence the fratricidal struggles between "quei ch'un muro ed una fossa serra" (*Purg.* VI, 84) (between those whom one wall and one moat shuts), between the cities and the neighboring villages, each aiming to overpower the other, and the anarchy that was to exhaust and overcome the life of the commune; while those dictatorships were forming that, consolidated in princedoms, had at least the merit of creating stable institutions, and of beginning the process of regional unification and the resolution of the antagonism between the old feudal class and the new bourgeoisie.

In the face of this grievous situation and of the disorder that was reigning in the world, what was the value of Dante's dream of restoring the empire?

Some have seen in it a pure and simple utopia, a hybrid mixture of sacred and profane: a dream, in short. But others think Dante's political theory was based on something that was not a dream but was actually existent in the Italian political consciousness and in the civil law—that is, in the conception still persisting of the empire. And that this idea of the empire was still alive in the consciousness of the glossators and civil lawyers has been solidly demonstrated beyond a doubt[2]; it is equally certain that the communes recognized the empire's supremacy even after Legnano, as did the lordships, which asked certificates and privileges of it and often swore fealty. But it is no less certain that the doctrine of imperial rights, affirmed by jurists at the end of the thirteenth century and into the next, had by this time fallen behind the course of political events, ever since France definitively withdrew from the empire's authority to the time when the Florentine commune resolutely took its position against Henry VII. As Dante himself acknowledges, after the death of Frederick II, imperial authority in Italy had become effectively null, so that Barbarossa's grandson was, for him, the last Roman emperor, even though Rudolph of Hapsburg, Adolph of Nassau, and Albert the German were elected after him. And what does a law unable to enforce itself count for? Henry VII himself, in order to be recognized and crowned by the pope, had to pledge fealty and submission to the church, as had Rudolph, Adolph, and Albert before him. So Dante's doctrine was utopian, no less than that of Bartolo and the other contemporary civil lawyers.

And it was utopian not only with regard to the present reality of Europe and of Italy in particular but equally so with regard to the past, that is, to the time of the Ottos and even Charlemagne, in fact even with regard to the epoch of the Antoninuses. For in this period of its greatest reach, the Roman Empire never coincided with the known world, and Germany, Persia, India, and Ethiopia (without counting the unknown and little-known lands) remained outside it.

Nor did the civil lawyers, such as Bartolo, push utopia as far as Dante did, who drew less support for his conceptions from juridical sources than from Virgil. It was from Virgil he heard that God had said: "To them—that is, to the Romans—I assign no limit to things nor of time. To them I have given empire without end."[3] And in the epistle to Henry VII he cited the lines from the *Aeneid* (I, 286–87):

> from that comely line
> The Trojan Caesar comes, to circumscribe
> Empire with ocean, fame with heaven's stars.

to prove that "the glorious dominion of the Romans is not confined either within the frontiers of Italy nor within the margins of three-cornered Europe. Although, constrained by violence, it has had to restrict its effective jurisdiction to a narrow space, it extends by inviolable right as far as Amphitrite's waves and scarcely allows itself to be circumscribed by the ineffectual waters of the ocean."[4]

And yet whoever reads the *Divine Comedy*, just as whoever reads Plato's *Republic*, or the *Gospel* where the advent of God's kingdom among men is shown imminent, he feels, beyond the utopian representation of unreal events, a sublime ethical and civil conception that resonates in the immortal song, as it does in Socrates' reasoning or in the Sermon on the Mount.

Dante's illusion lies in having shown in the course of time, time more or less near or far, an eternal idea, itself outside time, acting on human affairs only as an aspiration to surpass a limit. It can always be pushed further as long as we remain in the course of time, but it can never be surpassed. The "kingdom of God among men," as long as man is on this earth, as the theologians say, is no less utopian than the Dantean dream; Jesus himself admits it: "My kingdom is not of this world."

A universal monarchy founded on reason, ordered so as to restrain the relations among its lesser communities with justice, and to secure a perpetual peace fruitful of works; cities and kingdoms subject to the empire and intent on organizing civil life "by diverse duties" according to the different capacities and bents of the citizens; social classes distinguished on the "foundation that nature settles" and careful to ensure in just measure the wherewithal for its citizens' secure and peaceful life; a nobility founded on virtue rather than on birth or wealth, and such as to teach valor and courtesy to the populace by example; patriarchal families like the Florentine ones of Cacciaguida's time, when greed for profit and excess luxury had not yet spoiled them; and for all, a life that would not consume itself seeking material goods but would allow, to those capable, as much care for the perfection of the spirit through art and science, so as to realize the ideal of the happy life assigned to man in this world by Aristotle's *Ethics*. Finally, beside these institutions subject to the empire, the church of Christ, free of all earthly greed and solely bent upon its evangelical mission of showing the way to heaven to men, teaching detachment from earthly goods with doctrine and with example; and monastic orders at its service, as instruments for combating heresy, for spreading the light of the gospel through the world, for helping those who suffer with works of Christian charity, for alleviating sorrows unrecognized by all with words of hope and of comfort, for absolving him who has sinned, for raising the spirit, in the composure of solitude, to the contemplation of eternal life—all this is morally beautiful, and not only "they who in olden times sang," but souls thirsting for justice in all times, "perhaps on Parnassus" will dream of a like happy state of humanity.

But it is a dream that is in question because such a state of earthly happiness admits of greed not at all. Now greed, which Dante believed had been set free in the world by Lucifer's envy (*Inf.* I, 110–11), which in its juxtaposition to goodwill and charity (*Par.* XXVII, 121ff.), is the greatest obstacle to realizing justice and peace among men (*Monarchia* I, xi, 11–14), and the empire's universal lordship is only the mass of human desires arising from natural needs that drive man to provide for their satisfaction, Plato's *epithumia* (desire), the common and natural appetites of the *Nichomachean Ethics* (118b), which can and should be restrained by the virtue of continence but not eliminated. Greed makes up an essential and irrepressible moment of the dialectic of life, a force of history. Once eliminated, the same justice that was framed to restrain it comes to nothing, having no more reason for being. Had Adam not sinned, Christ could not have redeemed humanity; and if Christ was to die for the salvation of man, there had to be Jews to send him to death, as the Roman poet says. We can desire and strive that greed be restrained by justice, that political institutions coincide with ethics, the useful with the just, which is the aspiration of all times. But the fact that this is still an aspiration well away from fulfillment, and that continually we speak of "unjust" or "tyrannical" laws, and have continually in view civil institutions more perfect than the existing ones; the fact that we make every effort to see them realized, without ever succeeding entirely, so that after so much effort we are forced to cry out:—You alone are true, o ideal!—all this proves that every political system is inadequate to realize morality perfectly. Morality does not recognize the accommodations to which every political system is forced to resort.

Dante was a true prophet not because his intentions of political and ecclesiastical reform were realized (we recognize, in fact, that, given the natural course of events, they were unrealizable, as it proved) but because like all the great prophets he could lift his sight beyond the events that were occurring beneath his eyes and show an eternal ideal of justice as the criterion for measuring the moral stature of men and the value of their actions. Such an ideal also has its reality in the dialectical process of the spirit, which could not progress without setting an end for itself to tend toward. In the absoluteness of the idea, fixed beyond space and time, the spirit projects the infinity of thought and its unsated desire: "You made us, Lord, for Yourself and our hearts are unquiet until they rest in You."[5] And in the longing to reunite itself with God, the restless human soul aspires to free itself from the strictures of space and time, to return to the origin it finds not without, but within, itself: "To itself its movement returns, circling the deep mind,"[6] "like a wheel that is evenly moved" (Par. XXXIII, 144) around the pivot that supports it. In this unfolding of the soul upon itself to go back to the hidden sources of being, in this capacity to become abstracted from the mutable appearances of the senses, lies precisely what the ancients called rapture and ecstasy.

"Do not go forth, return within yourself, in the inner man dwells truth; and if you find you are mutable, transcend yourself . . . make for the place where the light of reason is kindled."[7]

The man who is used to giving ear to the low voices rising from the nether depth of consciousness and to fixing his gaze within the light shining in the innermost recesses of the soul is not dismayed if the external world shatters around him because he has found what is sufficient to him and cannot be taken from him: God.

Notes

1. The two major proponents of Dante's Thomism are G. M. Cornoldi, *La filosofia scolastica di S. Tommaso e di Dante* (Rome: Tip. Befani, 1887), and G. Busnelli, *Cosmogonia e antropogenesi secondo Dante e le sue fonti* (Rome: Civilta Cattolica, 1922).

2. F. Ercole, *Impero e papato nella tradizione giuridica bolognese e nel diritto pubblico italiano del Rinascimento* (Bologna: Zanichelli, 1911).

3. *Aeneid* I, 278–79; *Convivio* IV, iv, 11.

4. *Epistle* VII, 11–13.

5. St. Augustine, *Confessions*, I, 1.

6. Boethius, *The Consolation of Philosophy*, II, metre 9.

7. St. Augustine, *On the True Religion*, C, 39.

Dante's Place in History
Etienne Gilson[*]

The most laborious, but the surest and most profitable, way to estimate correctly the meaning and importance of Dante's political philosophy, particularly as regards the idea of philosophy implicit in it, is to place it in its proper historical and doctrinal perspective. It would be something of merely local importance, were it possible to conceive of a political philosophy which did not depend on any general philosophy. Such is not the case, and we shall shortly see that Dante's attitude to these problems involved him in a certain number of other questions, the exact determination of which is important for the understanding of his work.

It may be postulated as a historically verifiable philosophical law that *the manner in which one conceives the relationship of the State to the Church, that in which one conceives the relationship of philosophy to theology and that in which one conceives the relationship of nature to grace, are necessarily correlated.* Considered from this point of view, the political doctrines of the Middle Ages may be divided, roughly at least, into three main types. There can be no question of identifying any one of them with one of these types: the facts of history do not in their diversity permit themselves to be identified with pure doctrinal essences any more than individuals permit themselves to be identified with the essential type of their species. One may, however, relate particular doctrines to certain types, of which they are distinct individual realizations, and classify them according as the resemblance which they bear to one or another of them is more or less striking.

The first of these types is characterized by a dominating tendency to integrate the order of nature with the order of grace in the highest degree possible. Doctrines of this type may be recognized by the fact that in them the distinction between grace and nature tends to merge into the distinction between good and evil. The reason for this is obvious. These are essentially religious doctrines. Centering on the problem of healing fallen nature, these doctrines take into account only that part of nature which needs to be healed through grace, that is to say the wounds that have been inflicted on it by sin—in short, its corruption. If one is to appraise this attitude correctly, it is essential not to transform it into a philosophical doctrine. To do so would be tantamount to making those who adopt it say that nature is essentially evil. As Christians, they know, on the contrary, that all that is, in so far as it is, is good. When they speak of nature,

[*] Reprinted from Etienne Gilson, *Dante the Philosopher*, trans. David Moore (London, 1948), 201–24, by permission of the copyright owner; © 1948, 1978 by the Pontificial Institute of Mediaeval Studies, Toronto.

they do so not as philosophers whose purpose is to define its essence, but as doctors who regard it as a patient to be cured, or rather as priests who regard it as a creature to be saved. The *opus creationis* ("work of creation") interests the philosopher directly, but the *opus recreationis* ("work of re-creation") is the direct concern of the priest. The attitude to nature which we are describing is essentially a "priestly" attitude. As such, it is characterized by three features, whose permanence in history is remarkable: it tends to integrate the order of nature with the order of grace in the highest degree possible, to integrate the order of reason with that of faith in the highest degree possible, and to integrate the order of the State with that of the Church in the highest degree possible.

Since it is this third aspect of the problem that particularly engages our attention here, it will be enough to go back as far as St. Augustine to find its prototype. If there is anything that corresponds to the formula "political Augustinism," it should be said that, when it penetrates into political problems, Augustinism tends to integrate the State with the Church, by virtue of an internal logic which nothing in it can keep from reaching its conclusion. The two communities which Augustine took as special delight in describing and which include all others are the City of God and the Earthly City. Now both are supernatural and religious cities, designated by two "mystic" names, of which one, Jerusalem, designates the community of all the elect, past, present and future, while the other, Babylon, designates the community formed by all the damned, past, present and future. Strictly speaking, no earthly community can be identified with one or the other of these mystic cities; indeed, it cannot be said that the Church harbours only the elect, or even that it harbours all the elect; yet the Church is the most exact approximation on earth to the City of God, because it is the city of God's intention; as for Babylon, it is the worldly city and prototype of all pagan States, in so far as, in accordance with Pagan laws, their organization has in view ends that are not God's ends.[1]

In the form in which he left it, Augustine's doctrine contained an idea of capital importance: that of a universal religious city; but it said nothing of a universal temporal community of which, on the morrow of the sack of Rome by the Barbarians, the condition of the Roman Empire scarcely invited him to think. Augustine cannot, then, be represented as having absorbed the Empire into the Church. Undoubtedly he considers that a Christian Emperor can and should serve the Church, but the State itself, regarded as such, is in his eyes simply a variable quantity. If the State is essentially pagan, as had been the case with the old Roman Empire, it is essentially evil and may in fact be identified with Babylon, as the Church may be with Jerusalem. If the State is not exclusively pagan, but tolerates

Christian citizens, or is even governed by a Christian ruler, its members will be divided between the two mystic cities to which they owe allegiance: "Just as there is only one holy city—Jerusalem—so there is only one city of iniquity—Babylon. All the wicked belong to Babylon just as all the godly belong to Jerusalem" (Augustine, *Enarr. in Ps.* 86,6). As for the States themselves, they are no longer in either camp, for they can no longer be identified with Babylon and they have not yet become one with Jerusalem.

As soon as there was a Holy Roman Empire, its integration with the Church became, on the contrary, inevitable by virtue of the very principles which Augustine had laid down. If, in practice, a pagan State may be automatically identified with Babylon, a Christian State may be automatically identified with Jerusalem. After the reign of Charlemagne, during that of Louis the Pious, the integration of the State with the Church is an accomplished fact. Beginning from this time, indeed, we encounter with growing frequency examples of those distinctive formulas *in which the definition of the Church includes the State*. This is a new fact and one big with consequences. To tell the truth, from the very day that theologians and canonists first gave currency to a conception of the Church in which the temporal order was included as a matter of course, a reaction such as Dante's became inevitable. "The body of the Holy Church of God in its entirety divides to form principally two eminent persons," it was said as early as the ninth century, "the priestly and the royal." Likewise Jonas of Orleans: "All the faithful should know that the universal Church is the body of Christ, its head is this same Christ, and in it (*in ea*) we find, principally, two persons, to wit, the priestly and the royal, and the predominance of the priestly over the other is the greater inasmuch as it will have to render an account to God even of kings."[2]

Beginning from the moment when the temporal order itself was thus integrated with the Church, there remained, to be sure, a Church to represent the City of God, but there no longer remained a pagan Empire to represent the Earthly City. Thus, as a consequence at once surprising and inevitable, Jerusalem alone remained and Babylon disappeared. This is what Otto of Freising explicitly says in his celebrated *De duabus civitatibus*. Finding himself further from events than Augustine, Otto dates the disappearance of Babylon from the accession of Constantine. "In view of the fact that not only all men, but even the Emperors, with a few exceptions, were Catholics, it seems to me that, beginning from this time, I have written the history, not of two cities, but, so to speak, of only one, which I call the Church. For although the elect and the damned occupy a single dwelling, I can no longer call these cities two, as I have done above: I ought to say that they are really only one, although it is composite, for in it the grain is mixed with the tares."[3]

Thus, through identifying the City of God with the Church and the Earthly City with the State, men have gradually come to integrate the State with the Church, whose universality will henceforth embrace the temporal and spiritual domains alike. It is this same fundamental attitude that recurs in the thirteenth century—but this time enhanced and enriched by all the contributions made to it by contemporary philosophy and theology—in the doctrinal synthesis of Roger Bacon. Never has the priestly conception of the world been more clearly or more completely expressed than in the work of this Franciscan, who may be said to be in this matter the arch-adversary of Dante. The Baconian universe presupposes a dovetailing of the orders, wherein that which we call nature, or natural, finds sustenance and justification only through being integrated with the supernatural and the religious. All wisdom is contained in the Holy. Scriptures as the open hand is contained in the closed fist. What is called Philosophy, or Law, is merely an explanation, and, as it were, the development of what is implicit in the Scriptures. In other words, all that is valid and cogent in Philosophy or Law is virtually what may be gleaned from the Bible. Thus understood Christian Revelation is Wisdom itself, and it is this Wisdom, proclaimed, dispensed and applied by the Pope, that ensures the unity of the Church, governs the community of faithful peoples, ensures the conversion of infidel peoples and the destruction of those who cannot be converted. In short, since the treasure of Revelation, the law of the world, is in the Pope's power, so also is the world: *Habetis ecclesiam Dei in potestate vestra, et mundum totum habetis dirigere* ("You have the Church of God in your power, and you have the task of governing the entire world").[4]

We are therefore faced here with a unitary system of Wisdom, in which each science derives its principles from the science above it, while all alike derive their principles from Revelation, which contains them. In a corresponding, or rather an identical sense, we are faced with a unitary system as regards the social order, in which all Christian temporal communities, which together form the *respublica fidelium* ("republic of the faithful"), are included in the spiritual community that is the Church, just as the sciences are included in the Wisdom to which the Pope, custodian of the treasure of Revelation, holds the key. One Wisdom, one world, one goal.

Let us now imagine a doctrine like that of St. Thomas, in which the order of nature is really distinct from that of grace, but subordinate to it. In such a doctrine we ought to expect to find, together with a real distinction between natural wisdom and revealed wisdom, a real distinction between the temporal order and the spiritual order, between the State and the Church. However, since we have a hierarchical system, entailing the subordination of nature to grace, there will certainly have to be also a hierarchical system entailing the subordination of the temporal domain to the spiritual and of the State to the Church. Containing distinctions of a far more flexible kind and enjoying opportunities of agreement denied to that of Bacon, the Thomistic doctrine will not on that account be any the less antagonistic, in its ultimate conclusions, to that of Dante. Instead of the dovetailing and, so to speak, the telescoping of all the natural orders into the religious order, we shall have in St. Thomas's doctrine a linear hierarchy of the orders, based on a linear hierarchy of the *ultima*, which are all subordinate to the final goal of man. Now since this goal is the beatific vision, it is essentially religious. In Thomism, therefore, the Church will necessarily have direct authority over the State.

The tendency to-day, however, is to admit that St. Thomas, if he did not preach the doctrine of the "indirect" subordination of the temporal power to the spiritual, at any rate laid its foundations. It is easy to see why this expression has finally gained currency. Certain mediaeval theologians did in fact attribute to the Pope an absolute and universal power, which he, according to their theory, freely delegates to princes, and which the latter, since they derive it from him, only exercise under his supervision and by virtue of his authority. In such doctrines, therefore, the Pope, as a temporal sovereign, has direct temporal authority over all other temporal sovereigns. Now that is certainly not the teaching of St. Thomas, in whose eyes even the temporal authority of the Popes is essentially spiritual in origin as in purpose. Indeed, the Pope's duty and right of intervention in temporal matters is always bound up with a spiritual purpose, and is due to the fact that that purpose falls within his competence. The expression "indirect power" is therefore justified in so far as it indicates the important fact that, even in temporal matters, the pope remains a spiritual sovereign. King and priest, it is because he is a priest that he is a king.

This expression has, however, the disadvantage of fostering the belief that, because the temporal power of the Popes over princes is essentially spiritual, it is merely an advisory or corrective power, exercising no direct influence over the temporal authority of the prince as such—a power whose scope is strictly delimited by the celebrated formula *ratione peccati*. In order to see how foreign such a conception is to St. Thomas it is only necessary to reconsider the particular problem against its general background, which consists in the relations between nature and grace. It is because St. Thomas always makes a real distinction between the orders that, thus distinguished, they are directly subject to graduation on a hierarchical principle. Hence, the Pope, by reason of his eminence and his supreme spiritual authority, has temporal authority over princes. How far does this authority extend? To all of the prince's activities which, in any degree, concern man's final goal, which falls within the competence of the Pope. Thus, because the goal of the political order is designed with a view to the religious and supernatural goal of the Church, the ruler of the Church as such is the ruler of princes, even in temporal matters. It would, however, be a waste of time to try to determine *a priori*, by some general formula, when, why, how and to what extent the Pope has the right of intervention in the life of the State. It rests with the Pope alone to judge. He it is who speaks or does not speak and, according to the particular circumstances, exercises or does not exercise his right to intervene in temporal matters in order to ensure to men the attainment of the final goal which God has promised them, and to which, as the vicar of Jesus Christ on earth, he leads them.

Nothing could be more lucid in this connection than the comparison that St. Thomas himself has drawn between the pagan order, the Jewish order and the Christian order. It indicates with the utmost clarity the question which dominates the whole problem. Is man's final goal temporal or spiritual? If it is temporal, priests are subordinate to princes; if it is spiritual, princes are subordinate to priests. There is absolutely no question in all this of direct or indirect power; it is a question of the hierarchical subordination of the means to the end. That is why, in Christianity, and in Christianity alone, princes are subject to the priesthood in that the Pope, *qua* Pope, has supreme authority over princes *qua* princes. Here, incidentally, is a comparative table of these relations as it emerges from the *De regimine principum* of St. Thomas, Book I, Chapter 14:

Pagan Priesthood	Jewish Priesthood	Christian Priesthood
has as its goal the procurement of temporal goods from Spirits	has as its goal the procurement of earthly goods from God	has as its goal the procurement of heavenly goods from God
priests subject to kings	priests subject to kings	kings subject to priests

Such, then, in their nakedness, are St. Thomas's principle and its consequence. The principle: *Ei ad quem finis ultimi cura pertinet, subdi debent illi ad quos pertinet cura antecedentium finium et ejus imperio dirigi* ("Those who are in charge of the subordinate goals must be governed by his authority"); the consequence: *In lege Christi reges debent sacerdotibus esse subjecti* ("In the law of Christ kings must be subject to the priesthood"). Now, as St. Thomas repeated in Book I, Chapter 15, "the goal of life, which enables us to live righteously in this world, is heavenly beatitude; it is therefore an essential part of the king's function to organize the life of his people in a way that makes it easier for it to secure heavenly beatitude. The king should therefore prescribe that course which leads to heavenly beatitude, and forbid the contrary as far as possible." And how will the king get to know all this? By learning the divine law which priests are charged with teaching. There is, then, no break in the hierarchy of these powers: *Tanto est regimen sublimius, quanto ad finem ulteriorem ordinatur* ("The more remote the goal to which government is directed, the more sublime that same government"). Now man's final goal is the enjoyment of God; to lead man to this goal there must be a king who is himself not only man, but God—i.e., Jesus Christ or his successor, the Roman Pontiff, "to whom all the kings of the Christian people would be subject, as to our Lord Jesus Christ Himself." From whatever angle one regards this doctrine, one cannot make it say, as Dante says, that the Pope exercises no temporal authority over the Empire. Indeed, it says precisely the opposite, and not all the skill that is expended to bring the two doctrines into line can have the effect of reconciling them.

If this is correct, the doctrinal gulf that divides the champions of the Pope's temporal supremacy and their opponents is not fixed between Roger Bacon and Thomas Aquinas, but between Thomas Aquinas and Dante. Under the pressure of Dante's political passion, the unity of mediaeval Christendom, with its subservience to the Popes, has now been abruptly and utterly shattered. The emperor may henceforth pursue his special aim without looking to the head of the Church for anything but his blessing. Everywhere expelled from the temporal order, the authority of the Roman Pontiff finds itself confined exclusively to the order of grace. This Dantesque Pope who no longer deposes princes is therefore very different from the Pope of St. Thomas Aquinas.[5] The most remarkable thing about Dante's attitude, however, is that he understood, with a profundity of thought for which he must be commended, that *one cannot entirely withdraw the temporal world from the jurisdiction of the spiritual world without entirely withdrawing philosophy from the jurisdiction of theology*. It is because he clearly saw this fact and plainly indicated it that Dante occupies a cardinal position in the history of mediaeval political philosophy. For after all, if philosophic reason, by which the Emperor is guided, were to remain in the smallest degree subject to the authority of the theologians, the Pope would through their agency recover the authority over the Emperor which it is desired to take from him. By the very fact that he controlled reason, he would control the will that is guided by reason. Thus, the separation of Church and Empire necessarily presupposes the separation of theology and philosophy, and that is why, just as he split mediaeval Christendom into two camps, Dante also completely shatters the unity of Christian wisdom, the unifying principle and the bond of Christendom. In each of these vital matters this alleged Thomist struck a mortal blow at the doctrine of St. Thomas Aquinas.

Faced with these indisputable facts, one appreciates why some interpreters of Dante have resolutely taxed him with Averroism. And we are this time nearer the mark—but what is the Averroism in question? Is it Averroes himself? A primary reason for doubting it is that the principal passages in Averroes dealing with the place of religion in the State seem to have remained unknown to Dante and his contemporaries, owing to the fact that they had not been translated from the Arabic into Latin. Moreover, it is only necessary to refer to his treatise on the *Reconciliation of Religion and Philosophy* or to that part of the *Destructio destructionum* which deals with these problems to find oneself transported to a universe as different from Dante's as was his from those of Roger Bacon and St. Thomas Aquinas. It is a known fact that Averroes recognized no absolute truth apart from pure philosophical truth, discovered by means of the irrefutable demonstrations of reason. Below the extremely limited class of the philosophers, who alone are capable of aspiring to knowledge of this kind, Averroes placed the more numerous class of the theologians, folk who seize eagerly upon the probabilities indicated by dialectics, but are as incapable to irrefutable demonstrations as they are disinclined to aspire to them. Lower still comes the host of ordinary people, as blind to dialectical probability as to rational certainty, susceptible only to the persuasion of rhetoric and the artifices of orators with the ability to excite their imaginations and passions. In a doctrine of this kind, which has with reason been termed "the most profound commentary that has ever been forthcoming on that celebrated formula: *The people must have a religion,*" there can be no question for one moment of in any sense subordinating philosophy to religion. On the contrary, it is rather, indeed, religion that is subordinated to philosophy. The special role which then devolves upon religion—and in which there is no possible substitute for it, not even philosophy—consists in teaching the people myths capable of inducing them, by their implications of punishments or pleasures in store, to live orderly and virtuous lives. An example is the doctrine of the future life, with its chastisements or its rewards—a doctrine whose prevalence among so many different religious sects must have a profound significance. That significance is as follows. The philosophers may indeed prove by reason the necessity for men to live virtuous lives, but what effect will their proofs have on the immense host of people who cannot even understand them? Only religion can perform the miracle of teaching the mass of mankind just as much as they can understand of truth, and in the exact form required in order that they may be convinced of it. Accordingly, let the people be given full knowledge of the resurrection of the body, the pains and chastisements of the life to come, prayers, sacrifices and all that will be deemed necessary for their moral education, for that is the special function of religious doctrines—to enable the State to be well ordered by spreading enlightenment among its citizens.

That such a doctrine is completely unacceptable to a Christian is obvious, and that is why, even if he had been or was acquainted with it, Dante could not have accepted it. All his convictions rebelled against it—even his separatism. Nothing was capable of more deeply wounding his passionate feeling of respect for the complete independence of the orders than this Averroistic doctrine whereby the religious order was subordinated to the philosophical order and subjected to moral or political aims. Dante does not for one moment doubt that the noblest of human aims is to enjoy the beatific vision in a blessed eternity, or that the Church, whose sole head is the Pope, exists to lead us to it. No more than the author of the *Divine Comedy* does the author of the *Monarchy* regard the immortality of the soul, the resurrection of the body, Hell and Paradise as so many myths that help to further the ends pursued by politics and ethics. In short, there is in Dante's eyes a distinct supernatural order, existing in its own right, and all men, philosophers included, are equally bound by its special conditions, which are a means to its special end.

If there is any Averroism in Dante, and if it is not the Averroism of Averroes himself, is it not an attitude imitated from that of the Latin Averroists of the thirteenth century, such as Boethius of Dacia or Siger of Brabant? It is extremely difficult to answer "Yes" or "No" to the question so put, for the simple reason that, if Dante preached some sort of political Averroism, his *Monarchy* must be regarded, in the present state of our knowledge, as the first and perhaps the most perfect evidence of the existence of such a movement. No treatise on politics written by an Averroist and at present known to us is of earlier date than the *Monarchy*. This fact assuredly does not prove that Dante does not here draw his inspiration from Averroism. In the first place, it may be that Averroistic political writings of earlier date than his work will one day be discovered. Nor is it impossible that conversations, or even a teaching-campaign of which no written traces survive, may have exerted on Dante an influence of which the *Monarchy* is in this respect the fruit. In fact, in a passage that has often been quoted, Pierre Dubois informs us that Siger of Brabant had publicly debated in Paris a question taken from the *Politics* of Aristotle. Since we are ignorant of the duration, scope and content of this teaching, and since, moreover, we do not know if and how Dante may have been affected by it, nothing that we might say on this subject would be more than mere conjecture. Since our ignorance is complete, it is better to refrain from discussing the matter.

It is, on the other hand, legitimate to wonder whether, by virtue of the principles from which it draws its inspiration and the use to which it puts them, Dante's *Monarchy* is not itself in some way, and even, perhaps, in a very original way, one of the expressions of mediaeval Latin Averroism. In answering this question we must first of all remember that, in its very essence, Latin Averroism was confirmation of an actual disagreement between certain conclusions of philosophy, regarded as rationally necessary, and certain teachings of Christian Revelation, regarded as true on the authority of the word of God. Now we do not find in the *Monarchy*, any more than in the *Banquet*, proof that Dante ever accepted as rationally necessary a single philosophical conclusion that is at variance with Christian dogma. Not only did he never preach the eternity of the world and the unity of the active intellect, or deny the immortality of the soul and the penalties of the life to come, but he always maintained that the conclusions of philosophy, in so far, that is, as philosophy is competent in these matters, tend in the same direction as the teachings of Christian Revelation. Let us, moreover, note carefully that Dante could not have thought differently without destroying the balance of his own doctrine, since it rests entirely on the absolute certainty that all forms of authority, being equally derived from God, have only to develop in accordance with their respective natures in order to be assured of agreement. In fact, there is no more conflict between the faith and reason of Dante than between the faith and reason of St. Thomas Aquinas. Dante has less confidence than St. Thomas in the capacity of reason for furnishing proofs in matters of natural theology. He appeals to faith a little more readily than the theologian, but he does so in order to confirm or round off the conclusions of philosophy, never in order to deny them. If, then, the conflict commonly referred to as that of "twofold truth" is co-essential with Averroism, it is scarcely possible to call the doctrine of the *De Monarchia* Averroistic.

Why, then, in spite of everything, can we not re-read the final chapters of this treatise without thinking of the Latin Averroists? Undoubtedly because of the separatism of the orders which is there so vehemently affirmed and which, indeed, constitutes one of the characteristic features of Averroism. Yet, so far as Dante is concerned, what is involved is a form of separatism which is not only free from conflict, but which entails and assists the harmony of the orders thus separated. The influence exerted by Averroes was so vast, so profound and so multiform that we cannot say with certainty that Dante escaped it. History here clashes with psychology, which is one of its bounds. If one remembers the crisis of philosophism which the poet seems at one time to have experienced, and thinks of the place that later, in the *Divine Comedy*, he reserved for Siger of Brabant, one's inclination is to regard the formal separatism, unmarked by any opposition between its components, which Dante preached as a mild and very much attenuated form of the material separatism, abounding in conflicts, which was professed by the Latin Averroists of his time. Let us say, then, if it is desired, that Dante's attitude towards philosophy naturally finds a place in the history of mediaeval Aristotelianism between St. Thomas Aquinas and the Averroism condemned in 1277, in which, for personal reasons, the separatism of the orders is to his liking; but let us be careful to make it clear that if, in this precise particular, Dante was able to regard Averroism as an ally, his attitude is derived neither from the doctrine of Averroes nor from that of any of the Latin Averroists known to us.

In the first place, this Averroistic philosophy was not accepted by Dante. Again, if Dante's separatism was inspired by political-philosophical motives, no known Averroist seems to have gone before him along this road—indeed, none, to my knowledge seems to have followed him along it. There is nothing surprising in this. Since Dante's position necessarily implies that the philosophy of Averroes is false in so far as it contradicts the Christian faith, it is not clear how the influence of Averroes could have given rise to a political philosophy like Dante's. The same remark applies to Latin Averroism. The only reason for the excellent harmony existing between Church and Empire in Dante's thought is that the philosophy on which the Emperor bases his laws is in harmony with the theology that the Pope teaches. Since philosophy and theology do not harmonize in Latin Averroism, the unity of the Dantesque world can find neither foundations nor even acceptance in it.

We cannot, then, rule out the hypothesis that, having set himself a personal problem of political philosophy, Dante himself evolved its solution with the help of the materials placed at his disposal by Aristotle. The hypothesis commends itself to our notice all the more as Dante's attitude towards philosophy does not admit of identification with any other. Whatever the influences of which it bears the stamp, his doctrine is no more a second-hand doctrine than his answer to the problem of the Priesthood and the Empire is a second-hand answer. Now it is quite true that Aristotle could in no way help the author of the *Monarchy* to solve a problem which could not arise in a Greek civilization. Even if Dante read Aristotle's *Politics*, which is not certain, it cannot have dictated his answer to the problem he set himself. The same observation would, moreover, apply to the *Ethics ad Nicomachum*, which to our certain knowledge Dante read and meditated, together with the commentary provided by St. Thomas Aquinas. Yet the enthusiasm with which his reading of this work filled him is probably responsible for Dante's conception of his ideal of a temporal order independent of the Church and seeking its own final goal under the guidance of reason alone. Since Aristotle envisaged the possibility of temporal felicity secured through the natural virtue of justice, why should not this final goal of the Greek city still be, even in the fourteenth century, that of the Empire?

Now Dante was not only acquainted with the *Nicomachean Ethics,* but he treasured it.[6] He was himself so conscious of this predilection that in the *Divine Comedy* he made Virgil say to him: "la tua Etica" (*Inf.,* XI, 80). If, as all this work attests, Dante was animated by an ardent desire for justice and peace in the temporal sphere, it is understandable that this altogether admirable book, in which, even through St. Thomas's commentary with its Christian inspiration, the ideal of human temporal felicity secured entirely through the practice of the natural virtues was so clearly visible, was to him in a sense the Bible of the Lawgiver. What promises did Dante not hear echoing in the pregnant phrases in which St. Thomas summarized the authentic thought of Aristotle! *Finis politicae est humanum bonum, idest optimus in rebus humanis; . . . unde ad ipsam [artem civilem] maxime pertinet considerare finem ultimum humanae vitae, tanquam ad principalissimam.* ("The goal of politics is the good of humanity, in other words it is the loftiest goal in the realm of human affairs; . . . hence, the supreme function of this same [civil art], as the chief of all arts, is the consideration of the final goal of human life").[7] Is this not precisely that "final goal of human life," final although temporal, whose realization the *Monarchy* appeals to politics to ensure? Now what science lays the foundations of politics, if not ethics? And in what book do we find ethics, if not in the *Nicomachean Ethics?* Aristotle's thought is so clear that even the Christian amendments of St. Thomas never prevent it from emerging: "But we must know that Aristotle calls politics the very first of the sciences, not in an absolute sense, but in the category of the active sciences, dealing with human affairs, of which politics considers the final goal. For if the final goal of the whole universe is in question, it is the divine science that considers it, and *this* is the very first of all the sciences. But he says that it is the concern of politics to consider the final goal of human life, and if he defines the nature of that goal in this book [*on ethics*], the truth is that the teaching of this book contains the primary elements of political science."

St. Thomas's conscientiousness is admirable, for, while his duty as a theologian compels him to recall in good time that the supreme science can only be that of the supreme Goal, and hence theology, he nevertheless does not forget to conclude, like the objective commentator he is: *Dicit autem ad politicam pertinere considerationem altimi finis humanae vitae* ("Moreover, he says that the function of politics is the consideration of the final goal of human life"). Dante needed nothing more for the composition of his work. The rights of theology could wait their turn, in the certainty that they would be respected, so long as it was granted that of attributing to human life a final goal accessible by means of natural ethics and politics alone. Did St. Thomas's remarkable discretion as a commentator on Aristotle lead Dante to believe that even the Angel of the Schools acknowledged the existence of a "final goal" to human life attainable in this world through political and moral justice? Psychologically it is not impossible, but we shall never know. If we were to accept the theory, Dante's admiration for a St. Thomas thus interpreted would merely be the easier to explain. There is, however, no need to accept it. Even if he clearly saw what modifications St. Thomas effected in Aristotle's doctrine, Dante nonetheless found Aristotle's doctrine in this commentary, which is incomparably more luminous than the obscure Latin translation with which it deals, and it was this doctrine that he seized upon—neglecting the rest—as though it were a prize that was his by right.

If we admit the reality of this influence exerted by Aristotle's *Ethics* on the formation of Dante's political philosophy, its essential characteristics are easily explained. The striking external resemblance of Dante's attitude to that of the Latin Averroists is perhaps only one of those cases, like that of Erasmus and Luther, in which two adversaries agree in practice on a common attitude against a common foe, but for very different reasons. Such working agreements sometimes conceal profound dissensions, and these are not lacking between Dante and Averroism. We do not find, in the propositions condemned in 1227 by Etienne Tempier, any political thesis properly so called, but they contain more than two hundred physical, metaphysical and moral theses. Of these it cannot be said that Dante ever accepted a single one, but he explicitly rejected a certain number of them, and several were the very negation of his doctrine. Let us take, for example, Proposition 167: "Felicity is secured in this life, and not in another"; or Proposition 177: "There are no possible virtues apart from acquired or innate virtues"; or again, Proposition 157: "When a man is sufficiently disciplined in mind and feeling by the intellectual and moral virtues of which the Philosopher speaks in his *Ethics*, he is sufficiently prepared for eternal felicity." What such propositions express could in Dante's eyes only be a most horrible confusion of the orders. If these Averroistic propositions are true, Dante's whole doctrine is false. Moreover, if the dictum that the conclusions of philosophy are *always* in agreement with theology is called in question, the structure of the Dantesque world totters on its foundations, because peace, consisting in the spontaneous harmony of the three autonomous powers that govern it, is thereby made impossible.

The simplest course would therefore be to regard Dante's attitude not as a particular case of Latin Averroism but as an effort to base his political separatism on the moral philosophy of Aristotle. In this way we should understand why, instead of separating theology from philosophy in order to reconcile and unite them. Dante's universe remains thereby typically Christian, but it is so after his own fashion, and it does not admit of identification with any other known type of mediaeval Christian universe. Grace does not absorb nature, as in Roger Bacon, for example; it does not penetrate the inner nature, as in St. Thomas Aquinas; it is not eliminated to the advantage of nature, as in Averroes; it does not oppose nature, as in the Latin Averroists of the type of Siger of Brabant; indeed, one would say rather that it ranks above nature in dignity and beside it in authority, sure of a perfect harmony which nothing can disturb so long as grace and nature respect the limits set by God Himself to their domains. Dante's Emperor possesses the key to the Earthly Paradise, but the Pope alone holds the key that opens to men the Kingdom of Heaven. Even in this world the Pope's authority is no longer of this world: he dominates it without playing an active part in it.

Thus conceived, Dante's doctrine has the uniform flow of original thought, and we feel the presence of a personal initiative behind each of the theses of which it is composed. That, indeed, is why, properly speaking, it cannot be classified. The ideal of a universal monarchy, a universal philosophy and a universal faith, all three completely independent in their respective spheres, yet exhibiting perfect concord solely through the spontaneity of their individual action, has no parallel in the Middle Ages, or, for that matter, in any other epoch of history. It would be easy to find advocates to plead that there is concord among these three orders in the subordination of two of them to the third, but Dante desires that there should be a concord among them arising from their independence. One could also easily find by virtue of the incompatibility of their conclusions and even of their principles, but Dante desires that they should enjoy an independence arising from their independence. One could also easily find subscribers to the belief that the three orders enjoy independence by virtue of the incompatibility of their conclusions and even of their principles, but Dante desires that they should enjoy an independence arising from their concord. That is why the notion of justice is, as it were, the mainspring of his work, for such a social organization cannot survive for one moment unless each of the interested parties is firmly resolved to show scrupulous respect for the various forms of authority by which its own authority is restricted. Hence what characterizes Dante's ideal is his deep faith that the works of God will harmonize provided that they remain true to their nature. And so we see his desire for justice unceasingly accompanied by a boundless exaltation of freedom. In his eyes freedom is essentially the right of every being to act in accordance with his own nature, under the aegis of the beneficent authorities which protect him and enable him to attain his goal. For our will must be subject to that of the Emperor in order to be free from tyrants and Popes, just as our faith must be subject to the authority of the Pope in order to be free from that of tyrants and Emperors.

The singular character of Dante's doctrine is well indicated by the paradoxical interpretation that he has offered of the famous passage in Genesis, I, 16: *Fecitique Deus duo luminaria magna, luminare majus, ut praeesset diei; et luminare minus, ut praeesset nocti* ("And God made two great lights: the greater light to rule the day, and the lesser light to rule the night"). None could doubt that the reference there was to the sun and the moon, and there might well have been discussion aimed at discovering who was the sun—the Pope or the Emperor; but no one had ever thought of saying that God had created two suns—one to lighten the way of this world, the other to show us the way of God. Yet this is what the justly famous lines in *Purg.*, XVI, 106–108 say:

> Soleva Roma, che il buon mondo feo,
> due soli aver, che l'una e l'altra strada
> facean vedere, e nel mondo e di Deo.
> (*Purg.* XVI, 106–108)

[Rome, which made the world good, nor wont to have two suns, which made visible both the one road and the other, that of the world and that of God.]

These lines, which summarize exactly the separatism preached by Dante in the *Monarchy*, admirably express his doctrine's divergences from the recognized standpoints. The distinction between the road of the world and the road of God, each lightened by its own sun, is a faithful reflection of the distinction between the two final goals to which the Pope and the Emperor lead humanity in the *Monarchy*. We cannot, then, accuse Guido Vernani of having made a mistake about the doctrinal implications of the work when, at the end of his *De reprobatione Monarchiae*, he denounced its peculiar character. With a clumsiness that is only too noticeable, but with a proper sense of the crucial features of the doctrine, Guido accused Dante of assigning a separate form of beatitude to corruptible man, who can have neither virtue nor beatitude properly so called; with regarding man, in consequence, as being destined by God for this beatitude, conceived as a final goal distinct from heavenly beatitude; and with inferring that the Empire is not subject to the Papacy from the fact that both are directly subject to the will of God.[8] It is surprising that such theses, of which the last two at any rate are so obviously antagonistic to Thomism, can to-day be regarded as hardly different from those which St. Thomas propounded. Not only did the Dominican Guido Vernani and the Franciscan Guglielmo di Sarzana judge of them otherwise, but Pope John XXII condemned the *De Monarchia* to the flames in 1329 and the book was put on the Index in 1554. Although it was withdrawn during the course of the nineteenth century, it is hard to believe that the character of its doctrine changed between the sixteenth and the nineteenth centuries. Undoubtedly it was simply considered that political conditions had altered sufficiently for the doctrine to have lost much of its virulence, but it does not need a great effort of imagination to conceive of conditions under which it might recover it.

Yet however antagonistic Dante's political philosophy may be to Thomism, it does not seem to have been marshalled against it from abstract motives, whether religious or metaphysical. To seek the inspiration of the *Monarchy* along these lines is probably to steer clear of the one quarter in which one has any chance of finding it. Indeed, Dante here is rather carrying out his special mission as a political reformer and a righter of wrongs. What he desires first and foremost is to abolish the monstrous injustice which in his eyes is constituted by the Papacy's usurpation of the Empire. Already, in the "covetous" and the Decretalists attacked in the *Monarchy*, we have those whom the *Divine Comedy* is presently to situate in Hell, for these men betray not only the authority on which they encroach, but even that which they represent. Like the tyrant who puts power to a personal use, the cleric who puts Revelation to a temporal use commits a crime; he even commits the supreme crime—the betrayal of the Holy Spirit: *O summum facinus, etiamsi contingat in somniis, aeterni Spiritus intentione abuti!* ("O most heinous of crimes [even if it be committed in dreams]—abuse of the eternal Spirit's intentions!")[9] Dante's conception of the nature and role of philosophy was such a personal one precisely because it was required for the solution of the essentially personal problem that he set himself in the *Monarchy*. It should therefore be interpreted not in terms of Averroes' or St. Thomas's doctrine, but in terms of his ideal of a universal Empire.

PHILOSOPHY IN THE *DIVINE COMEDY*

The study of Dante's attitude towards philosophy in the *Divine Comedy* inevitably brings one up against the problem that is raised by the presence in Paradise of the Averroistic philosopher Siger of Brabant. One might easily devote a large volume to a critical examination of the answers already suggested. It would take a very gifted writer, however, to make such a book readable; while it requires considerable temerity to re-open a question that has been debated so often, and with so little profit.

Indeed, strictly speaking, the problem does not admit of solution. Its principal data are two unknowns, and historians spend their time reproaching one another with arbitrarily determining the value of one in terms of the supposed value which they ascribe to the other. In other words, if we were sure, on the one hand of Dante's thought, on the other of Siger of Brabant's, it would be easy enough to discover what Dante may have thought of Siger. But we are not. It may therefore be proved with equal ease either that Dante was an Averroist, since he put a notorious Averroist in Paradise, or that Siger was no longer an Averroist when Dante put him in Paradise, since Dante was not an Averroist and yet put him there. Thus every historian will accuse his neighbour either of choosing the Siger he needs to justify his Dante, or of inventing the Dante he needs to justify his Siger. By itself this would still mean nothing. Every historian will undertake to prove that all his opponents make that mistake which he alone has avoided. In that case, it will be said, why refer again to a question which cannot even be formulated? And my answer will be: Because it is unfortunately inevitable once we seek to define Dante's attitude towards philosophy, which we *must* do if we wish to ascribe a precise meaning to the *Monarchy* and the *Banquet.* That is why, having defined the mistakes made by the majority of my predecessors, I am about to offer you my own.

I. Dante's Thomism

On the threshold of this new problem we encounter once again, and more inevitably than ever, the weighty Dantesque synthesis of Father Mandonnet. What makes it here singularly interesting is the fact that, unlike his fellows, this excellent historian has not begun by loading the dice. Hence, equally certain that Dante was a Thomist and Siger an Averroist, he has come up against the problem in the uncompromising form of a paradox, which, as it stands, would seem to be insoluble. This is not to deny that Dante's general philosophical attitude in the *Divine Comedy* is known, for it amounts to an admission that his attitude in that work was, on the whole, that of a Thomist, and that Dante's approval of Siger cannot be attributed to sympathy with his Averroism.

This makes it necessary to deal—finally, directly and for its own sake—with the proof of Dante's Thomism which has repeatedly been furnished Father Mandonnet. Now this proof is in his writings bound up with, embedded in, a regular system of symbolic interpretation. If Dante is to be a Thomist there must be only three principal actors in the *Divine Comedy;* if there are to be only three of these actors their number must be determined by the symbolism of the Trinity; if their number is to be so determined this symbolism must dominate the *Divine Comedy* down to the last detail. Now no one dreams of disputing that Dante many a time had recourse to symbolism. Not only does he himself say that he did so, but it is obvious.[10] It will not even be disputed that, like all who have recourse to symbolism, Dante is capable of representing anything by any symbol. We have already come across notable examples of this, and it would be possible to add others. If, then, I am to discuss the cases of symbolism alleged by Father Mandonnet, the truth is not that I consider them unlikely in themselves, for, in this field, nothing is unlikely; nor is it that Dante seems to me incapable of them, for, in this field, he was capable of anything. The true aim of this discussion is to show that we are not entitled, just because all symbolism is arbitrary, to ascribe to Dante symbolist arguments for which we are not sure that he was in fact responsible. We may reckon with his arbitrary symbolism whenever we are certain that it exists, but to his let us not add our own. Above all, let us not attribute to him precisely the arbitrary symbolism needed to justify the personal interpretation of his thought whose accuracy we are seeking to verify. Once having started along this road, we should be lost. To free oneself from the spell of Father Mandonnet's symbolist dialectics, one is absolutely bound to examine the data on which his arguments rest and to estimate their exact value. A doubly thankless task, in truth. Since no symbolism is impossible, we shall never prove that Dante did not accept, or would not have accepted, those forms of symbolism which are attributed to him. What I shall attempt, therefore, is to show that, instead of basing his thesis on the symbolism which he has found in Dante, Father Mandonnet has too often found in Dante the symbolism needed to prove his thesis.

. . . .

C. The Symbolism of Intelletto

Dante, adds Father Mandonnet, "also in the *Comedy*, uses the word *intelletto* 30 times: six times in the *Inferno*, 12 in the *Purgatorio*, 12 in the *Paradiso*. The reason is that the understanding of the damned is deprived of the *ben dell'intelletto*. On the other hand, 30, as we know, is the symbol of Philosophy; now the sciences are the property and the appanage of the human understanding: hence the number of mentions."[11]

Once more, Father Mandonnet gives no references. Now Scartazzini's Concordance notes only 28 examples of the use of *Intelletto* in the *Divine Comedy*:[12] five in the *Inferno*, 12 in the *Purgatorio* and 11 in the *Paradiso*. Let us assume, however, that Father Mandonnet's figures are accurate; how shall we explain Dante's decision to symbolize the fact that the understanding of the damned is deprived of the sight of God by the number 6, a multiple of the perfect number, which is 3? At a pinch we might have understood his using *intelletto* once in Hell to symbolize the intellect in its natural state. Even better should we have understood his not using the word at all, as in the case with "will"; but there is here no conceivable significance implicit in the number 6, and Father Mandonnet himself does not suggest any. The same may be said of the number 12 which applies to the *Purgatorio* and the *Paradiso* alike. Assuming that there is any sense in naming the intellect six times in Hell in order to indicate that it is there deprived of the sight of God, it is not clear why it should be named 12 times in Purgatory, where it does not yet enjoy that sight, and, again, why it should once more be named 12 times in Paradise, where it enjoys the sight of God. A sequence such as 1, 6, 9 would have been understandable; the sequence of 6, 12, 12 is absolutely the reverse. If, as is probable, the correct figures are Scartazzini's (5, 12, 11) the problem does not even arise.

D. The Symbolism of "Will"

"Like a good Thomist," continues Father Mandonnet, "Dante uses the word 'will' only ten times: that is to say one third as many times; for the understanding is the dominating faculty. The will is not mentioned in Hell, because the damned and the devils no longer have the will to make for their goal. They blaspheme God and do not desire Him, but hate Him. The will is named once in Purgatory: it has not achieved its object. It is named nine times in Paradise."[13]

This time the reader's perplexity is greater than ever, for not only does Father Mandonnet give us no references, but he does not even tell us what Italian word he translates by the French *volonte*. We have, in fact, a choice of three forms: *volonta, volontade* and *volontate*. Which is the relevant one? We cannot be sure. Father Mandonnet simply tells us in a note to look in SCARTAZZINI *Enciclopedia dantesca*. We must conclude from this that Scartazzini's Encyclopaedia is not at one with his Concordance. If we refer to this latter work we find seven examples of *volonta*, one of which is the variant *volontate*. If we ignored the variants and totalled up the three forms, we should obtain 13 examples, and not ten. If we totalled up the examples of *volonta* and *volontade*, we should have two in the *Purgatorio* and eight in the *Paradiso*, which is not one and nine. If we totalled up the examples of *volontade* and *volontate*, we should have one in the *Purgatorio* and five in the *Paradiso*: one and five are not one and nine.[14] However we go about it, we cannot arrive at Father Mandonnet's figures.

Once more, however, let us pretend to accept the figures that are given us. We wonder what they can really mean. *Sorridere* appears once in the *Inferno* because laughter is the peculiar attribute of man. *Intelletto* is used six times because in Hell the intellect is deprived of the sight of God. And now we are told that *will* is not used at all because the will of the damned is rooted in evil. Yet certainly the damned still have a will, otherwise they could not hate God. It should therefore be mentioned either once, like the "peculiar attribute of man," or six times, like the intellect. The same remark applies to the single mention of the will in Purgatory. True, it has not there achieved its object, but neither has the intellect of the souls in Purgatory; why, when should the intellect be mentioned there six times and the will only once, seeing that these two faculties are in the same state? Of the sequence 0, 1, 9 as of the previous ones, it may be said that strictly it does not signify anything. The fact that Father Mandonnet's thesis triumphs, whatever the figures, entitles us to conclude that any number may symbolize anything.

Notes

1. For the sake of greater brevity, I venture at this point to refer the reader to my *The Christian Philosophy of Saint Augustine*, trans. L. S. M. Lynch (New York: Vintage Books, 1967).

2. The first passage is taken from a Letter addressed by the bishops of the Empire in 829 (Council of Paris) to the Emperor Louis the Pious. See R. W. Carlyle, *A History of Mediaeval Political Theory in the West* (London: W. Blackwood and Son, 1903), I, pp. 254 and 190–191. For the passage from Jonas of Orleans, see Carlyle, I, p. 254.

3. Otto of Freising, *Chronicon*, lib. V, Prol.; lib. VII, Prol; lib. VIII, Prol. On the work of Otto see the excellent Introduction by Charles Christopher Mierow to his translation of *The Two Cities. A Chronicle of Universal History to the Year 1146 A.D. by Otto Bishop of Freising* (New York: Columbia Univ. Press, 1928).

4. Roger Bacon, *Opus Tertium*, cap. XXIV, ed. J. S. Brewer (London: Longman & Green, 1859), p. 87.

5. By the very fact that he restricts the authority of the Church to the purely spiritual domain Dante is seen to be naturally in sympathy with all who have in any sense striven to detemporalize the Church—as, for example, St. Bernard (see the excellent study by E. Jordan, "Dante et saint Bernard" in the *Bulletin du Comite francais catholique pour la celebration du sixieme centenaire de la mort de Dante Alighieri*, 4 (Oct. 1921), pp. 267–330. Yet his attitude need not be identical with theirs, for the Spiritualists are concerned above all with the purity of the Church, whereas Dante is concerned at least as much with the independence of the Empire.

6. Cf. A. H. Gilbert, "Had Dante Read the *Politics* of Aristotle?" *Publications of the Modern Language Association of America*, 43.3 (Sept. 1928), pp. 602–613. The author does not, incidentally, claim to establish that Dante did not read the *Politics*, but that his quotations from it may be explained away as excerpts from Egidio Colonna and Thomas Aquinas. . . . Quotations from the *Politics* occur in the following passages of the *Monarchia:* I, 3, 5, 12; II, 3, 7, 8; The *Ethics* is cited in I, 3, 11, 13, 14, 15; II, 2, 3, 8, 12; III, 10, 12.

7. St. Thomas Aquinas, *Commentary on the Nichomachean Ethics*, Lect. II, ed. Angelo Pirotta (Turin: Marietti, 1934), no. 29 and no. 30.

8. Guido Vernani, *De reprobatione Monarchiae*, ed. Jarro (Guido Piccini) (Florence-Rome, 1906), pp. 200–201.

9. *Monarchia* III, 4.

10. Dante, *Epistle X*, sect. 7.

11. P. Mandonnet, *Dante le Theologien: Introduction a l'intelligence de la vie, des oeuvres et de l'art de Dante Alighieri* (Paris: Desclee De Brouwer, 1935), p. 189.

12. A. Scartazzini, *Concordanza della Divina Commedia di Dante Alighieri* (Leipzig: Brockhaus, 1901), p. 74.

13. P. Mandonnet, *Dante le Theologien*, pp. 189–190.

14. A. Scartazzini, *Concordanza*, p. 166.

Allegory

Charles S. Singleton*

In his *Letter to Cangrande*, where he explains that his poem is "polysemous" and that its subject is twofold, Dante does not point to the allegory of a journey in the *Comedy*. More senses than one and duality of subject he explains with respect rather to things seen beyond. The subject, he says, taken in the literal sense, is the "state of souls after death"; whereas, allegorically, it is (to reduce his longer statement of it) God's justice as that may be seen in the state of souls after death.

We take him to mean this: the literal subject, so defined, will point beyond itself in the manner that we may in fact see it everywhere doing as we read the poem. Here are Francesca and Paolo, forever without peace, tossed on an infernal storm. This is the simple and literal fact, such is their state after death. But in the literal fact we may behold the justice of God: for their state, which is a punishment, bears witness to its sufficient reason, its justice. The passion of lust is itself such a storm; peace is forever denied it. It is proper, it is just, that the condition of the lustful after death should be the condition of lust itself; even as in Paradise, that the state of those who are in charity should be the very condition of charity. And so everywhere: in the hemisphere of light surrounding the virtuous pagans in Limbo, in the eternal rending and cleaving of schismatics, in their sewn eyelids of the envious, man's just deserts and God's justice are beheld. Nor is this offered as a justification of God's ways to men. Here is no pleading of a case for God. In His will these things are so, and that is our peace if not always theirs.

* From Charles S. Singleton, *Commedia: Elements of Structure* (Cambridge: Harvard University Press, 1954), 1–17.

Thus, in the *Letter* at this point, Dante is attending to a dimension of the poem to all readings most familiar and most prized, its great dimension in height and depth, a vertical scale in which a gaze of centuries turned inward on the human soul has found the way to objectify itself in vision: a vision so organically one that Dante's own division of it into two senses is very much open to question. But such is the discursive mode of his *Letter*. And such at the moment is ours. It was evidently his hope that thus by division his noble patron and others might see his subject, in this respect, more clearly. It is our present hope that his subject, in yet another respect, may likewise be better seen and better understood.

In spite of Dante's own terminology in the *Letter*, we might somewhat help a prevailing and growing critical confusion in these matters if we could agree to call this aspect of them, the state of souls after death along with its "other" meaning, symbolism rather than allegory. We may consider that had Dante, like Milton, couched his poem merely in terms of things seen and known under inspiration of the heavenly Muse, with no narrative of a journey to God and with no protagonist moving as our post of observation within the field of vision, we might still have his twofold subject as he explains it in the *Letter*. In this way, for instance, we should see Virgil dwelling with his companions in Limbo in the hemisphere of light, we should see Beatrice sitting beside ancient Rachel in the light of glory. Virgil and Beatrice, in that case, would exemplify the twofold subject as the *Letter* presents it: their particular state after death and man's deserts under God's justice.

But Beatrice does not keep to her seat, nor does Virgil stay in Limbo. And when Beatrice moves and comes to Virgil in Limbo, she is recognized by him at once for what we are to know her to be as the poem unfolds:

> O donna di virtu sola per cui
> l'umana specie eccede ogni contento
> di quel ciel c'ha minor li cerchi sui.
> *Inferno* II. 76–78

O lady of virtue through whom alone mankind arises above all that is contained by that heaven which has its circlings least (i.e., the sphere of the moon within which all things are transitory).

Beatrice had come to dispatch Virgil to rescue her lover from the slope of the Hill where his way was blocked by the Wolf. And from assurances already given by Virgil in the first canto, we know that her role will be to lead her lover from that point in the upward way beyond which Virgil may not go. But here Virgil knows her at once as a guide to more than this one man. She (and she alone) is that lady by means of whom mankind, "l'umana specie," ascends.

Beatrice's role as guide, and hence her meaning, extends beyond any one man's journey to God. She has a role in mankind's journey to God, which must mean a journey here in this life. Thus already, at the beginning of the poem, in the terms of her recognition by Virgil, a dual journey in which she has a part is put before us. A "journey" there, as well as the "state of souls" there, can point beyond itself.

Here, then, is yet another dimension of the poem which we meet in the poem at the start. If Dante said little about it in the *Letter*, that was probably because he could take it more for granted than we may; and because to dwell upon allegory in this aspect would have meant to focus upon a certain wayfarer at the center of this subject—and it is not praiseworthy, he tells us elsewhere, to speak of oneself. At a point near the end of the *Letter*, to be sure, he does refer to those who may carp and question his going to Paradise. But let these persons, he says, read certain works of Augustine and Richard of St. Victor and Bernard of Clairvaux.[1] We are certainly not inclined to question his going; but if we do read the particular works referred to, we see at once that they all treat of the possibility of a journey to God even in this life, a journey of the mind and heart, a possibility ideally open to "umana specie." Without calling it allegory, Dante in the *Letter* is here pointing to the outline of a twofold journey visible in his poem.

Take Virgil. No one, in the poem, announces or declares his role as guide in a twofold journey, as Virgil at once does for Beatrice, yet the poem has ways of pointing to his similar and cooperative role. When, for instance, Virgil must rebuke his charge for lingering too long over the vulgar spat between Maestro Adamo and Sinon, he says:

> e fa ragion ch'io ti sia sempre a lato
> se piu avvien che fortuna t'accoglia
> dove sien genti in simigliante piato.
> (*Inf.* XXX, 145–147)

And see to it that I be ever at your side if Fortune should bring you again where there are people in any such dispute.

We can hardly take Virgil to mean (or to mean merely) that this is likely to happen again in the journey there. Virgil means, of course, in the journey here, the journey of our life to which Dante must return. It is here that he must make sure, in the future, that Virgil be at his side. Thus Virgil, like Beatrice, has a dual role as guide, in a journey there and in a journey here.

We take note of obvious things. And these, clearly, are touches which, though they point to a journey here, in themselves give no clear idea of what that journey is. They are signals pointing to some scheme doctrinal or philosophical which, were there no more than this given within the poem, would lie quite outside the work. But the poem has not left outside itself the more precise pattern of that journey. It bears it within itself in such a way that when it points to it, it can be pointing to a pattern objective within the structure.

We may observe the manner in which this can happen at that point in *Inferno* when a knotted cord is thrown into the abyss to summon Geryon out of the Eighth Circle: a cord which, we are now told, Dante has been wearing as a girdle:

> Io avea una corda intorno cinta
> e con essa pensai alcuna volta
> prender la lonza alle pelle dipinta.
> (*Inf.* XVI, 106–108)

I had a cord about my waist and with it once thought to catch the leopard with the painted hide.

Plainly we are here referred back to a moment in the opening scene of the first canto of the poem when this wayfarer, on the dark slope of the mountain, had met the leopard, first of the three beasts which had beset his path there. And if we have come to see (as it may be hoped that by now we have) that the three beasts represent the three major areas of sin in Hell, we glimpse a correspondence between the journey through Hell and the journey as given in that first scene. The leopard is for fraud. And here now, at precisely the moment when we are entering the area of fraud in Hell, we are reminded of the moment back there before the beast. There are other particulars in this connection which could be examined at this point. Let this however suffice as an instance of the way in which the dual pattern of a journey can emerge in Hell.

At no point in the whole of the journey beyond this life are we more unmistakably referred back to the scene in Canto I *Inferno* than in Canto I *Purgatorio*. Here the wayfarer girds himself again, here the ascent may finally begin. It is daybreak and, as the light dawns, a scene comes clear in outline which returns us by direct reflection to the situation in the first canto of the poem. We sense at once the striking resemblance. Dominant in both scenes is the outline of a mountain: a mountain to be climbed, for there, at the summit, in both instances, lies happiness and peace. At its base and below, in the one scene, is bitter darkness, a wild wood and the path to Hell; in the other, there is Hell itself which has but now been left behind. By a mountain to be ascended the way of a journey is given, upward or downward as it may be, between the two poles of light and darkness.

When the poem is unfolded in its entirety and we may stand back from it for a comprehensive view of these matters, we realize

that the opening scene in Canto I *Inferno* figured and forecast, as
well as any single scene might do, the whole configuration of the
journey beyond. There is a special reason why we should feel the
reflected presence of that first scene most clearly at the beginning
of *Purgatorio;* for in *Inferno* I, in the central focus, a mountain rises
as it does in *Purgatorio* I, a mountain at whose summit (as we shall
know later) lies the first of two goals. The way of Purgatory is in
fact central in the whole of the journey beyond, and is so given in
the first scene. The other regions, at the extremities of the way, are
suggested here rather than given in outline: Paradise by the light
above, Hell by the darkness below. Details in the first scene, not
well understood at the moment, will reveal their meaning in the
developing journey. Thus, at the beginning, the crest of the mountain
is lighted by a planet "which leads man aright by whatever way";
and at the summit of the purgatorial mountain, in the journey beyond,
it is Beatrice who comes to fulfill the forecast, coming in the figure
of a rising sun.

It is, therefore, small wonder that at the beginning of Purgatory
we have a sense of return somehow to a place and to a way already
familiar. And there are verses here to signal this:

> Noi andavam per lo solingo piano
> com'om che torna alla perduta strada.
> *(Purgatorio* I, 118–119)

We were going over the solitary plain as one who returns to a way
that was lost.

* * *

If we have not always seen this quite as clearly as we might, it
may be because we have had our difficulties with the opening scene
of the poem. Things here do seem to stand in a kind of half-light
which does not generally prevail in the rest of the work, even in the
dimness of Hell. Here at the beginning, things both are and are not
what they seem, as Benedetto Croce notes, beginning his reading of
the poem.[2] We move in a kind of double vision. Only, in observing
the fact, Croce does what the modern reader is too often tempted
to do: to put off on Dante his own inability or his own refusal to
accustom his eyes to this light, and say rather that Dante at the outset
is under some strain and special labor to get his poem under way.
But the labor and the strain are Croce's and the modern reader's.
The poet is not striving for single vision (as a later Aesthetics would
hold that he ought to be doing if he means to write poetry). The
poet is deliberately leading the reader into double vision, to place
him on what he had every right to assume would be the most familiar

of scenes. There is this about that landscape at the beginning: we may not mark its whereabouts on any map. And, when we stand at the doorway of Hell and look back to where we were before, if we ask ourselves where that was, we know that we may not exactly say. We cannot locate that first scene. But that is not the important point. The point is that the scene was designed to locate us. This language of metaphor (for all the poet could anticipate of his readers) could hardly be more familiar, nor these figures more worn by use. Here, simply, is the way of our life. And Augustine's exclamation, centuries before, over this way of speaking of it, could really have registered, even in his time, little of the surprise of novelty. Yet it can help us to sharpen our view:

> To whom shall I tell, how shall I tell, of the weight of cupidity how it presses us down that steep abyss and how charity lifts us up by Your spirit which moved over the waters? To whom shall I tell it? How shall I tell it? For it is in no space-occupying place that we sink and out of which we rise again. What could be more like and what more unlike? These are affections, these are loves, these are the uncleanness of our own spirits that flow down with the weight of the cares we are so attached to; and it is Your sanctity that bears us upward by our attachment to freedom from these cares: so that we lift up our hearts to You where Your spirit moved over the waters and we come to supreme peace when our soul has passed beyond these waters where there is no standing ground.[3]

We were noting a matter of close correspondence between the scene at the beginning and that in *Purgatorio* I. There is more to be observed. When Dante and Virgil have come forth to see the stars again, we know they stand not only on what is the lower slope of a mountain, but on what is, by virtue of the presence of real water there, a shore as well. Ulysses, as the poem reminds us at this point, had tried to navigate this sea before and had failed to reach the dry land where Dante and Virgil stand. Now, in this particular detail of a "shore," we might say, looking back, that correspondence is at least lacking here between the two scenes. But if we do say this, we show either that we are not close readers of a poem or that we are intolerant of a poem's ways. For water on the first scene there is. Looking down from Heaven, Santa Lucia had pointed to it there, as she urged Beatrice to behold the plight of her lover on the dark slope, struggling before the Wolf:

> Beatrice, loda di Dio vera,
>   che non, soccorri quei che t'amò tanto
>   ch'uscì per te della volgare schiera?
> Non odi la pieta del suo pianto?
>   Non vedi tu la morte che'l combatte
>   sulla fiumana ove'l mar non ha vanto?

(*Inf.* II, 103–108)

Beatrice, true praise of God, why do you not help him who loved
you so much that he left the common herd? Do you not hear how
piteous his cry? Do you not see how death struggles against him
there over that river of which the sea has no boast?

The commentators are in some doubt here. Is this "fiumana"
Acheron? Or is it a "mere" metaphor? And what does the modifier
"over which the sea has no boast" mean? The commentators are
having their difficulties with the focus; and a reading course for some
of them would be in order, too, in a language of metaphor from St.
Augustine to St. Bernard, a language which the poet had thought he
could count on to place the reader. No, this is not Acheron (neither
is it a "mere" metaphor if Lucia can see this stream and point to it
from Heaven). And if the sea has no vaunt over it, that is because
this flood does not flow into any sea. Our primer in metaphor would
contain a passage from Hugh of St. Victor (d. 1141) on the Ark:

> . . . let us understand that there are two worlds, the visible and
> invisible. The visible, of course, is this physical universe which we
> see with the eyes of our body, and the invisible is the heart of man
> which we cannot see. And as in the days of Noah the waters of
> the flood covered the whole earth, and only the ark was borne up
> by the waters, and not only could it not be covered, but the more
> the waters rose, the higher it was raised. And now let us understand
> the concupiscence of this world that is in the heart of man as waters
> of the flood; but understand the ark which is lifted above them as
> the faith of Christ which treads upon transitory pleasure and aspires
> to eternal goods which are above. For concupiscence of this world
> is compared to waters because it flows and glides, and like water
> flows downward, always seeking the depths. . . . If a man were to
> enter his own heart he would be able to see how concupiscence
> always flows downward to those things that are transitory.[4]

In a sense it might be regretted that somehow a curtain does
not fall at the end of Canto II *Inferno* to mark off the first two cantos
of the poem for the prologue which they are. Such a marker would
serve to point up some fundamental distinctions as to time and place
in the poem, distinctions which must be grasped if we are to see the
true nature and outline of its allegory. Just there, at that point, some
such device would help us to realize that in the prologue scene we
are set up on the stage of this life; that on this first stage we may
speak of the actor or actors in the first person plural, as "we," even
as the poem suggests in its first adjective. This is the way of our life,
the life of soul, this is our predicament. It ought to be the scene we
know best, the most familiar scene in the world—and in the poem.
Here lies the way of our life. The features of it, the things here that

we can make out; a hill, a wood, these beasts, all have their existence there where the "fiumana" runs which Lucia sees from Heaven. Where that is, Augustine and Hugh have helped us to see. Here we are in no space-occupying place. Then: curtain—to rise again on the first act of this play, on a scene before the doorway to Hell which is an abyss that is space-occupying and which, on Dante's map, may be located. The change in scene is not only a change in place. Time has changed. For we do not forget that this is a remembered journey (and hence may not really be given in dramatic form). The man who went that way has now returned. His journey was *there* and it was *then*. And time in yet another sense has changed. Of the scene and of the journey in the prologue we might say "our life." Not so beyond the door. The journey beyond is too exceptional an event to bear any but a singular possessive. It was then, and there, and it was his journey. Whereas in the prologue (even though the tense is past) in so far as we might see this as "our" journey, it takes place, as to time, in a kind of "ever-present," with Everyman as actor.

And yet, no sooner have we imagined a curtain at this point than we could wish it away. It might help us with certain essential distinctions. But the poet has not wanted there any such discontinuity as it might suggest. His problem was not Augustine's "how shall I tell of movements of soul in concrete images." His language is already given to the poet and he uses it with full assurance. His problem is to manage to leave this scene, which is not space-occupying, and to attain to that scene which is; to remove a wayfarer from this scene, where he functions in a mode open to a plural "we," on to a scene and a journey where his role is a most singular one. "Our" journey must become "his" journey, "his" must arise out of "our." A literal and very real journey of a living man, a man in a body of flesh and bone, is to be launched forth from a place that does not occupy space. A curtain cannot help, indeed can only defeat. Only a movement within poetic ambiguity at its fullest power could bring about an organic transition in these terms. But this is not all. The journey to the scene of which we may say "then" and "there" and "his" will leave behind it another of which we may speak in terms of "here" and "now" and "our," leave it and yet not lose touch with it. For his journey beyond will remain potentially open to our journey here, between the two there will be a bridge not cut by any divider, an organic tie, a living way back to metaphor.

Even in the prologue, in "our journey," the birth of a literal sense, "his journey," takes place. Not many verses after the first verse of the poem, in fact, we may see this begin to happen. It is part of the necessary work achieved here in ambiguity that even while the prologue scene is locating us, it is launching him:

> Allor fu la paura un poco queta
>   che nel lago del cor m'era durata
>   la notte ch'io passai con tanta pieta.
> E come quei che con lena affannata
>   uscito fuor del pelago alla riva
>   si volge a l'acqua perigliosa e guata,
> così l'animo mio ch'ancor fuggiva
>   si volse a retro a rimirar lo passo
>   che non lasciò giammai persona viva.
> Poi ch'ei posato un poco il corpo lasso,
>   ripresi via per la piaggia diserta. . . .
>   (*Inf.* I, 19–29)

Then was the fear somewhat quieted that had prevailed in the lake of my heart through the night that I had passed so piteously. And as one who has come from the deep to the shore, gasping for breath, turns to gaze back at the perilous water, so my soul which was fleeing yet, turned back to look upon that pass which never left anyone in life. When I had rested my tired body a while, I set out once more across the lonely slope [and/or *shore*].

Coming through the verses preceding the simile we move in the recognizable terms of the prologue. Here movement is *moto spirituale* and the simile will further the action as such. With the "pelago" of its first term, we may admire the way the figure has made use of the "lago del cor" just before. And with the "animo" fleeing and then turning, the comparison is resolved in a mode commensurate with the prologue scene. Thus my soul, *moto spirituale.* All is smooth here.

So smooth indeed that we may fail to remark the extraordinary strategy of the two verses which follow immediately: "When I had rested my tired body a while." A body here? How is that? Is this body to be taken as the hill and the other features on this scene, to be understood as we have learned to understand those things? Have we begun another metaphor here? Not so. This body is no metaphor. As it emerges, a curious bifurcation is taking place. A dual journey is born. The figure that we see here now, standing in the body on this "shore," is beginning to move (before we know this) toward a doorway of Hell that is no metaphor and toward a journey that is likewise no metaphor.

The strategy is subtle. We note that by this figure a "piaggia" (which means "shore" as well as "slope") is put here, which later in the opening scene of Purgatory will find its correspondence, as will the act of coming forth from the "pelago" to stand on a shore. But of that, enough. I would note rather that we accept this new thing, this body on this scene, because it is a tired body, even though or perhaps rather because we do not pause to put the question: how or why would it be tired? If we do, there is clearly only one answer (and if we evade that answer we confess to our inability to face a poet's way of bringing this mysterious incarnation about within the scene). The body is tired from the struggle out of the "pelago"! But the "pelago," but that water, is not really there on the scene at all, it is only part of a comparison, it is only in the first term of a simile. No matter. This body is tired from the struggle out of that water; and when it moves on across the deserted shore (shore!) it may no longer be recalled or reduced to metaphor. We are moving now beyond a condition imposed by words. If, in the grammar of rhetoric, we had some term to describe this, some term, say, to match a verb "trasumanar" as it later applies to another "going beyond" in Paradiso, we could make good use of it here.

The whole journey beyond exceeds metaphor. It is irreducible to the kind of allegory in which it had its origin. As this figure of a living man, this whole person soul and body, moves through the doorway to Hell, the poem quits the recognizable and familiar double vision in which it began, to come into single and most singular vision, that is, into single journey; to embodied vision, having a substance and a persuasion that could not have been expected from this beginning. There unfolds the line of a literal journey given as real, and it is the body beyond, the flesh brought into these realms of spirit there, that like a catalyst precipitates everywhere the fleshed, the embodied and incarnate. This man's feet on a slope coming down to a river of blood dislodge stones so that a centaur on guard here draws an arrow from his quiver and with it pushes back his beard to utter his amazement. This man must be carried across the river (since it is boiling) on the back of another centaur, for "he is no spirit that can go through the air." Things seen and touched become what living eyes can see and living hands can touch. "Trattando l'ombre come cose salda" (treating the shades like a firm) (Purg. XXI, 136). His foot strikes the frozen face of a sinner stuck fast in the ice of Cocito, his hands pull chunks of hair from the head of another. This Florentine can walk along with another Florentine under a rain of fire and talk (as to tone) as though this were Florence still. By his speech he will be recognized as Florentine by other fellow citizens. His great-great-grandfather rejoices at his coming. The particular, the individual, the concrete, the fleshed, the incarnate, is everywhere with the strength of reality and the irreducibility of reality itself. Here is vision truly made flesh. And the possibility of it arose and was born back there in the prologue. We shall not exhaust the mystery of it for all our scrutiny.

It is because this is so that we have never before known an allegory like Dante's allegory. For in this poem, the embodied, the real and literal, the irreducible journey, "his" journey beyond, will time and again recall that other journey where the prologue scene placed us, our journey here. And will do this, not by inviting us to "undo" the journey there, but by permitting us to see through the event there as if it were not there, not by washing out the literal; but by a kind of recall more common in musical structure by which a theme, known in a prelude, but then left behind, emerges within another theme in its progressing development. There is no literary allegory to compare with this. Our references to Bunyan and to the *Romance of the Rose* have missed the point completely. We have Bunyan, if you will, in the prologue scene. But beyond the prologue (we are driven to desperate comparisons) we have Milton. We have, that is, an action as surely given in terms of the literal and the historical as Milton's is. These events are what they are, these things happened—there, then, once in time. Thus we should have to put Bunyan and Milton together (may we be forgiven the violence of these deeds hereafter!) to get Dante. But even this composite would not yet give us Dante's allegory. In order to have that, Milton's historical sense, at certain appointed places, would have to open up to Bunyan, recall and reflect *Pilgrim's Progress* with which we would have begun. We have seen in the *Comedy* how this does happen. And we see it best there because we can really see it nowhere else but there, where a poet has managed these things in organic structure.

* * *

Nowhere else. But if we are willing to take time to remember a kind of allegory which we have pretty well forgotten, we may be helped to see better how Dante has constructed his. This is the allegory of Holy Scripture. We may well feel justified in turning to it. Dante, in the *Letter to Cangrande,* cites from Psalm 113 (Vulgate) the familiar example and offers the accepted view:

> . . . for it is one sense which we get through the letter, and another which we get through the thing the letter signifies; and the first is called literal, but the second either allegorical or moral or anagogical. And this mode, for its better manifestation, may be considered in these verses: "When Israel came out of Egypt, and the house of Jacob from a people of strange speech, Judea became his sanctification, Israel his power." Now if we attend to the letter alone, the departure of the children of Israel from Egypt in the time of Moses is presented to us; if the allegory, our redemption wrought by Christ; if the moral sense, the conversion of the soul from the grief and misery of sin to the state of grace; if the anagogical, the departure of the holy soul from slavery of this corruption to the liberty of eternal glory. And although these mystic senses have each

their special denominations, they may all in general be called allegorical, since they differ from the literal and historical. . . .

In the *Convivio*, Dante speaks again of this kind of allegory to
distinguish it from another which he there calls the "allegory of
poets." By the difference between the two we may better see the
essential features of scriptural allegory. The radical difference lies in
the nature of the literal sense in the one and in the other. The
"allegory of poets," which is that of fable, of parable (and hence is
also to be found in the Scriptures), is a mode in which the first and
literal sense is one devised, fashioned (*fictio* in its original meaning)
in order to conceal, and in concealing to convey, a truth. Not so in
the other mode, as we may see from the example cited. There the
first sense is historical, as Dante says it is, and not "fiction." The
children of Israel did depart from Egypt in the time of Moses.
Whatever the other senses may be, this first sense abides, stands
quite on its own, is not devised "for the sake of." Indeed it was
generally recognized that in Holy Scripture the historical sense might
at times be the only sense there. These things have been so; they
have happened in time. This is the record of them.

If Dante's model for the allegory which he built into his *Comedy*
is to be seen here in this conception of scriptural allegory (and I am
convinced that it is) then the primary importance of that fact lies
not so much in what it says about his second or mystic sense as in
what is says about his first or literal. For we can readily see that the
nature of the literal in the model can confirm our sense and understanding of the literal in the *Comedy*: namely, that in the poem, as
in the mode of scriptural allegory, the literal sense is given as an
historical sense standing in its own right, like Milton's, say—not
devised in order to convey a hidden truth, but given in the focus of
single vision. (Nothing of more importance could happen in Dante
criticism at present than a general recognition of this fact.)

Then, as we look in the example at the other sense of scriptural
allegory, we see how Dante has built here too according to his model.
In Scripture, as we noted, the historical sense, keeping its full force
as such, can and does yield another sense. It may do this, indeed it
will do this, intermittently. And note the nature of the second sense
in the model. In the event there, the Exodus, is signified another
event; in the journey there we see meanings which bring to mind
our journey here. All of the "other" meanings in the example of the
Exodus have our journey, the movement of soul in the way of salvation,
in common. Dante has followed his model closely.

When the other sense is there in Scripture, it is there simply
because intended there by God. Hence, there was general agreement
that only God could write in this mode of allegory, wherein the event

signified by the words in its turn signifies the "other" meaning, and only God could use events as words, causing them to point beyond themselves, only He could make Exodus there (the real event) signify our journey here. And this is of course as it should be. The Word of God was given us for our salvation; it is proper that the events recorded therein should now and then look to that matter. There is this, moreover, to be said: the Word of God can count on the eye of a faithful reader who will be reading for his salvation, ever mindful of our journey here while he reads a Psalm of the Exodus.

A poet has not God's power and may not presume to write as He can. But he may *imitate* God's way of writing. He may construct a literal historical sense, a journey beyond (it too happens to be an Exodus!) to be, in the make-believe of his poem, as God's literal sense is in His book (and with God's help he will have power to make it real). And he will make his allegorical or mystic, his other sense, even as God's: a sense concerning our journey, our way of salvation, here in this life. But there would still be a gap to be filled. The poet is at a disadvantage. His work may not assume the reader's attitude that was sure to be brought to God's: the eye of the faithful ever concerned with our journey here. A poet will lay provision as God's word need not do. This the poet will do by so arranging his poem that the reader comes to his literal sense by first passing through the sense that is to be the second and reflected sense; so that our journey here may then be recalled and reflected along the line of a journey there. The poet will provide in a special way; with a prologue, putting the journey to be reflected where, within his poem and organically, he can control the reflection.

Notes

1. See *Letter to CanGrande,* paragraph 28, in this collection. The texts referred to are *On the Quantity of the Soul* by St. Augustine, available in English as *The Measure of the Soul,* trans. F. E. Tourscher (Philadelphia: The Peter Reilly Co., 1934); Richard of St. Victor, *De Contemplatione,* available in English as *The Mystical Ark* in Richard of St. Victor, *The Twelve Patriarchs,* trans. G. A. Zinn (New York: Paulist Press, 1979); finally St. Bernard, *De Consideratione,* available as *On Consideration,* trans. G. Lewis (Oxford: Clarendon Press, 1908).

2. Benedetto Croce, *La Poesia di Dante* (Bari: Laterza, 1921), p. 73.

3. St. Augustine, *Confessions,* trans. F. J. Sheed (New York: Sheed and Ward, 1943), XIII, 7.

4. Hugh of St. Victor, *De Arca Noe Morali,* I, vi in *Patrologia Latina,* 176, 672. The English text is from Hugh of St. Victor, *Selected Spiritual Writings* (New York: Harper and Row, 1962).

Dante's Katabasis and Mission   Gian Roberto Sarolli°

Dante's creative task has been defined as of "superhuman difficulty." This is clearly discernible in the language of the poem; for although the *Commedia*, considered as a whole, seems astonishingly light and simple—thanks to its clear and orderly structure—there is no single passage that does not reflect tension and effort; one is left with the impression that the work at every step demanded of Dante a boundless devotion, an unstinting expenditure of himself. No less devotion, no less unstinting expenditure of self is demanded of Dante scholars when they are faced by the difficult question of whether or not it is prophetic.

Bruno Nardi, following in the footsteps of Pietrobono and Barbi, has stressed that:

> Just as Dante considers the Journey of Aeneas "sive in corpore nescio, sive extra corpus nescio, deus scit," granted by God to the Trojan hero, equal to St. Paul's rapture to the Third heaven ("Whether in the body or out of the body I do not know, God knows"), so does he consider the prophetic vision granted to him a special grace of God, who has chosen him to denounce both the "reason that has made the world wicked" and the divine plan for the making green again of the tree of Paradise spoiled a second time.[1]

The opposite theory is adhered to by Alessandro Passerin D'Entreves who repeats the opinion of the great historian James Bryce that the *Monarchia* (and consequently the *Divina Commedia*) must be considered the epitaph of the Holy Roman Empire rather than a prophecy. Passerin d'Entreves, aware of what we might call the Hamletic doubt in Dante studies, points out further that the " 'glorious dream of Dante' [Gentile] has been hailed as a prophecy or described as a mirage."[2]

An idea similar to that of Bryce is expressed, mutatis mutandis, in Ernst Curtius' classic *European Literature and the Latin Middle Ages.* The renowned German scholar pointed out that the central message of the *Divina Commedia* can be grasped when it is recognized that Beatrice as well as the 3 beasts defeated by the *Veltro* and the *DXV* represent a theological system transformed into a prophetic one. Curtius states that this message:

> concerns a prophecy whose fulfillment he [Dante] expected in the immediate future. When he died at 56, his certainty was presumably still unshaken. Had he reached the "perfect" age of 81 (*Conv.* IV, xxiv, 6), he would perhaps have been obliged to admit the collapse

° From Gian Roberto Sarolli, *Prolegomena alla "Divina Commedia"* (Florence: Olschki, 1971), 381–89.

of his historical construction. But he could not retract his work. His imperious spirit believed that it could command even the future. A future, however, which could envisage only fourteenth-century Italy. . . . Even if we could interpret his prophecy, that would give it no meaning for us. What Dante hid, Dante scholarship need not now unriddle. But it must take seriously the fact that Dante believed that he had an apocalyptic mission.[3]

Although the arduous task of solving the enigmas and difficult lines of Dante's work has met with the disapproval and mockery of almost all the critics, I believe that it is essential for the general interpretation of the *Divina Commedia* and of Dante's life. As an illustration, let me refer to my suggestion, and repeatedly discussed, that the hidden meaning of both the *Veltro* and the *DXV* lies in a well-known christological symbol applicable, in terms of political theology, to Christ himself as well as to the Emperor as a *typus Christi,* in accordance with the view of Kantorowicz. Thus, Curtius' presentation of the problem, and the solution of the famous enigma enable us to arrive at the central message of the *Divina Commedia* and the very core of Dante's hope and mission. It is my opinion, and Barbi's as well, that the whole structure of the *Divina Commedia* is based upon the prophetic urgency, and that, without the prophecy, the unsurpassed poem would achieve a less powerful immediacy of meaning. The above-mentioned political theology must be considered as an indispensable Ariadne guiding us through the apparent labyrinth of Dante's poetry. This can readily be understood if we consider the famous Canto XXV of the *Paradiso* in which the word *ritornero* (I shall return), significant because Dante never used words idly, reveals his twofold meaning, the double katabasis, the return to earth after his fateful journey, as St. Peter will say in *Paradiso* XXVII, 64–65: "E tu, figliuol, che per lo mortal pondo / ancor giú *tornerai*" (my italics)—before and / or after the exile to Florence, which is merely suggested in the *Paradiso* (XXV, 8–9): "*ritorneró* poeta; ed in sul fonte / del mio battesmo prendero 'l cappelo" (my italics)—and to God, *nunc* and *sub specie aeternitatis.*

Canto XXV of the *Paradiso* is well known but let us have before us its most significant passages:

> Se mai continga che 'l poema sacro
> al quale ha posto mano e cielo e
> terra,
> sì che m'ha fatto per più anni macro,
> vinca la crudeltà che fuor mi serra
> del bello ovile ov'io dormi' agnello,
> nimico ai lupi che li danno guerra;
> con altra voce omai, con altro vello
> ritornerò poeta; ed in sul fonte

del mio battesmo prenderò 'l cappello;
però che ne la fede, che fa conte
l'anime a Dio, quivi intra'io, e poi
Petro per lei si mi girò la fronte.
. . . .
E quella pia che guidò le penne
de la mie ali a così alto volo,
a la risposta cosagi mi prevenne:
"La Chiesa militante alcun figliuolo
non ha con più speranza, com'è
scritto
nel sol che raggia tutto nostro stuolo:
però li è conceduto che d'Egitto
vegna in Ierusalemme per vedere,
anzi che 'l militar li sia prescritto."
. . . .
Ahi quanto ne la mente mi commossi,
quando mi volsi per veder Beatrice,
per non poter veder, benchè io fossi
presso di lei, e nel mondo felice!
(*Par.* XXV, 1–12; 49–57; 136–139)

If ever it come to pass that the sacred poem to which heaven and
earth have so set hand that it has made me lean for many years
should overcome the cruelty which bars me from the fair sheepfold
where I slept as a lamb, an enemy to the wolves which war on it,
with changed voice now and with changed fleece a poet will I
return, and at the font of my baptism will I take the crown; because
there I entered into the Faith that makes souls known to God; and
afterward Peter, for its sake, thus encircled my brow. . . .

And that compassionate one, who had guided the feathers of my
wings to such lofty flight, anticipated my reply thus, "The Church
Militant has not any child possessed of more hope, as is written in
the Sun which irradiates all our host; therefore is it granted him
to come from Egypt to Jerusalem, that he may see, before his term
of warfare is completed. . . .

Ah! how greatly was I stirred in my mind when I turned to see
Beatrice, at not being able to see, although I was near her, and in
the world of bliss.

There are many key words in these stanzas, but the most important are *contingere* and *fede* in the first part, *speranza* and *militare*
in the second, and *vedere* both in the second part and at the end.
Dante scholars, misled by the opening conjunction "if" emphatically
stressed by the adverb "ever," have overlooked the significance of
the verb *contingere*, having always accepted its most banal meaning
"to happen," as a result of a *lectio facilior*. It will be sufficient to
mention Sapegno as representing the Italian tradition, and Grandgent,

the Anglo-American one. In addition, Niccolo Rodolico, in his *Lettura Dantesca*, states " 'If ever!' The first words of the canto reveal the uncertainty in the coming about of what the poet most hopes for; it's a longing for eternal happiness; it is a doubt precisely there where one cannot be under the burden of doubts. It is the contrast between hope, as it appears doubtful to men, and the certain hope of glory."[4]

Rodolico would probably have better understood this passage had he realized that Dante was using a typical example of *argumentatio necessaria*, a rhetorical device codified by Cicero and underlined by Boethius and by Marius Victorinus, in order to focus our attention on the following bare Latinism *contingere*. There is an obvious connection with St. Thomas Aquinas' distinction between *contingentia* and *necessitas (Summa Theol.* I, q. 22, a. 4; q. 14, a. 13), or, perhaps better, between "contingens" and "necessarius" in the *Summa Contra Gentiles* (I, 67). In the quoted passage the great Soul of the poet is expressing in pure Christian terms not his doubt, but what I would like to call his theological humility, which finds its counterpart in his stylistic and rhetorical humility, his careful choice, according to the *rota Virgili*, of the very *humiles* (elegiac) words (and let us not forget that the messianic prophecy of Virgil is contained in the well-known Eclogue): *agnello* and *ovile*, for example, and *cappello* for laurel (or something else that I shall advance later on as my own hypothesis). His theological humility can be interpreted as a certainty provided that such a certainty was written in the great book of the Universe, in the Mind of God, the macrocosm corresponding perfectly to the microcosm represented at one and the same time by Dante and the *Divina Commedia*. Of course one cannot deny that the verb "continga" at first glance appears to have no special connotation of fulfillment in Dante's passage; rather, it seems to reflect the poet's uncertainty in his hope. But it is used in this same Canto XXV when Dante is undergoing the examination in hope by St. James, and when Dante himself is defined by Beatrice as the hope of the Militant Church (vv. 51–53), and this is the only occasion it is used in the whole vernacular *corpus* of the poet. For all these reasons, one cannot accept the *lectio facilior* without first examining the historical development of the word, and the wide range of associations contained in it.

Contingere had many meanings during the classical and mediaeval period, and at least one of these meanings underwent considerable development at the hands of the scholastic philosophers, particularly St. Thomas Aquinas. As a transitive verb, *contingo (con + tango =* I touch; the *Catholicon*, for example, offers glosses, especially for *contactus)* most frequently meant "to touch physically," sometimes in a hostile fashion, or to touch with something, as in anointing. In a more figurative sense it denoted "to arrive at," "to reach something," "to border on something," "to be concerned with," or "to belong to."

In this latter sense we find the words of the prodigal son, "da mihi portionem substantiae quae me contingit" (Luke XV, 22). *Contingere* as "belong to" would appear to have some relation to Dante's use of the term—"if ever it would belong, be appropriate to, the sacred poem . . . to defeat cruelty"—except for the fact that Dante used the verb intransitively, and a transitive meaning must be considered incompatible. *Contingere* was widely used as an intransitive verb during the classical and mediaeval period, and it is from this usage that modern Dante commentators derive their interpretation. Intransitively it was synonymous with *obvenire, venire, accidere, concedere,* and *competere,* all of which denote "to happen" or "to befall." Priscian and Isidore of Seville agreed with these meanings. Since either good or evil could follow indifferently after *contingere,* nothing new has been added to the established meaning of the verb.

Perhaps Aristotle's works on logic provide the basic meaning that ultimately influenced Dante. In his *On Interpretation* and the *Prior Analysis* he discussed the nature and varieties of syllogisms, and drew a distinction between the necessary and "the possible" (the contingent). The expression "to be possible" may be used in two ways:

> In one, it means to happen generally and fall short of necessity, e.g., man's turning grey or growing or decaying, or generally what naturally belongs to a thing. . . . In another sense the expression means the indefinite, which can be both thus and not thus, e.g. an animal's walking or an earthquake's taking place while it is walking, or generally what happens by chance: for none of these inclines by nature in the one way more than in the opposite.[5]

It is in the works of Aquinas that the ideal of contingency is removed from the syllogism and placed within the realm of Divine Providence. It would not be surprising if Dante, in opening his canto of hope, chose a verb that would echo his hope in Providence. In the *Summa Contra Gentiles* (I, 67), Aquinas distinguished the contingent from the necessary in a way that would have been quite intelligible to Aristotle. The contingent and the necessary differ according to their relationship to their cause. The necessary can only be, that is, must follow from its cause. The contingent can either be or not be—it can happen or not happen. In the *Summa Theologica* St. Thomas discussed whether God can know future contingent things: concluding that God does know these, he distinguished between the contingent in act now and the contingent respecting the future (from man's point of view). Man can know only the present contingent with certain knowledge. God's way of knowing is basically different. "And although contingent things became actual successively, nevertheless God knows contingent things not successively, as they are in their own being, as we do; but simultaneously (*S.T.* Ie, 1, 9, 14, a. 13)."

This is because his knowledge is eternal, and all things in time are present to him from eternity. God's knowledge is certain; man, who knows only the causes of contingent things, has only a conjectural knowledge of future contingents.

Aquinas re-emphasized the role of Providence in Question 22, Article 4 of the *Summa Theologica,* which deals with whether Providence imposes any necessity on things foreseen. He asserted that necessity is imposed on some things, but not all. Everything aims toward divine goodness, which is an extrinsic end to all things; after this, "the principal good in things themselves is the perfection of the universe; which would not be, were not all grades of being found in things. Whence it pertains to divine providence to produce every grade of being." Divine Providence has prepared causes that follow infallibly and of necessity for some things, and contingent causes for others, "according to the nature of their proximate causes." Effects follow from contingent things if they are not prevented in some way. God knows not only the causes and results of contingents, but also knows how contingent causes may be impeded.[6]

Placing contingent events under the care of Divine Providence puts Dante's words ("Se mai continga") in a new light. If we accept Beatrice's judgment that "La Chiesa militante alcun figliuolo / non ha con piu speranza, *com'è scritto* / nel sol . . ." (*Par.* XXV, 52–54; italics mine) (The Church militant has no other child possessed of more hope, as is written in the Sun), then we may make the barest suggestion that Dante was indeed rich in the virtue of Hope, and would have been optimistic rather than pessimistic about the fate of his poem, his literary militancy, as I have elsewhere pointed out, as well as of his mission. The fact that *continga, qua* verb, is a *hapax legomenon* in the *Divina Commedia,* and especially in this very peculiar passage, may well indicate that the poet intended it to have a very extraordinary meaning applicable here alone: "If it should fulfil the design of Divine Providence that the sacred poem should defeat the cruelty. . . ." This meaning seems to confirm the reason for which the name of the Poet, Dante, ought to be recorded "by necessity," in *Purgatorio* XXX, 55. Therefore *contingere* and *necessitas* in the *Divina Commedia* ought to be considered interdependent and providential.

Notes

1. Bruno Nardi, *Dante e la cultura medievale* (Bari: Laterza, 1942), p. 123.

2. A. Passerin D'Entreves, *Dante as a Political Thinker* (Oxford: Clarendon Press, 1952), p. 2.

3. E. R. Curtius, *European Literature and the Latin Middle Ages,* trans. Willard R. Trask (New York: Harper and Row, 1963), p. 377.

4. Cf. *La Divina Commedia*, ed. N. Sapegno (Milan-Naples: Ricciardi, 1957) *ad hoc; La Divina Commedia* ed. C. H. Grandgent (Boston: D. C. Heath and Co., 1933) *ad hoc;* N. Rodolico, "Canto XXC," in *Letture dantesche. Paradiso*, ed. G. Getto (Florence: Le Monnier, 1961), p. 134.

5. *Prior Analytics* I, 13 in *The Works of Aristotle* (Oxford: Clarendon Press, 1928), vol. I.

6. The English quotations from the *Summa Theologica* (referred to also as *S.T.*) are from the translation by the Fathers of the English Dominican Province (2d ed., London, 1920).

The Dance of the Stars:
Paradiso X
John Freccero°

In the fourth canto of the *Paradiso*, Beatrice enunciates the principle upon which much of the metaphoric structure of the *cantica* depends. She tells the pilgrim that the display of souls distributed throughout the heavenly spheres is a celestial command performance in his honor, devised to enable him to perceive in spatial terms the spiritual gradations of blessedness:

Così parlar conviensi al vostro ingegno,
però che solo da sensato apprende
ciò che fa poscia d'intelletto degno.
(Par. IV, 40–42)

It is needful to speak thus to your faculty, since only through sense perception does it apprehend that which it afterwards makes fit for the intellect.

At the same time, it is clear by the inexorable logic of the story (whose principal theme is how the story came to be written) that what applies to the dramatic action applies to the poem itself; that is, heaven's condescension to the pilgrim is matched by the poet's condescension to us. In the poem, the descent of the divine to the human is for the benefit of a pilgrim whose ultimate goal is presumably to transcend the need for any such compromise, except of course (and the whole of the poem is contained in this exception) in order to tell others of his journey. Heaven's metaphor for the state of blessedness is in fact the poet's metaphor for a spiritual experience that transcends the human, an *exemplus* of what it means to *trasu-*

° From John Freccero, *"Paradiso* X: The Dance of the Stars," *Dante Studies* 86 (1968): 85–111, and now reprinted as "The Dance of the Stars: *Paradiso* X," in *Dante: The Poetics of Conversion* (Cambridge: Harvard University Press, 1986), 221–44.

manare: "l'essemplo basti / a cui esperienza grazia serba" (*Par.* I, 70) (let the example suffice any for whom grace reserves that experience).

The extraordinary poetic implication of Beatrice's words is that, unlike any other part of the poem, the *Paradiso* at this point can claim no more than a purely *ad hoc* reality. When the pilgrim's ascent to the celestial rose is completed, the blessed return to their seats in the heavenly amphitheater and the heavenly bodies are left to travel in their respective spheres unaccompanied by the family of the elect—no Farinata strikes an attitude here for all eternity. This amounts to saying that the representation points to no reality, however fictive, beyond itself. The structure of the *cantica* depends, not upon a principle of *mimesis,* but rather upon metaphor: the creation of a totally new reality out of elements so disparate as to seem contradictory by any logic other than that of poetry. What is more, some of the elements represent fragments of world systems long since abandoned by Dante's time and fused together only long enough to attempt a rendering in images of what cannot be imagined. The concession of a command performance to the pilgrim within the fiction of the story stands for a poetic *tour de force* whereby Dante reconciles Christian images of the heaven with a neoplatonic cosmic vision in a synthesis which, for all of its reputedly "medieval" flavor, seems almost baroque in its daring and fragility. It is the poignancy of the *Paradiso,* as it is of baroque poetry, that the synthesis is dissipated by the poem's ending:

> Così la neve al sol si disigilla;
> così al vento ne le foglie levi
> si perdea la sentenza di Si-
> billa.
>
> (*Par.* XXXIII, 64–66)

Thus is the snow unsealed by the sun; thus in the wind, on the light leaves, the Sibyl's oracle was lost.

Whether the reader is left, like Dante, with an ineffable sweetness in his heart, or with what a baroque theorist called "the taste of ashes"[1] is a question that transcends the limits of poetry.

We can, however, set out to identify the various elements that make up the kaleidoscopic structure of the *Paradiso* with a view to understanding not only how they fit together, but also their metaphoric relationship to the spiritual reality they were chosen to represent. It is my intention to examine a very small portion of the *Paradiso* with these ends in view. Specifically, I should like to identify some of the elements of symbolic cosmology contained in Dante's description of the Heaven of the Sun and to discuss some of the themes that make possible in these cantos the translation of beatitude into astronomical terms.

Before proceeding, however, it would be well to identify, in Dante's terms, the process whereby he pieces together his spatial metaphor for beatitude. It is characteristic of the poet that at the moment of his striking *tour de force* he should invoke the authority of the Bible for his accommodation of spiritual reality to human faculties. Immediately after telling Dante about the descent of the blessed to the planetary spheres, Beatrice says:

> Per questo la Scrittura condescende
> a vostra facultate, e piedi e mano
> attribuisce a Dio e altro intende . . .
> *(Par.* IV, 43–45)

For this reason Scripture condescends to your capacity, and attributes hands and feet to God, having other meaning . . .

We have already noted that the accommodation of heaven to the senses of the pilgrim stands for the accommodation of the poet's experience *per verba* to us, but the pattern for all such accommodation was established by the Bible, the eternal witness of God's accommodation—his Word—to man. Thus, at precisely the point in the *Paradiso* where Dante seems to depart most radically from the Christian tradition, he implies that his accomplishment is essentially an imitation of the Bible. This passage might well serve as confirmation (if confirmation were still required) of Singleton's thesis[2] that Dante consciously chose to write an allegory which he took to be biblical even in those passages where we are inclined to see more of Plato, Servius, and Macrobius than of the Holy Spirit.

Nevertheless, the Christian mystery underlying Dante's representation seems to be clothed in Platonic myth. Beatrice's words in the fourth canto are occasioned by what the pilgrim assumes to be a resemblance of the *Paradise* to Plato's *Timaeus,* inasmuch as the blessed souls seem to dwell eternally in the stars, "secondo la sentenza di Platone" (v. 24). If Plato's text means what it says, Beatrice denies that the resemblance can be real. If, on the other hand,

> e forse sua sentenza è d'altra guisa
> che la voce non suona, ed esser puote
> con intenzion da non esser derisa.
> *(Par.* IV, 55–57)

But perhaps his opinion is other than his words sound, and may be of a meaning not to be derided.

The implication is that if Plato intends his account to be read as myth, then it may be taken to bear a resemblance to the representation of the *Paradiso.* Whatever this implied resemblance suggests for the interpretation of Plato, it certainly seems to reinforce the suggestion that the descent of the blessed to the heavenly spheres is in fact a dramatization of the process of myth-making and, as such, is an extended figure for what the poet is himself doing as he writes his poem. The relationship of the true home of the blessed in the Empyrean to the temporary positions they occupy in the celestial spheres is exactly the relationship between Plato's presumed meaning and his mythical account of it in the *Timaeus*. Paradoxically then, in this most theological of *cantiche*, Dante seems to fashion his representation according to what might be called the allegory of poets (for Plato is surely a poet in this respect); yet the paradox is compounded and thus, perhaps, resolved by the suggestion that, while the technique and the terms of the figure may be Platonic, the inspiration is essentially biblical. The biblical representation of divine reality in anthropomorphic terms would seem to be the exemplar of all such verbal accommodations, in which the letter says one thing "ed altro intende."

It should be noted in passing that Beatrice's theory about the possible meaning of the Platonic myth concerning the stellar origins and the stellar destiny of the human soul may indirectly shed some light on the question of how extensive was Dante's knowledge of the *Timaeus* tradition.[3] She suggests that the myth really refers to the doctrine of stellar influences:

> S'elli intende tornare a queste ruote
> l'onor de la influenza e 'l biasmo, forse
> in alcun vero suo arco percuote.
> Questo principio, male inteso, torse
> già tutto il mondo quasi, sì che Giove,
> Mercurio e Marte a nominar trascorse.
> (*Par.* IV, 58–63)

If he means that the honor of their influence and the blame returns to these wheels, perhaps his bow hits some truth. This principle, ill-understood, once misled almost the entire world, so that it ran astray in naming Jove and Mercury and Mars.

It happens that this explanation of the myth as an "integumentum" for describing stellar influence occurs in twelfth-century apologetics for Plato associated with the School of Chartres.[4] In particular, Guillaume de Conches, in his glosses on the *Timaeus*, not only ascribes this kind of meaning to Plato, but immediately follows his interpretation with a qualification, lest he be accused of an heretical astrological determinism. Similarly, in his glosses on the meter of Boethius which alludes to the Platonic myth, he puts forward the same interpretation and a similar qualification:

> God assigned the souls to the stars, that is, He made souls of such a nature that they have their bodily existence according to the influence of the stars. For heat comes from the stars, and without

it there is no life, nor can the soul exist; not because, as they say, all things that come to pass come from the stars, but certain things, such as heat and cold, and certain infirmities and the like. And if someone should say, "Aren't these things created by God?" the response would be: they come into existence from God, but through the influence of the stars.[5]

Beatrice's similar interpretation of the passage from the *Timaeus*, with its corresponding qualification about the limits of astrological influence, implies a knowledge on the part of the poet that is more than casual of both the text and the interpretation, which made the theme acceptable to Christian philosophers.

It is quite clear that Beatrice's interpretation cannot provide us with a literary explanation of why Dante chose to structure his *ad hoc* poetical representation so as to resemble the Platonic myth. We have seen that the extended metaphor of the *Paradiso*, established by the command performance of the elect for the benefit of the pilgrim, is in fact a poetic reconciliation of the Platonic myth of the stellar souls with the Christian conception of heaven. And, constructing his representation, Dante seemed to be imitating the technique of both Plato and the Bible. I should now like to discuss other facets of the significance attributed to the Platonic myth in the Middle Ages, not mentioned by Beatrice, but nonetheless crucial for understanding how this theme from the *Timaeus* functions within the extended metaphor of the paradisiac representation. This will lead us directly into an examination of the Heaven of the Sun, our example of metaphoric structure in the *Paradiso*.

In a number of other essays . . . I have tried to show that the tradition established by the *Timaeus*, according to which the spiritual development of the soul was represented by corporeal movement, is the ultimate (although not necessarily proximate) source of Dante's own allegorical journey in the poem. For Plato, the most perfect of all corporeal motion was that exemplified by the regular, diurnal circulation of the stars. The stars, that is, perfect rationality, represent at once the soul's birthright and its destiny; education is the process whereby the star-soul, fallen to earth, struggles to regain its celestial home. So in Dante's poem, the stars represent the goal of the itinerary of the mind: a goal barely glimpsed at the end of the *Inferno*, within reach by the end of the *Purgatorio*, and achieved at journey's end (*Inf.* XXXIV, 139; *Purg.* XXXIII, 145; *Par.* XXXIII, 145).

This allegorical significance of stellar movement is probably implicit in the somewhat obscure etymology of the Latin word *consideratio* (*cum* plus *siderare*, to move with the stars?) which was given technical force in the mystical theology of St. Bernard. Such a resonance seems to come very close to the surface in the verse that Dante uses to describe the soul of Richard of St. Victor, "che a considerar fu piu che viro" (*Par.* X, 132) (who in contemplation was more than man). Given the profusion of comparisons of the "spiriti sapienti" to the stars and the fact these blessed souls represent most particularly the intellectual perfection for which the pilgrim strives, it does not seem too much to suppose that Dante intended to give the word a Platonic force whether or not that force is demonstrably part of the semantic tradition.[6] At any rate, it is clear to the most casual reader of the *Paradiso* that the souls of the Heaven of the Sun, as well as those of Mars, Jupiter, and Saturn are repeatedly compared to the fixed stars.

On the face of it, this comparison of the souls to stars would seem to create a poetic difficulty somewhat analogous to the difficulty of reconciling the immaterial Christian paradise with the Platonic heavenly spheres, at least as far as the representation of the Heaven of the Sun is concerned. Put most simply, that representation raises the question of what stars are doing in the sphere of the sun. The blessed souls have achieved the spiritual perfection toward which the pilgrim strives by degrees; the fiction of their temporary descent to the heavenly spheres makes it possible for the pilgrim to see and talk with them while he is still short of his goal. In imagistic terms, the perfection toward which he strives and which they have achieved is expressed in terms of the fixed stars. Under what circumstances can stars be said to "descend" to the sun? The rules of physics or of logic admittedly do not apply to poetic representations; once having accepted the fact that Dante's representation is not meant to represent any recognizable material reality, we are inclined to accept without question a *stellar* display, the souls of the "spiriti sapienti," in the sphere of the *sun,* especially since we do not believe in a *sphere* of the sun and are inclined to take a post-Galilean view of astronomical imagery anyway. A contemporary of the poet with an equal amount of astronomical learning, however, would not have failed to see that there is in the Heaven of the Sun an image mediating between the solar and stellar elements of the poet's metaphor, thus binding them together into the kind of coherence that one would expect of a metaphor that seeks to establish a new reality.

The poet sets forth the controlling image of his representation by beginning the canto with one of his most imperious and most famous addresses to the reader, inviting him to look up, neither to the stars nor to the sun, but to a point on the Zodiac, the sun's apparent path through the stars:

> Leva dunque, lettore, a l'altre rote
> meco la vista, dritto a quella parte
> dove l'un moto e l'altro si percuote;
> e lì comincia a vagheggiar ne l'arte

> di quel maestro che dentro a sè l'ama,
> tanto che mai da lei l'occhio non parte.
>   (*Par.* X, 7–12)

Lift then your sight with me, reader, to the lofty wheels, straight
to that part where the one motion strikes the other; and amorously
there begin to gaze upon that Master's art who within Himself so
loves it that His eye never turns from it.

This mention of the Zodiac, which may at first seem somewhat
irrelevant, in fact invites the reader to consider that part of the
heavens which, because of traditional associations, probably suggested
to the poet the scene that he describes in the rest of the canto.

In any other poet, a similar scene might strike us as bizarre or
at least undignified. The twelve spirits form a circle around the poet
and his guide and begin their dance:

> Poi, sì cantando, quelli ardenti soli
>   si fuor girati intorno a noi tre volte,
>   come stelle vicine a' fermi poli,
> donne mi parver, non da ballo sciolte,
>   ma che s'arrestin tacite, ascoltando
>   fin che le nove note hanno ricolte.
>   (X, 76–81)

When, so singing, those blazing suns had circled three times round
about us, like stars neighboring the fixed poles, they seemed as
ladies not released from the dance, but who stop silent, listening
till they have caught the new notes.

The consummate artistry of these lines temporarily suppresses the
astonishment that one experiences in retrospect when one realizes
that these twelve stars are among the greatest heros of Christian
philosophy and theology. The masterstroke of the second terzina, the
pause before the continuation of the dance, both sets the scene
dramatically for the speech that is to follow and allows the reader
the time to contemplate the *tour de force;* it is in fact a subtle
underscoring of what I have been referring to as the "command
performance" quality of the *cantica*—in the normal course of things,
the circumpolar dance of the stars awaits no man. In spite of the
reader's sense of shock in reading these lines, however, it happens
that they depend in part upon a very precise tradition, an examination
of which may help us to see that the dance is in fact zodiacal.

The origins of the theme of what I shall call the "zodiacal dance"
of wisemen are doubtless lost in antiquity and are at any rate not
immediately relevant. For our purposes, the earliest and best text I
am able to offer is gnostic in origin, was known to St. Augustine,[7]
and was transmitted in the apocryphal Acts of John. On close in-
spection, it seems to reveal many of the elements present in the

Dantesque scene. After recounting several incidents of his disciple-ship, the pseudo-John tells us that the Savior one day called the apostles together and commanded them to form a ring around him and to sing and dance:

> So He commanded us to make as it were a ring, holding one another's hands and Himself standing in the middle. He said, "Respond 'Amen' to me." He began, then, to sing a hymn and so say: "Glory to Thee, Father!" And we, going abut in a ring, said: "Amen."
> Glory to Thee, Word! Glory to Thee, Grace!
> Amen . . .
> I would wash myself and I would wash. Amen.
> Grace is dancing.
> I would pipe, dance all of you! Amen
> I would mourn, lament all of you! Amen.
> And Ogdoad is singing with us! Amen.
> The Twelfth number is dancing above. Amen.
> And the Whole that can dance. Amen . . .[8]

Nowhere is the astronomical imagery explicit in this hymn, but without it, the last three lines are incomprehensible. The "Ogdoad" is the number eight, the favorite of the Gnostics, standing for, among other things, the eight celestial spheres.[9] "The Whole that can dance" seems in fact to be a reference to the cosmos, whose rotation is the eternal dance to the "harmony of the spheres." Finally, the "twelfth number" that dances above, the emblem of these twelve disciples who dance below (and the ancestor of the twelve spirits who dance in the Heaven of the Sun), is the Zodiac, whose twelve constellations were represented, in a tradition that goes as far back as the Chaldeans,[10] surrounding the most important of all heavenly bodies. In short, the hymn depends upon one of the most ancient of Christian mysteries: Christ is the Sun.[11] As the twelve constellations surround what Dante calls the "sole sensible," so the twelve disciples turn about Christ, whom Dante calls the "Sole de li Angeli) (Par. X, 53). It is one of the ironies of intellectual history that the cult of the sun, adapted eventually to the exigencies of Christian symbolism, should have reached its highest point within a Ptolemaic world-view, when its centrality was regarded as purely symbolic.

The comparison of the twelve disciples to the twelve signs of the Zodiac is not simply an inference from an isolated text. The theme has been carefully documented by Jean Danielou, who has traced it from Judaeo-Hellenic antiquity (the comparison of the twelve tribes to the Zodiac) to fourth-century Christianity, although he does not mention the hymn quoted above.[12] The persistence of the theme throughout the Middle Ages has been previously traced by F. Piper in the nineteenth century.[13] To sum up their findings, we may say that the associations arose because of the importance of the number twelve in both the astronomical (twelve hours in the day, twelve months in the year, twelve signs of the Zodiac) and the biblical (twelve tribes of Israel, twelve gates of the temple, twelve apostles, etc.) traditions. Indeed, some historians of comparative religion trace the rise of the latter to the former. The exegetical tradition centered the association on those biblical passages which seemed to identify Christ as the "Day of the Lord" (Ps. 117:24) and as the "Year of the Lord" (Is. 61:2).

It may seem like forcing the text to invoke this tradition for an explanation of the scene in the *Paradiso*. If twelve theologians and philosophers are easily assimilable to twelve apostles, can the same be said for the signifiers of the respective comparisons? That is, could Dante have assimilated a whole zodiacal sign or a whole constellation with a single star? A biblical passage which has little relevance for Danielou's exposition but which is central to ours enables us to answer in the affirmative. In a passage from the Apocalypse which is probably of some importance for understanding the imagery of *Paradiso* XXIII (and such an understanding does seem to be required for all but the Crocean reading of the poem), there appear to be twelve stars which the exegetical tradition assimilated to the theme under discussion: "And there appeared a great wonder in heaven; a woman clothed with sun, and the moon under her feet, and upon her head a crown of twelve stars" (Apoc. 12:1). The sun in this portrait was invariably glossed as a reference to Christ and the twelve stars as his disciples. The motif of the crown of stars is explicitly recalled in the tradition studied by Danielou (Ps. 64:12: "Benedices coronae anni begignitatis tuae") as it is by Dante (*Par.* X, 65, 92; XIII, 13–15). The passage from the Apocalypse supplies the complement to the zodiacal theme required for an account of Dante's representation.

There is another passage in *Paradiso* X which, when interpreted in the light of this central theme, gains considerably in coherence. It is not in itself obscure, yet its presence in the poem is difficult to understand until we consider the central astronomical figure which binds it to the rest of the canto—an organizing principle, as it were, at the imagistic level. I refer to the exquisite image of the mechanical clock at the end of the canto. For all of its familiarity to us, it must have startled contemporaries, most of whom had undoubtedly never seen any such device. It serves as an example of how radically juxtaposed elements, in this case the most ancient ideas of astronomic speculation and the most modern of mechanical inventions, are fused together in Dante's synthesis, much as Solomon and Siger of Brabant both find a place in his cast of characters:

> Indi, come orologio che ne chiami
> ne l'ora che la sposa di Dio surge

> a mattinar lo sposo perche l'ami,
>   che l'una parte e l'altra tira e urge,
>   tin tin sonando . . .
>   (*Par.* X, 139–143)

Then, like a clock which calls us at the hour when the Bride of God rises to sing her matins to her Bridegroom, that he may love her, in which the one part draws or drives the other, sounding ting! ting!

Of the many themes alluded to in this dense and beautiful passage—the sun and the liturgy,[14] the Church and Christ as Bride and Bridegroom, the dawn song of lovers—I should like to single out just one: the aptness of comparing the "spiriti sapienti" to an instrument for measuring the diurnal course of the sun. We have seen from the discussion of Danielou's work that solar imagery applied to Christ in both of his symbolic roles, as both the Day and the Year of the Lord. Because the sun measures both the day and the year (it is for this reason "lo ministro magior de la natura"—*Par.* X, 28), its path, the Zodiac, may be said to mark both the hours and the months. The manifestation of the number twelve would thus compress universal history—the span of history represented by the "spiriti sapienti," the hours and the years—into the eternal now of the "dance" in the Empyrean of which this is a foreshadowing. A text from St. Ambrose will serve as an example of the tradition: "If the whole in duration of the world is like a single day, its hours mark off centuries: in other words, the centuries are its hours. Now there are twelve hours in the day. Therefore, in the mystic sense, the Day is indeed Christ. He has his twelve Apostles, who shone with the light of heaven, in which Grace has its distinct phases."[15] So in Dante's *Paradiso*, the souls of the blessed take in all of history by gazing into history's center: "Mirando il punto / a cui tutti li tempi son presenti" (*Par.* XVII, 17–18) (Gazing upon the point to which all times are present).

Because this is a foreshadowing of the movement of the blessed souls in the Empyrean, the center of this circular dance is not occupied by the *Sol salutis*, but simply by the pilgrim and his guide. Beatrice clearly contrasts this representation with the paradisiac original when she juxtaposes this material sun with the "Sole de li Angeli." There is, however, one comparison that suggests Beatrice's role in the representation; her position in the center of the circular dance is very much like that of a heavenly body—not the sun, but the moon:

> Io vidi più folgor vivi e vincenti
>   far di noi centre e di se far corona,
>   più dolci in voce che in vista lucenti:
> cosi cinger la figlia di Latona
>   vedem talvolta, quando l'aere e pregno,

sì che ritenga il fil che fa la zona.
                    (*Par.* X, 64–69)

I saw many flashing lights of surpassing brightness make of us a
center and of themselves a crown, more sweet in voice than shining
in aspect. Thus girt we sometimes see Latona's daughter when the
air is so impregnate that it holds the thread which makes her zone.

This passage cannot be dismissed as merely decorative or merely
metaphoric, for the comparison it suggests between Beatrice and the
pilgrim on one hand and the moon on the other has been rigorously
prepared by the verses which immediately precede it. Beatrice tells
the pilgrim to thank God, whom she describes as the Sun, for having
given him the grace to ascend to the sphere of the material sun. He
does so with such concentration that he forgets Beatrice for the
moment: "E sì tutto il mio amore in lui si mise / che Beatrice eclissò
ne l'oblio" (*Par.* X, 59–60) (and all my love was so set in Him that
it eclipsed Beatrice in oblivion). The word "eclipse" here does not
signify a darkening, but rather a blotting out by a greater light, as
Benvenuto da Imola observed: "[Beatrix] exlipsata est, idest, nubilata
in luce."[16] It is a commonplace of symbolic astronomy that the moon
regularly endures such an "eclipse" as it approaches the light of the
sun, which for this reason is thought of as a lover embracing his
beloved. This submerged significance of Beatrice's "eclipse" by God
comes to the surface in the lines immediately following, when she
is indirectly compared to the moon.

The phenomenon of the halo around the moon (sometimes referred to in the Middle Ages as *Iris,* like the rainbow to which Dante
later compares the spirits in *Par.* XII, 10ff.) is a substitute for an
astronomical spectacle, the sun surrounded by the stars, which no
mortal eye can ever see. We may presume, then, that it stands to
the sun as the human to the divine or, to use Dante's own language,
as the "essemplo" to the "essemplare" (*Par.* XXVIII, 55–56). It is
abundantly clear that the sun is here a symbol for divinity and that
Beatrice is associated with the moon; it remains for us to establish
the sense in which she may be said to substitute for the referent of
the solar image whose history we have discussed. It will come as no
surprise in the context of Hugo Rahner's "Christian Mystery" of the
sun and the moon, if we suggest that Beatrice's role here is meant
to be emblematic of the Church guiding the faithful.[17] Put more
simply, we may say that if the twelve apostles are the Zodiac of *Sol
Christi,* then the twelve philosophers and theologians are the "corona"
of *Luna Ecclesiae.*

From the earliest days of Christianity, as Rahner has shown, "it
is as though Helios and Selene were only created in order—to quote
Origen—'to carry out their stately dance for the salvation of the

world.' "[18] The ancient world had already characterized the relationship between sun and moon as that of lovers; it remained only to apply the teaching of Paul about the heavenly Bridegroom and his Bride to that ancient image-complex in order to see in the *mysterium Lunae* the whole drama of the Church. The waxing and waning of the moon, the derivation of its light from the sun, its illumination in darkness and its fading in the light of day all seemed perfect allegories of the relationship of Christ to the Church. The woman "clothed with the sun" on Apoc. 12 (quoted above) became the *locus classicus* for discussions of this kind which, according to Rahner, were perfected in the writings of Augustine. Rahner ends his discussion by citing *Paradiso* XXIII, Dante's direct treatment of the theme:

> Quale ne' plenilunii sereni
>   Trivia ride tra le ninfe etterne
>   che dipingon lo ciel per tutti i seni,
> vid' i' sopra migliaia di lucerne
>   un sol the tutte quante l'accendea,
>   come fa 'l nostro le viste superne . . .
>   (*Par.* XXIII, 25–30)

As in the clear skies at the full moon Trivia smiles among the eternal nymphs that deck heaven through all its depths, I saw, above thousands of lamps, a Sun which kindled each one of them as does our own the things we see above . . .

If, as a recent critic has suggested, the function of this metaphor is "purely emotional,"[19] then it must be said that the emotion is that of all of Christendom, occasioned by the fulfillment of universal history. This moment in the poem marks the shift in the metaphor we have been discussing and in many others as well—perhaps of all the astronomical metaphors of the *Paradiso* up to this point. The contrast is still between the "Sole de li Angeli" ("Un Sole") and the "sole sensibile" ("il nostro") but this time their functions are reversed: for the first time in the poem, the *Sol Christi* may be beheld by the pilgrim while the material sun is simply a memory of the sphere and the world below. If that transcendent sun is compared to the moon (Diana—Trivia) and the stars *(ninfe)* here in our world, it is because the *mysterium Lunae*, the Church, is all we have on this side of the frontiers of material reality to foreshadow the triumph of Christ; a contingent, provisional image, like those of *Paradiso* X, until the break of eternal Day.

I have tried to show that the traditional image of the apostles and the Zodiac may be taken as the background for the controlling theme of *Paradiso* X and that the shift from the apostles to theologians and philosophers finds its counterpart in a shifting of the center from the sun to Beatrice and the pilgrim or, according to one of the comparisons, the moon. There are two additional reasons that can be adduced to support the hypothesis that this shift is implicitly from Christ to a traditional image for the Church. The first of these is that the comparison to the moon surrounded by water vapor (expressed in terms subtly suggestive of generation and maternity: *cingere, pregno, zona*), like the faint suggestion of flowers and fields noticed by Aldo Scaglione in the *Trivia* image ("le ninfe etterne / che dipingon lo ciel . . . ' ' "; cf. "le piante [di] questa ghirlanda," *Par*. X, 91) underscores precisely the elements of moon imagery which enabled early exegetes to identify the heavenly body with the Church. Rahner makes the point:

> What causes the Sun's light to grow more mild is that Selene mingles the fire of Helios with the water of her own being, and I might as well at this stage tell you more about the rioting fancies of Greek thought on the subject of "heavenly moonwater." Poets and nature-mystics produced an abundance of ideas about it, ideas which lingered on for a thousand years. . . . Selene becomes a giver of water, dew is created which she causes to drip down . . . it is a begetter of life upon the earth; it brings about the growth of the grass and the growth of beasts and makes it possible for human mothers to bear their children. . . . In view of what has been said, it is not surprising that in seeking to give expression to her own beliefs the Christian should have made use of this lunar imagery with which the whole Hellenistic world was familiar.[20]

Then he goes on to demonstrate how this imagery seemed perfect for conveying ideas about spiritual rebirth and the water of baptism associated with the Church. The virgin goddess Diana (or "Trivia," to use Dante's name for her) was transformed by Christianity from moon mother into the *Mater Ecclesia*.

The second, much more obvious reason for thinking that the triumph of the theologians and philosophers is a triumph of the Church foreshadowing the triumph of *Sol Christi* has already been mentioned, although in passing. It is simply this: the harmonic song produced by the dance of the philosophers and theologians is compared by the poet at the culminating point of the canto to the liturgical song of the Church, the eternal present marked by the hours of the day. By referring to this song in erotic terms ("la sposa di Dio surge / a mattinar lo sposo perche l'ami") the poet binds into a single stunning unity not only Christ and his Church, sun and moon, apostles and theologians, but also his own longing relationship to God, through the mediation of Beatrice. It would be foolhardy to generalize this mediation into an identification. We may say only that the mediation on the personal level, this man's salvation, finds its counterpart in human society in the role of the Church and for this reason Dante chose to use the traditional imagery of mediation to describe her. It is in this sense, as the relationship of incarnate reality to salvation history, that Beatrice may be said in this canto to be a *figura Ecclesiae*.

The ending of the narrative and therefore of the canto calls our attention to Christ, the second person of the Trinity and the exemplar of all wisdom—*Somma Sapienza*. The propriety of such an ending in the canto of the "spiriti sapienti" is too obvious to require extensive commentary. What is equally obvious, however, is that the beginning of the canto seems to have little to do with this ending, for all of the didactic insistence of the involved address to the reader. The opening lines of the canto hint at some of the most complicated of all problems of medieval thought: the inner life of the Trinity, its role in the creation, the relationship of the heavens to generation and corruption on earth and, finally, the relationship of all of these problems to the moral life. After touching upon all of these themes, the poet somewhat impatiently dismisses his reader:

> Or it riman, lettor, sovra 'l tuo banco,
> dietro pensando a ciò che si preliba,
> s'esser vuoi lieto assai prima che stanco.
> Messo t'ho innanzi; omai per te ti ciba;
> che a se torce tutta la mia cura
> quella materia ond' io son fatto scriba.
>
> (*Par.* X, 22–27)

Now remain, reader, upon your bench, reflecting on this of which you have a foretaste, if you would be glad far sooner than weary. I have set before you; now feed yourself, because that matter of which I am made the scribe wrests to itself all my care.

It would take more than a lifetime to complete the task set for us in these lines and certainly more than these pages to sketch out how this doctrinal passage serves to introduce not only the tenth canto, but the next four as well. To conclude, however, I should like simply to point to a few elements of the opening verses that relate to the translation of beatitude into astronomical terms. This will require first of all a return to our discussion of the relevance of the Platonic tradition to the canto's theme.

The theme of the circular dance of the stars is a familiar one in the *Timaeus*. The phrase "choreae stellarum" used in the translation of Chalcidius is already a figurative application of the word meaning "choral dance" to the exigencies of astronomical description. In the commentary of Guillaume de Conches a definition is offered of the movement of the starry spheres that might equally well describe the dance of the "spiriti sapienti";

And the dance is a circular motion accompanied by harmonious sound. For this reason the philosophers say that the stars perform *(facere)* a dance, because they move in a circle, and from their motion they produce *(reddunt)* a harmonious sound.[21]

Elsewhere, Guillaume identifies the music specifically as *cantus*.[22] The song produced by the stellar dance is of course the music of the spheres, the music produced by the varying movements of the heavenly bodies, inaudible to mortal ears.[23] The music of the Heaven of the Sun, "voce a voce in tempra," seems to have the same transcendent quality, for the poet twice insists that it cannot be heard here below (vv. 75 and 146). Of more importance for the association of these ancient, admittedly general themes with the tenth canto is the fact that it is the sun, according to the *Timaeus*, that sets the standard of motion for all of the heavens by measuring time:

> And in order that there might be a conspicuous measure for the relative speed and slowness with which they moved in their eight revolutions *(chorea)*, the god kindled a light in the . . . Sun—in order that he might fill the whole heaven with his shining and that all living things for whom it was meet might possess number, learning it from the revolution of the same and uniform. Thus and for these reasons day and night came into being, the period of the single and most intelligent revolution.[24]

It should be observed that the sun has an equally regulatory function in Dante's metaphoric universe even down to the detail of the motion which it induces in the "spiriti sapienti." When their rank is doubled and the poet asks us to imagine two garlands circling about a center, the description he gives us of their motion, as if "l'uno andasse al prima e l'altro al poi" *(Par.* XIII, 18) (one went first and the other after), is part of the definition of time: "numero di movimento [celestiale] secondo prima e poi"[25] (number of heavenly motion according to a 'before' and an 'after'). Time may have its roots in the *Primum Mobile*, but its measure in hours and years is determined by the sun.

The centrality of the sun and its essential role in the cosmos led very early, possibly with the Stoics, to the idea that it represented the location of the world-soul, the *anima mundi*, whose varied history in the Middle Ages, including identification with the Holy Spirit and then finally with the goddess Natura, has been traced by Tullio Gregory.[26] By Dante's time, of course, no Aristotelian could take the idea of a world soul seriously, but a poet was perfectly free to do so and survivals of the idea remain in Dante's poem. . . . In the present context, I should like simply to point out a poetic survival, not explicitly stated, in the form of an associative principle that binds together the introduction of the tenth canto with the narrative contained within it and relates both to the moral imperative of the journey. That associative principle finds its expression precisely in the address to the reader; when Dante asks the reader to look up at the critical point in the Zodiac he is in fact asking us to contemplate not only the image which underlies the narrative of the canto, as we have seen, but also the complex of themes traditionally associated with the Zodiac in the tradition of symbolic cosmology.[27] The Zodiac was traditionally believed to be the emblem of the Creator's mark on the world and the seal of rationality both on man and on the heavens. So in the tenth canto, it is the sign of "quanto per mente e per loco si gira" (v. 4).

The text that first associated the circular movement of rationality *(per mente)* and of the heavens *(per loco)* with the circularity of divinity was Plato's *Timaeus*. It was obvious to subsequent commentators on Plato's text that the motions of the world-soul, for all of their apparently mythical character, were in fact derived from the two motions observable in the heavens: the diurnal circling of the sun from east to west, marking the hours of the day, and the annual circling of the sun in the opposite direction along the Zodiac, marking the months of the year. When the sun crossed the equator at its point of intersection with the ecliptic, "dove l'un moto e l'altro si percuote," it was thought to mark the spot where the Platonic Demiurge had set into motion both the soul of the world and the soul of man.[28] Boethius' *Consolation of Philosophy* (III, 9) provided the Middle Ages with a most concise statement of the manner in which the universe bears the image of the *anima mundi:* "You release the World-Soul throughout the harmonious parts of the universe . . . to give motion to all things. That soul, thus divided, pursues its revolving course in two circles, and, returning to itself, embraces the profound mind and *transforms heaven to its own image.*"[29] It remained only to identify the Demiurge with the Father, the profound mind with the Son and the world-soul with Holy Spirit in order for Christians to see in both the heavens and the human mind the image of the Trinity.

The history of the assimilation of the three persons of the Trinity to their Platonic counterparts is of course a substantial part of the history of Christian philosophy in the Middle Ages and especially in the twelfth century.[30] What is of more concern to us here, however, is the assimilation of Platonic imagery to the Christian revelation. From the earliest days of Christianity, the Platonic emblem of the Demiurge's creative act, the letter "chi" corresponding to the intersection of celestial movement that Dante asks his reader to contemplate, was associated with the emblem of Christ and of his redemptive act: the cross. Wilhelm Bousset has traced the history of that association.[31] Among the passages he cites, one is of particular interest to us, for it brings together the theme of wisdom in the person of Christ and the theme of celestial harmony. The passage comes from the apocryphal Acts of John, quoted above in relation to the dance of the disciples. The Lord appears to John and shows him a celestial "cross of light" specifically distinguished from the true cross:

> This cross of light . . . is the marking off of all things and the uplifting and the foundation of these things that are fixed and were unsettled, and the harmony of the wisdom—and indeed the wisdom of the harmony. . . . This, then, is the cross which fixed all things apart by the Word, and marked off the things from birth and below it, and then compacted all into one.[32]

In his commentary, Bousset has shown that this passage reflects a blending of the cosmological theme from the *Timaeus* with elements of the Gospel and of the sapiential books of the Old Testament. He goes on to document the diffusion of the idea throughout the Patristic era and we may add to his findings that it survived well into the Middle Ages, for the association of the Platonic "X" with the cross reappears in the work of Peter Abelard.[33] The general relevance of these Christian accommodations of Plato's text to a reading of the *Paradiso* is probably considerable—the cross of light of the Acts of John, for example, seems particularly suggestive for an interpretation of Dante's representation in the heaven of Mars. In the present context, however, the relevance is simply this: the history traced by Bousset provides an analogue to the opening verses of the tenth canto, wherein a glance up at the celestial "X" ("the intersection of the equator and the ecliptic of the Zodiac) also serves to evoke the central mysteries of Christianity, through the mediation of Platonic myth.

If both the movement of mind (*per mente:* the "spiriti sapienti") and the vital principle of the universe (the heavens and the "mondo che li chiama"—v. 15) can be encompassed by the same astronomical motif (the sun and Zodiac), it is by virtue of the Christianization of the Platonic theme of the *anima mundi*. The Platonic theme and its Christian elaboration, together with the glance up at the Zodiac which exemplifies the concepts they represent, provide us with a sufficient background for interpreting the entire introduction to the canto.

The opening of the canto sets forth the twofold movement of the threefold Deity:

> Guardanto nel suo Figlio con l'Amore
>   che l'uno e l'altro etternalmente spira,
>   lo primo e ineffabile Valore
> quanto per mente e per loco si gira
>   con tant' ordine fè ch'esser non puote
>   sanza gustar di lui chi ciò rimira.
>   (*Par.* X, 1–6)

Looking upon His Son with the love which the One and the Other
eternally breathe forth, the primal and ineffable Power made everything that revolves through the mind or through space with such
order that he who contemplates it cannot but taste of Him.

Were it not for the standard Christian effort to re-establish equality
in the hierarchical relationship of the One, Mind and Soul in a
neoplatonic system, this opening might well be a paraphrase of Macrobius.[34] At any rate, Dante intends here to set forth the two motions
of the Trinity or, as he puts it in v. 51, "mostrando come *spira* e
come *figlia.*" These two motions, intellectual generation and the
spiration of love, volition, are the two motions in the Trinity which
find their counterpart in the cosmos, "dove l'un moto e l'altro si
percuote" insofar as the cosmos can reflect the inner life of the
Trinity. Because of the way in which these two motions along the
Zodiac affect all of creation, they are the instruments of God's Providence in the world (vv. 13–21). More than that, however, because
of the parallelism previously mentioned, the motions are the exemplar
of all created mind as well: whatever rotates *per mente* or *per loco.*
It is for this reason that all mind and all of the heavens offer a
foretaste of the Trinity.

This, I take it, is the force of the word "dunque" in the address
to the reader: "Leva *dunque,* lettor, a l'alte ruote / meco la vista"
(vv. 7–8). The call to look up at the heavens to contemplate the
wonders of the creation is of course a familiar religious theme, but
it is also a Platonic theme that fits in very well with the microcosmic-
macrocosmic context of the opening lines. It is exactly in the context
of the passage in Macrobius referred to above, reminiscent of the
poet's trinitarian opening, that the significance of the motif is clearly
enunciated:

> Human bodies . . . were found to be capable of sustaining, with
> difficulty, a small part of it [the divinity of Mind], and only they,
> since they alone seemed to be erect—reaching toward heaven and
> shunning earth, as it were—and since only the erect can always
> gaze with ease at the heavens; furthermore they alone have in their
> heads a likeness of a sphere . . . the only one capable of containing
> mind.[35]

The glance up at the heavens is in this sense the fulfillment of human
rationality.

To conclude, and at the same time to show the ways in which
my findings may be generalized to extend to the entire representation
of the Heaven of the Sun, I should like for the last time to mention
the circular dance of the star-souls. There are of course two motions
described when all of the "spiriti sapienti" finally appear. We have
discussed the twofold motion of the Trinity, whereby it *figlia* and

spira, with intellect and volition. We have suggested its analogies with the twofold motion of the sun along the Zodiac. It seems reasonable to assume that the Trinity is also the exemplar upon which the movement of the heavenly garlands is based. The repeatedly parallel syntax used to describe each pair of motions—"che l'uno e l'altro etternalmente spira," (X, 2) (the One and the Other eternally breathe forth); "dove l'un moto e l'altro si percuote" (X, 9) (where the one motion strikes the other); "e l'un ne l'altro aver li raggi suoi" (XIII, 16) (and one to have its rays within the other)—leads one to suspect that the poet intends to associate the movement of the "spiriti sapienti" with the twofold movement of the Trinity, comparing both to the two movements of the Zodiac. The suspicion is confirmed by the descriptions of the two wheels. The two movements of the Trinity (the generation of the word and the spiration of love) represent respectively an act of intelligence and an act of will. However else one divides the cast of characters in the Heaven of the Sun, there seems general agreement that the first circle represents intellectuals who shone with "cherubic splendor" and the second represents lovers who burned with "seraphic ardor," exemplifying respectively intelligence and will.

The evidence of the Zodiacal nature of the imagery beyond the tenth canto is equally clear, although perhaps not as widely recognized. First of all, as soon as the second circle appears, Dante describes the movement as that of a "mola" (XII, 3), a millstone, the same word that he used in the *Convivio* in order specifically to distinguish zodiacal motion from generically circular motion.[36] Again, he refers to the song of the souls as more beautiful than that of "nostre muse / nostre serene" (XII, 7–8), the mythological goddesses who presided over the turning of the spheres. We have seen that the phrase "l'uno andasse al prima e l'altro al poi" (XIII, 18) (one should go first and the other after) recalls the measurement of time by celestial motion. Most convincing of all, perhaps, is the fact that the two accounts of the lives of the saints, obviously constructed in parallel, make reference to the course of the sun at precisely the same verse—the "rising" of Francis is associated with the rising of the sun, while the "rising" of Dominic is associated with its setting. At verse 51 of *Paradiso* XI, Dante describes Francis' birth as a sun coming to the world, "come fa questo tal volta di Gange" (even as this [sun] is wont to rise from Ganges). At verse 51 of *Paradiso* XXI, he describes the birth of Dominic as taking place near where "lo sol tal volta ad ogni uom si nasconde" (where the sun sometimes hides himself from every man). This evidence would seem to indicate that the twofold zodiacal motion constitutes the patterns even of the narrative portions of the succeeding cantos.

E sì come al salir di prima sera
comincian per lo ciel nove parvenze,
sì che la vista pare e non par vera,
(*Par.* XIV, 70–71)

And as, at rise of early evening, new lights begin to show in heaven,
so that the sight does, and yet does not, seem real.

The pilgrim ascends almost immediately to the next heaven, as if he
were not quite ready to see this celestial, but not yet paradisiac
triune light. In this metaphoric area that is Dante's own creation,
somewhere between the daylight of earth and the daylight of eternity,
the sun with his two motions sets the scene for the revelation that
is to follow. It is clear here, as it was in the Convivio, what that
revelation will be, for, as Dante put it, "Nullo sensibile in tutto lo
mondo e piu degno di farsi essemplo di Dio che 'l sole" (No object
of sense in all the world is more fit to be made the symbol of God
than the sun).[37]

Notes

1. Emanuele Tesauro, *Il Cannocchiale aristotelico* (Venice, 1655), p. 493, quoted
by Eugenio Donato, "Tesauro's Poetics: Through the Looking Glass," *MLN*, 77 (Jan.
1963), 19: "Reduced to this level of reality, the concepts expressed by the metaphor
are nothing but 'argomenti urbanamente fallaci,' because 'ad udirle sorprendono l'intelletto, parendo concludenti di primo incontro, ma esaminate si risolvono in una vana
fallacia: come le mele nel Mar Negro, di veduta son belle e colorite, ma se le mordi,
ti lasciano le fauci piene di cenere e di fumo.' "
2. Charles S. Singleton, *Dante Studies I: Commedia, Elements of Structure* (Cambridge: Harvard Univ. Press, 1957), chap. 1.
3. G. Fraccaroli, trans. *Il Timeo* (Turin: Bocca, 1906); "Dante e il *Timeo*," pp.
291–324. Fraccaroli is certain that Dante knew the text in the translation of Chalcidius
and possibly a commentator. For a more recent view of the diffusion of the *Timaeus*
in Dante's time, see Guillaume de Conches, *Glosae super Platonem*, ed. E. Jeauneau
(*Textes philosophiques du Moyen Age*, 13 [Paris: Vrin, 1965]), pp. 29–31.
4. E. Jeauneau, "L'usage de la notion d'*integumentum* a travers les glosses de
Guillaume de Conches," *Archives d'histoire doctrinale et litteraire du moyen age*, 24
(Paris, 1957), pp. 35–100.
5. Guillaume de Conches, *Commentary on Boethius*, III, m. 9. Ms. Troyes 138,
fol. 57, published in part by C. Jourdain, "Des Commentaires inedits," *Notices et
extraits de la Bibliotheque Imperiale* XX (Paris, 1865), pp. 77–78.
6. Ernout and Meillet, in the *Dictionnaire Etymologique de la langue latine* (Paris:
Klincksiek, 1951) *s.v.* acknowledge that "A *sidus* les anciens rattachaient deja *considerare, desiderare.*" The Pythagorean idea of the intellectual quality of sidereal movement as enunciated by Timaeus (*Temaeus* 40a ff.) seems to me a more plausible
hypothesis, indicating a familiar *moral* distinction: *desiderare* = a fall to *temporalia.*
. . . St. Bernard's treatise, *De Consideratione* (*PL* 182, 727), gave the word the technical
force that is surely has, resonances apart, in Dante's description of Richard of St.
Victor, for whom, however, the key word was *contemplatio*. See Richard of St. Victor,

Selected Writings on Contemplation, trans. C. Kirchberger (London: Faber and Faber, 1957), pp. 269ff.

7. St. Augustine, Letter to Ceretius (*PL* 33, 1034ff.), referred to by Theodor Zahn, *Acta Ioannis* (Erlangen: Deichert, 1880), p. 220.

8. *Acta Ioannis*, ed. Zahn, p. 220, trans. B. Pick, *The Apocryphal Acts of Paul, Peter, John, Andrew and Thomas* (Chicago: Open Court, 1909), p. 181. For gnostic sources, see R. A. Lipsius, *Die Apokryphen Apostelgeschichten und Apostellegenden* (Braunschweig: Schwetschke, 1883), I, 520. For similar dances in antiquity, see Lipsius' notes as well as Erwin Rohde, *Psyche*, trans. A. Reymond (Paris: Payot, 1928), pp. 270ff., and Robert Eisler, *Weltenmantel und Himmelzeit* (Munchen: Beck, 1910), pp. 462 and 472, where "star-dances" of antiquity are cited.

9. For the number 8, its significance and its sources, see Hugo Rahner, who quotes the saying "all things are eight," *Greek Myths and Christian Mystery*, trans. B. Battershaw (London: Burns and Oates, 1957), pp. 74–78 and bibliography.

10. For a full bibliography, see J. Baltrusaitis, "L'image du monde Celeste du IXᵉ au XIIᵉ siecle," *Gazette des Beaux-Arts*, 20 (1938), 138, n. 1.

11. The wealth of citations from the Old and New Testaments, classical and gnostic sources are brought together in Franz Dolger's *Sol Salutis* (Munster: Aschendorff, 1925), pp. 445ff., as well as "Sonne und Sonnenstrahl als Gleichnis in der Logostheologie des Christlichen Altertums," *Antike und Christentum* (1929), 271.

12. Jean Danielou, "Les Douze Apotres et le Zodiaque," *Vigiliae Christianae*, 13 (1959), 14ff.

13. F. Piper, *Mythologie und Symbolik der christlichen Kunst* (Weimar: Londesindustrie-comptoir, 1847–1851), II, 292ff. See in particular his tables on pp. 305 and 306, listing the transformation of the significance of the various signs of the Zodiac.

14. For the liturgical day, see Odon Casel, *Le Mystere du culte* (Paris: Editions du Cerf, 1946), chap. 5, and Dolger, *Sol Salutis*, chap. 22.

15. *In Lucam* VII, 222, *Sources Chretiennes*, p. 92, quoted by Danielou, pp. 14–15.

16. Benevenuti de Rambaldis de Imola, *Comentum super Dantis Aldigherij Comoediam*, ed. Lacaita (Florence: Barbera, 1887), V, *ad loc.*

17. Rahner, chap. 4.

18. Ibid., p. 111, quoting Origen, *On Prayer*, p. 7.

19. Aldo Scaglione, "Imagery and Thematic Patterns in *Paradiso* XXXIII," *From Time to Eternity*, ed. T. Bergin (New Haven: Yale Univ. Press, 1967), p. 163.

20. Rahner, p. 160.

21. *Timaeus a Calcidio translatus*, ed. J. H. Waszink (*Plato latinus*, IV; Leyden: Brill, 1962), p. 33; *Timaeus* 40c.

22. *Glosae*, p. 186.

23. On the theme of harmony, see Leo Spitzer, *Classical and Christian Ideas of World Harmony*, ed. A. G. Hatcher (Baltimore: The Johns Hopkins Univ. Press, 1963).

24. *Timaeus* 39b. Francis Cornford, *Plato's Cosmology* (New York: Liberal Arts Press, 1957), p. 115.

25. *Convivio* IV, ii, 5–6.

26. Tullio Gregory, *Anima mundi* (Florence: Sansoni, 1955), esp. p. 123.

27. For an outline of the apparent movement of the sun along the Zodiac, see M. A. Orr, *Dante and the Early Astronomers*, 2nd ed. (London: Wingate, 1956), pp. 172–81.

28. *Timaeus* 36b ff. and Cornford's notes *ad hoc.*

29. Boethius, *Consolation of Philosophy* (New York: Liberal Arts Press, 1962), p. 72.

30. Z. Hayes, *The General Doctrine of Creation in the Thirteenth Century* (Munchen: Schoningh, 1964), p. 88.

31. "Platons Weltseele und das Kreuz Christi," *Zeitschift fur die Neutestamentliche Wissenschaft*, 14 (1913), 273.

32. Pick, *Acta Joannis*, p. 184.

33. *Theologia Christiana in Petri Abaelardi Opera*, ed. V. Cousin (Paris: Durand, 1859), II, 406–407.

34. Macrobius (I, 14) is a *locus classicus* for a resume of the neoplatonic doctrine of emanation and creation. See Macrobius, *Commentary on the Dream of Scipio*, trans. W. H. Stahl (New York: Columbia Univ. Press, 1952), pp. 142–148 and Stahl's notes.

35. Macrobius I, 14; Stahl, p. 144. In this chapter Macrobius derives *contemplatio* from "the temple of God"; see Stahl, p. 142 and notes. Dante echoes the tradition in *Paradiso* XXVIII, 53: "questo miro e angelico templo." Cf. *Convivio* III, v, 22.

36. "[Conviene] esso sole girare lo mondo intorno giu a la terra . . . come una mola de la quale non paia piu che mezo lo corpo suo." *Conv.* III, v, 14.

37. *Conv.* III, xii, 6. For the importance of the Sun in Aries as an *essemplo* of Christ, see Rahner, *Greek Myths*, pp. 109–112.

A Commentary upon the First Canto of the *Inferno*
Giuseppe Ungaretti[*]

The first impression given by the *Divine Comedy*, because of the anxiety running through it from beginning to end, is of marvelous inexorableness. Above all, there is God to be proclaimed: not a fetish, but the Supremest Intellect, to whom Man is eternally present, the order of the universe relying on God's judgment. Man's heroism and man's abjection, all human actions, when measured from the summit, appear to be placed forever in their proper and true reality. No representation of justice in European literature, after Plato's *Gorgias*, stemmed from a more precise and vast knowledge, and was animated by a more poetic, strenuous, and, I dare say, fanatical faith. The heedful beholding of his active justice arouses the spiritual music that ascends to its utmost liberation and purity. . . .

> fell
> Erichto, sorceress, who compell'd the shades
> Back to their bodies.

In order to know himself, man, as Dante knows, tends to clarify his own experience according to the earthly limits of space and time,

[*] From Giuseppe Ungaretti, "Canto I," in *Letture Dantesche. Inferno*, ed. Giovanni Getto (Florence: Sansoni, 1965), 5–23. Translated for this volume by Massimo M. Pesaresi.

the "sensible" and "corruptible" limits of nature; and also—Erichto being in ourselves—man will be first of all aware of time, the tragic sense of which, from within his secret, from spark to death, scans his individual existence; but in order to become aware of it, in order to perceive its shadows in the darkness of night, man must possess a human measure of space.

In the first part of the first canto, therefore, Dante is primarily concerned with showing how all things are naturally attracted by the physical revelation produced by the rising sun, and how man is likewise attracted by the divine grace too, which, abiding in the beautiful harmony of the universe, will appear to him through space, after the rising of the sun. Space naturally awakes man's first poetic impulse, by arousing his aspiration to freedom.

Man's first mode of knowing is, therefore, poetry: it is his inborn mode of becoming aware of what in his own nature is immortal and also it will be his supreme mode, when, in the fullness of his interior light, man will become one with poetry and, having attained moral strength and limpid understanding, will be free. In the beginning, the word was poetry to man; and when, all evil suffered, proclaimed, isolated, and overcome, man will be clad in the original robe of musical purity, the word will be, more than ever, light and poetry to him.

✹ ✹ ✹

In the first canto, the sense of time has its initial quivering in the consciousness of man when the three beasts appear in the equivocal shifting of forms characteristic of that moment of the day in which light seems to be a blemish in darkness, and the night can delude us as a forgery of light. In that moment, when a fiendish and monstrous influence dims the power of nature, we suddenly encounter an apocalyptic image: "Impell'd me where the sun in silence rests."

Is the sun silent? The sun speaks indeed, and now it is time to talk about the value that Dante bestows upon the word. The world is void: there is only the initial perspective movement of the canto with blurred shadows in pure stillness; there is only the perennial Aeneas reaching land; there is only a man to be sung, the new Aeneas in his still dark fate, and with him are, as shadows among shadows, the ancient Aeneas, still unnamed, and Virgil, the master who, through the *Divine Comedy*, will bind with the spell of poetry the two protagonists of history.

> And as a man, with difficult short breathy
> Forespent with toiling, 'scaped from sea to shore,
> Turns to the perilous wide waste, and stands
> At gaze; . . .

But the hour is still devoid of history, unless it be latent; the shipwrecked is still to himself only the shipwrecked who has not yet gathered his spirits after struggling in the storm; he is still the sleepy ("pien di sonno") one, who is extricating himself from the night, surprised by his own awakening. This is the desert hour in which a man, alone, stands. And in this desolate, intricate, blind solitude the sun unveils the intricateness, the desolation, the blindness: it gradually spreads its light among crowding hesitations. Meanwhile, the objects slowly find their proper modes of appearance: the things that grow impatient and urge the man to utter their individual names, to speak in their stead; and the things that talk and cry in man's place, even before he can see them and his tongue be loosed. Later, a few decades after Dante, we will learn that man had filled the void nature by making her human, by crowding her with names as if he himself were the creator of the world. This boast was not unknown to man's pride: there had been Cavalcanti, whom Dante used to listen to although he disapproved of some ideas of his. What if Dante had foreseen the baroque age and centuries of even darker despair, and that one day from the intricateness of contradictions the belief would rise that names are mere accidents? The word that for Dante is the soaring sign of the intellect and the hard tool of moral passion comes to initiate him to humanity and poetry: deep in the mystery of nature, the word, sacred, preceding man himself, is the very substance of conscience, although it will be uttered by man—and will be audible to him—only as the human instrument of history.

". . . The sun in silence rests," senses and consciousness are abruptly put together with no time left to duration, and such an immediacy is affirmed exactly when history is coming to the scenery of the mind.

Such is the word for Dante: although wise, it impetuously comes to the foreground, devouring and abolishing what is alien to the revelation it brings. Thus, sudden and irretrievable, it condensed and petrified with the spell and horror of the three heraldic beasts at the moment when he was divining them.

In Dante's words, human activity will find its lasting definition even through history and melancholy, which his time—Guido Cavalcanti's time—starts acknowledging; the melancholy brought by history, because time cannot avoid its condition of being itself the sign of perishing: the melancholy of history, as it appears in the evocation of "fell Erichto."

* * *

In the background of the first canto, emerging from the night, imbued with night, and almost made timid with the horror of the night the objects of space are seen, and shaped forever, in the perennial change that the fleeting moment brings: the intensity of change, the precise and delicate certainty with which change is perceived, may persuade us that to Dante's fame may suffice his perfection in depicting (vying with the sun) the physical hues of any fleeting moment; but ". . . the sun in silence rests."

In the background, the man, coming to the light of the rising sun, perceives it as any other living creature does; his lot, however, is to feel another light, to see that in front of him the abyss is coming to nothing; to see that he himself has emerged from the dissolving chasm, and all around a high order, the harmony of a beautiful work, is taking place. The aim of man is vertically drawn from the deepest abyss to the Empyrean, and man's first motion is a thirst for becoming, through order and light, part of the harmony and beauty of the universe: hope of the height. For one of those secrets that poetry— and Dante's poetry in particular—shares, a landscape, described in its successive phases, moves from unconscious sleep to involved drowsiness, and to uncertain dawn. All is suddenly mingled and transfused in the very rising of man hopeful of the height, who manifests himself by showing how the universe around us is but a perpetual variation all allusions to the human condition, and, therefore, can but teach to be human, to establish again a relation between the ephemeral and the eternal. . . .

The moment Virgil appears to Dante is precisely the moment chosen by Dante to indicate the relation between the sensible and the temporal experience, when the need for linking feeling with will and action is patent in man. In his poetic logic Dante imagines to be able to see Virgil only at that moment, although Virgil had been present from the beginning of the canto—when Dante finds himself "in a gloomy wood," bearing in himself—in his senses, feelings, imagination, and intellect—the figure of the new Aeneas, who had risen on earth in the fullness of time. Thirteen hundred years could be the "midway of this our mortal life," with the new era having such a solidity of frame, sharpness of features, and overall such a finely wrought texture of civilization.

The appearance of Virgil, eventually loosened from the shadows, is the third moment of great poetry in this canto. The first moment was the allusion to the ancient Aeneas, setting down on his promised land:

> And as a man, with difficult short breath,
> Forespent with toiling, 'scaped from sea to shore,
> Turns to the perilous wide waste, and stands

At gaze; e'en so my spirit, that yet fail'd,
Struggling with terror, turn'd to view the straits
That none hath pass'd and lived.

º º º

This was the oscillation between the horror of the fleeting night and the stupefaction at the still secret, yet already present, day. In this appalling flight of darkness, perturbed by the receding shadows of a near past; in this confusion of things and thoughts, which, at a presage of light, see in themselves the lingering night in the shape of a wandering of shadows, of a reluctant perplexity, here comes that verse—event of timbre and rhythm—in which the calming of things and thoughts in the pervading light is told:

My weary frame
After short pause recomforted, . . .

The second moment is when the man, discovering his aim through sensible experience, conceives "of the height all hope"; while the sight of "the gay skin of that swift animal" conspired to fill him with joyous hope, because the light, revealing her to his eager senses, revealed to his soul "of the height all hope":

The hour was morning's prime, and on his way
Aloft the sun ascended with those stars,
That with him rose when Love divine first moved
Those its fair works: so that with joyous hope
All things conspired to fill me, the gay skin
Of that swift animal, the matin dawn,
And the sweet season.

The pleasant sights of a space beguiling to disorder and chaos were naturally balanced in space itself by the harmony of creation as it shone in the springtime of the world:

The hour was morning's prime, and on his way
Aloft the sun ascended with those stars,
That with him rose when Love divine first moved
Those its fair works . . .

The very fact that the poetic illumination, in order to be perceptible to the mind, resorts to an antithetical comparison shows that the perception of human tragedy begins. In spite of the immortality of the soul, this tragic experience takes place in the dimension of passing away: in duration, in corruptibleness, in tragedy, in history, in the shaping of one's relations to oneself and society in a way reminiscent of the original beauty proper to the divine idea of Man, the human responsibility of every individual is expressed. . . .

The third moment of poetic beauty is when Dante is presented with the natural notion of eternity through the light of historical experience:

> While to the lower space with backward step
> I fell, my ken discern'd the form of one
> Whose voice seem'd faint through long disuse of speech
> When him in that great desert I espied,
> "Have mercy on me," cried I aloud,
> "Spirit! or living man! what'er thou be."

The world is ruined again, rent by obscurity and "fear"; the little light is riven by darkness because even the utmost bestiality partakes of some light, and the poet's mind collapses in that ruin from the height of hope. But in that moment he realizes the presence—the second miracle of the light—of one who had faintly appeared. . . .

>   one
> Whose voice seem'd faint through long disuse of speech . . .

has appeared, and such a "spirit or living man" has appeared in that great desert. Formerly, the poet had called "lonely steep" the place where the three beasts were about to appear, and he meant to express a void not yet vast, the solitude, not entirely discovered, of early morning: the desert vale and the shoulders of the hill, unrobed of darkness, and now clad in the sunbeams. At the bouncing of light from darkness, at the new progression of daybreak, the hesitations between light and shade have been pushed forward, and vast—vast, this time—is the desert, yawning from a millennial distance before the poet. Light has drawn her breath more freely this time. Inadvertently, this solitude lies open down to the poet, and from one thousand years distance a great experience is gleaming: the grand mode of history, which "seem'd faint through long disuse of speech," in poetry. . . .

In order to make the temporal light—light of history and light of memory—sensible, Dante turned it first into spatial light. . . . The apparition is dimly lighted: "faint" for the great distance, wherefrom it emerges and whereto the eyes reach because of the disclosed horizon. "Faint," says the poet, referring both to the dim light and to the feeble call in the distance; and in order to give the adjective greater intensity he enlarges the perspective encompassing the whole horizon and, catching his breath, adds: "him in that great desert I espied."

. . . In this canto, and in the entire *Divine Comedy*, the poet is deeply aware that everyone is alone in the presence of one's own destiny; that everyone, in boundless solitude, decides of one's own actions, through which the soul, being the form of the body, shows its features. The successive apparitions in solitude prepare the great solitude of the soul which, in the next canto, will feel its weakness, and in the secrecy of its bewilderment and the anxiety of loneliness, will receive Grace; and, feeling ready to the sacred initiation, will go like "Silvius' sire,"

> Yet clothed in corruptible flesh, among
> The immortal tribes had entrance . . .

and "sensibly present." Thus will begin the moral experience which will make history clear to Dante. . . .

✲ ✲ ✲

The shadow of Virgil must touch upon memory and the poet must recognize it in his mind, and talk to it, and eventually listen to and utter audible words; it is necessary that Virgil intervene between Dante and the she-wolf, namely that the illustrious historical experience chanted by Virgil intervene, for the new Aeneas to prophesy the *Veltro*, who will assault the she-wolf

> That never sated is her ravenous will,
> Still after food more craving than before. . . .

and "and shall destroy / Her with sharp pain."

We have come to the promise of the terrible appearance and elegant fury of the *Veltro*.

Apart from idle conjectures, the *Veltro* should be considered a form of the temporal energy, which, in the tragic experience of life, shall oppose the evil forces of such energy, wholly compromised in mundane interests; and shall manifest his—beneficial—will to power. The *Veltro* signifies primarily the necessity of fighting the earthly temporal energies with a temporal energy and also a precise distinction between history and eternity. The *Veltro* will be a temporal force, formed and guided in his relentless hunt by the aims of history: aims of a humanity endeavoring to affirm the eternal idea of Man. The *Veltro* will be a political force, yet bent to humbly pursuing "love, wisdom, and virtue."

The False Problem of Ugolino   Jorge Luis Borges*

I have not read (no one has) all the commentaries on Dante, but I suspect that, in the case of the famous line 75 of the penultimate

---

* From Jorge Luis Borges, *Nueve ensayos dantescos*, ed. Barnatan and Arce (Madrid: Espasa-Calpe, 1982), 205–11. Translated for this volume by Nicoletta Alegi.

canto on *Inferno*, they have created a problem that reflects a confusion between art and reality. In that line Ugolino of Pisa, while recounting the death of his children in the Tower of Hunger, says that hunger was more powerful than grief ("Poscia, piu che 'l dolor, pote il digiuno"). I must exclude the ancient commentaries from this reproach. For them the line is not problematic, and in fact they interpret it to say that grief could not kill Ugolino, but hunger could. Even Geoffrey Chaucer understands it in these terms in the bleak summary of the episode that he intercalated in the *Canterbury Tales*.

Let us reconsider the scene. In the icy bottom of the ninth circle, Ugolino gnaws endlessly the nape of Ruggieri degli Ubaldini and wipes his bloody mouth with the hair of the condemned soul. He raises his mouth, but not the face, from the bestial meal and recounts that Ruggieri betrayed him and put him in jail with his children. Through the narrow opening of the cell he saw many moons wax and wane until the night in which he dreamed that Ruggieri, with hungry mastiffs, hunted on the slope of a mountain a wolf and its wolf cubs. At dawn he hears the hammer nailing shut the entrance to the tower. A day and a night go by in silence. Ugolino, moved by grief, bites his hands; his children think that he does so out of hunger and offer him their own bodies, which he generated. Between the fifth and sixth day he sees them die, one after the other. Afterward, he goes blind and speaks to his dead ones and weeps and feels them in the dark. Later, hunger could more than grief.

I have stated the meaning that the first commentators gave to this passage. Rambaldi da Imola in the fourteenth century says as follows: "he says that the hunger prevailed on one who could not be conquered and killed by grief." Among the modern commentators Francesco Torraca, Guido Vitali, and Tommaso Casini follow this opinion. The first of the three sees bewilderment and remorse in the words of Ugolino ended up by eating the flesh of his children, a conjecture contrary to nature and to history. Benedetto Croce agrees and holds that of the two interpretations, the more plausible and verisimilar is the traditional one. Bianchi, very reasonably, glosses: "some understand that Ugolino ate the flesh of his children—an improbable interpretation which however is not legitimate to discard." Luigi Pietrobono (to whose ideas I shall return) says that the line is deliberately enigmatic.

Before joining, in my turn, in the *useless controversy*, I wish to linger a moment on the unanimous offering of the children. They pray their father that he take back those bodies that he had generated:

> tu ne vestisti
> queste misere carni, e tu le spoglia
> (*Inferno* XXXIII, 62–63).

[You dressed us in these miserable bodies, and you undress us.]

I suspect that this speech causes a growing uneasiness in those who admire it. De Sanctis *(Storia della letteratura italiana)* ponders the unforeseen conjunction of heterogeneous images; D'Ovidio admits that "this bold and rich exposition of a filial impetuousness almost disarms all critics." As to myself I think that here we are dealing with one of the very few falsehoods present in the *Comedia*. I judge it less worthy of Dante's work than of the pen of Malvezzi or of Gracian. Dante, I say, could not but feel its falseness, which is made more serious, without doubt, by the circumstance of the four children simultaneously toasting to the ravenous banquet. Some will insinuate that we are dealing with a lie of Ugolino, concocted to justify (to suggest) the previous crime.

The historical problem as to whether Ugolino practiced cannibalism in the first days of February 1289, is, clearly, insoluble. The aesthetic or literary problem is of a very different nature. It is possible to enunciate as follows: "Did Dante wish that we should think that Ugolino (the Ugolino of his *Inferno*, not that of history) ate the flesh of his children?" I shall risk the reply: Dante has not wished that we should think it but that we should suspect it. The ambiguity is part of his design. Ugolino gnaws the brain of the Archbishop; Ugolino dreams of dogs with sharp fangs, which tear the flanks of the wolf. Ugolino, moved by grief, bites his hands; Ugolino hears his children making the unverisimilar offer of their flesh; Ugolino, after uttering the ambiguous line, returns to gnaw the brain of the Archbishop. Such acts suggest or symbolize the atrocious deed. They fulfill a doubt function: we take them to be part of the history, and they are prophecies.

Robert Louis Stevenson remarks that the characters of a book are woven with words; however blasphemous this may appear, this is what Aquiles and Peter Gynt, Robinson Crusoe and Don Quixote are reduced to. To this are reduced also the powerful ones who govern the earth: Alexander is a series of words, and Attila is another. We must say of Ugolino that he is a verbal texture, that he consists of some 30 tercets. Must we include in that texture the notion of cannibalism? I repeat that we must suspect it with uncertainty and fear. To deny or to assert the monstrous crime of Ugolino is less terrifying than to be dazzled by it.

The statement "a book is the words that compose it" runs the risk of seeming an insipid axiom. However, we all are inclined to believe that there is a form separable from the content, and 10 minutes of conversation with Henry James would reveal to us the true argument of *The Turn of the Screw*. I think that this is not the case; I think that Dante did not know much more about Ugolino than his tercets explain to us. Schopenhauer declared that the first volume of his capital work consists of only one thought and that he did not find a shorter way to communicate it. Dante, on the contrary, would say that however much he imagined of Ugolino is in those debated tercets.

In real time, in history, each time that a man confronts different alternatives, he opts for one and eliminates and loses the others. It is not so in the ambiguous time of art, which is similar to that of hope and that of forgetfulness. Hamlet, in that time, is both sane and mad. In the darkness of his Tower of Hunger, Ugolino devours and does not devour the beloved corpses. That wavering imprecision, that uncertainty, is the strange matter of which he is made. Thus, with two possible agonies, Dante dreamed him and thus will dream him the generations to come.

The Light of Venus and the
Poetry of Dante   Giuseppe Mazzotta*

My title refers to the passage in the *Convivio* in which Dante classifies the seven liberal arts according to a conventional hierarchy of knowledge. Grammar, dialectic, rhetoric, music, geometry, arithmetic, and astronomy are the disciplines of the *trivium* and *quadrivium*, and each of them is linked to one of the planets in the Ptolemaic cosmology (*Convivio* 2.12.13–14). Venus is the planet identified with Rhetoric because the attributes of Venus, like those of rhetoric, are

> la chiarezza del suo aspetto, che e soavissima a vedere più che altra stella; l'altra si e la sua apparenza, ora da mane ora da sera. E queste due proprietadi sono ne la Rettorica: che la Rettorica è soavissima di tutte le altre scienze, però che a ciò principalmente intende; e appare da mane, quando dinanzi al viso de l'uditore lo rettorico parla, appare da sera, cioè retro, quando da lettera, per la parte remote, si parla per lo rettorico (*Conv.* 2.12.13–14).

> The clarity of its figure, that is sweeter to behold than any other star; the other is its appearance, now in the morning and now in the evening. And these two properties are in rhetoric: for rhetoric is sweeter than all the other sciences, since it is chiefly to this, that it is ordained; and it appears in the morning when the rhetorician addresses directly the listener; it appears in the evening, that is to say, behind, when the rhetorician speaks by letter from afar.

The definition alludes, as is generally acknowledged, to the tra-

* Giuseppe Mazzotta, "The Light of Venus and the Poetry of Dante." Reprinted by permission of the publisher from *Magister Regis: Studies in Honor of Robert Earl Kaske* (New York: Fordham University Press, 1986), 147–69.

ditional double function of rhetoric, oratory and the *ars dictaminis* or letter-writing.[1] What the definition also contains is the notion of the *ornatus*, the techniques of style or ornamentation whereby rhetoric is said to be the art that produces beautiful appearances.[2] The term "chiarezza," one might add, translates *claritas*, the light that St. Thomas Aquinas conceives to be the substance of beauty and the means of its disclosure.

In the *Convivio*, Dante does not really worry about the issue of the beautiful as an autonomous aesthetic category. Although the beautiful can be an attribute of philosophy (Dante speaks, for instance, of "la bellissima Filosofia" (*Conv.* 2.12.9) or the synonym of morality, the importance of both the beautiful and rhetoric is decisively circumscribed in this speculative text of moral philosophy. To grasp the reduced value conferred on rhetoric in the *Convivio*, where it is made to provide decorative imagery, one should only remember its centrality in the *De vulgari eloquentia*. The treatise, which straddles medieval poetics and rhetoric, was written with the explicit aim of teaching those poets who have so far versified "casualiter" to compose "regulariter" by the observance of rules and by the imitation of the great poets of antiquity (*De vulgari eloquentia, II.iv.1-3*). This aim reverses, may I suggest in passing, Matthew of Vendome's judgment. In his *Ars versificatoria*, Matthew dismisses the lore of the ancient poets, their rhetorical figures and metaphors, as useless and unworthy of emulation: "hoc autem modernis non licet" (*Ars versificatoria*, 4.5). But for Dante rhetoric, which begins with the Greeks, is the very equivalent of poetry, or as he puts it, "fictio rhetorica musicaque poita" ("A rhetorical fiction set to music," *De vul. El.* 2.4.2-3). The concern with style and taste, which occupy a large portion of the *De vulgari eloquentia*, dramatizes the identification of rhetoric and poetry. At the same time, as the art of discourse, the art of pleading political or juridical causes, rhetoric is also in the *De vulgari eloquentia* the tool for the establishment of political, legal, and moral authority. In this sense, Dante's notion of rhetoric re-enacts the concerns of a cultural tradition that ranges from Cicero to Brunetto Latini.

It comes as something of a surprise that scholars, who have been remarkably zealous in mapping the complex implications of rhetoric in the *De vulgari eloquentia*, have not given equal attention to its role in Dante's other major works. In the case of the other texts, rhetoric is treated as a repertory of figures, but not as a category of knowledge with unique claims about authority and power. The statement, in truth, ought to be tempered somewhat in the light of the extensive debates to which the question of allegory in both the *Convivio* and the *Divine Comedy* has been subjected. Yet even then the relationship between rhetoric and the other arts or the way in which rhetoric engenders reliable knowledge and may even dissimulate its strategies is not always adequately probed.[3] It is not my intention to review here the research that scholars such as Schiaffini, Pazzaglia, Tateo, Baldwin, and others have carried out on various influences on Dante's thinking about rhetoric, or their systematic analyses of the places in Dante's *oeuvre* where rhetoric is explicitly mentioned. I shall focus instead on the *Convivio*, the *Vita nuova*, and *Inferno* 27 to show how rhetoric works itself out in these texts, but I will also submit new evidence that might shed light on Dante's position in the liberal arts, namely, thirteenth-century polemics involving the secular masters of theology at the University of Paris and the anti-academicism of the early Franciscans.

There is no significant trace of this polemic in the *Convivio*. The point of departure for this unfinished treatise, and the principle that shapes its articulation, is the authority of Aristotle, who in his *Metaphysics*, which Dante calls "la Prima Filosofia," states that, "tutti li uomini naturalmente desiderano di sapere" (*Conv.* 1.1.1). The reference to Aristotle may well be an enactment of the technique of the exordium which rhetorical conventions prescribe. But the reference also announces what turns out to be the central preoccupation of the four books: namely, that knowledge is made available by and through the light of natural reason. This recognition of man's rationality allows Dante to argue that it can be the choice of man to pursue the way to achieve the good life on this earth. In spite of the initial *sententia*, the *Convivio* is explicitly modeled not on Aristotle's *Metaphysics*, which deals with pure theoretical knowledge such as the knowledge of spiritual entities, but on Aristotle's *Ethics*. This is, as Isidore of Seville refers to it, the practical "ars bene vivendi," which casts man in the here and now of his historical existence and which demands that man exercise the choices (without which no ethics can be conceived) appropriate to a moral agent.

It is this philosophical optimism about human rationality that accounts for the thematic configuration of the *Convivio*. The narrative is punctuated, for instance, with references to one's own natural language as preferable to Latin, which is at some remove from one's own life; it is clustered with insistent discussions of the moral virtues and whether or not nobility is contingent on birth, wealth, or customs; it focuses on the value of political life and the justice which the Roman Empire, a product of human history, managed to establish in the world (*Conv.* 4.4). What sustains the textual movement is above all a belief in the allegory of poets as a technique that affords the thorough interpretability of the indirections of poetic language. Running parallel to the notion that poetry can be the object of a full philosophical investigation, there is an insistence on the knowability of the moral and rational operations of man.

This acceptance of the natural order is the principle that lies at the heart of two related and crucial gestures which shape the intellectual structure of the *Convivio*. The first, as Gilson has argued, is the revolutionary re-arrangement, within the confines of the *Convivio*, of the dignity of aims: ethics rather than metaphysics is placed as the *summum bonum*.[4] The second is the subordination of rhetoric to ethics. This statement needs clarification. The first treatise. actually begins by explaining Dante's own shift away from the *Vita nuova* to the *Convivio*:

> Non si concede pere li retorici alcuno di sé medesimo sanza necessaria cagione parlare, e da ció è l'uomo rimosso perchè parlare d'alcuno non si può che il parladore non lodi o non biasimi quelli di cui elli parla: . . . Veramente . . . per necessarie cagioni lo parlare di sè è conceduto: . . . L'una è quando sanza ragionare di se grande infamia o pericolo, non si può cessare; . . . E questa necessitate mosse Boezio di sè medesimo parlare, acciò che sotto pretesto di consolazione escusasse la perputuale infamia del suo essilio. . . . L'altra è quando, per ragionare di sè, grandissima utilitade ne segue altrui per via di dottrina; e questa ragione mosse Agustino ne le sue Confessioni a parlare di sè, che per lo processo de la sua vita, . . . ne diede essemplo e dottrina. . . .(*Conv.* 1.2–12)

Rhetoricians do not allow anyone to speak of himself except of necessity. And this is forbidden because when speaking of someone, the speaker must either praise or blame the man of whom he speaks: . . . Truly . . . a man may be permitted to speak of himself for necessary reasons: . . . One may do so when by not speaking of oneself great infamy or peril cannot be avoided; . . . It is necessity that moved Boethius to speak of himself in order that under the pretext of finding consolation he might ease the perpetual disgrace of his exile. . . . The other is when, by speaking of oneself, great utility to others results from such speech. This reason moved Augustine in his *Confessions* to speak of himself, so that by means of the process of his life . . . he presented an example and lesson. . . .

The passage is primarily a dismissal of what is known as epideictic rhetoric, one of the three classical divisions—along with the deliberative and the forensic—of rhetoric proper. Epideictic rhetoric, says Cicero in *De inventione*, is the branch of oratory which casts praise or vituperation on some person. (*De Inventione*, 1.5.7). This epideictic mode, quite clearly, is identified with the autobiographical writing of Boethius and St. Augustine. But for all the acknowledgment of the utility and exemplariness of the *Confessions*, Dante's passage is overtly anti-Augustinian: the point of the *Convivio* is that the natural order, of which St. Augustine had too narrow an appreciation, is the locus of a possible moral-social project. More importantly, the passage marks an anti-Augustinian phase in Dante because it signals the limitations of auto-biographical writing in favor of a philosophical discourse that would transcend private concerns and squarely grapple, as the *Convivio* will do, with the issue of the authority of intellectual knowledge and its relationship to political power.

The departure from the *Confessions* is in reality Dante's way of distancing himself from his own Augustinian text, the *Vita nuova*, and its rhetoric. It could be pointed out that in the *Vita nuova* there is an occasional resistance to the excesses of self-staging: "converrebbe essere me laudatore di me medesimo, la quale cosa e al postutto biasimevole a chi lo fae" (it would not be proper for me to praise myself, for self-praise would be reprehensible, *Vita nuova* 28.2). Yet the rhetoric of the self remains the path through which the poet's own imaginative search is carried out. The exordium of the *Vita nuova* consistently stresses the autobiographical boundaries of the experiences about to be related:

> In quella parte del libro de la mia memoria dinanzi a la quale poco si potrebbe leggere, si trova una rubrica la quale dice: *Incipit vita nova*. Sotto la quale rubrica io trovo scritte le parole le quali e mio intendimento d'assemplare in questo libello; e se non tutte, almeno la loro sentenzia (1.1).

> In that part of the book of my memory before which there is little to read, one finds a rubric which says: *Incipit vita nova*. Under this rubric I find written words which is my intention to copy in this little book; and if not all the words, at least their sentence.

The exordium is a proem, as Dante will call it later in the narrative, in the technical sense of a *captatio benevolentiae*. One could also point out the technical resonance of the term "sententia." Although the *Glossarium* of Du Cange refers only to the juridical sense of the word and neglects the meaning of moral lesson, which one can find in the *Rhetorica ad Herennium*, it hints that the text is also a plea for oneself in the presence of one's beloved. But what is central in the proem is the textual presence, which has gone unnoticed by the editors, of Guido Cavalcanti's "Donna me prega."

As is well known, Cavalcanti wrote his poem in response to the physician Guido Orlandi's query about the origin of love. Orlandi's sonnet "Onde si move e donde nasce amore?" ("Whence does love come and grow?") proceeds to ask where love dwells, whether it is *sustanzia, accidente,* or *memora,* and what feeds love; it climaxes with a series of questions as to whether love has its own figural representation or whether it goes around disguised. Cavalcanti replies that love takes its dwelling place in that part where memory is, "in quella parte dove sta memora / prende suo stato" ("in that part where memory is, it takes its being"), a formulation which Dante's exordium, "in quella parte del libro de la mia memoria," unequivocally echoes.

The echo compels us to place the *Vita nuova* as conceived from the start in the shadow of Cavalcanti's poetry, but it does not mean that the two texts are telling the same story. The most fundamental difference between them is their antithetical views of rhetoric and the nature of the aesthetic experience. For Guido, memory—which is in the sensitive faculty of the soul—is the place where love literally resides. In his skeptical materialism there is no room for a vision that might relieve one's dark desires.[5] The deeper truth—so runs Cavalcanti's argument—is imageless, and Guido's steady effort in the poem is to unsettle any possible bonds between poetic images and love, or love and the order of the rational soul. The scientism of "Donna me prega" literalizes desire and makes it part of the night: its poetry, with its overt anti-metaphysical strains, paradoxically turns against poetry and assigns truth to the idealized realm of philosophical speculation.

For Dante, on the contrary, the truth of love is to be the child of time—as Venus is—and hence under the sway of mutability and death. The temporality of desire links it unavoidably to memory, but memory is here—and this is the main departure from Cavalcanti— a book or the "memoria artificialis," which is one of the five parts of rhetoric. The parts are usually identified as *inventio, dispositio, elocutio, memoria,* and *pronuntiatio;* memory is defined as "firma animi rerum ac verborum perceptio" (*De Inventione,* 1.7.9). The rhetoricity of memory turns the quest of the *Vita nuova* into an interrogation of the value of figures. More precisely, memory is not the refuge of a deluded self, the *a priori* recognition of appearances as illusive shapes, the way Cavalcanti would have it. For Dante, memory is the visionary faculty, the imagination through which the poet can question the phenomena of natural existence and urge them to release their hidden secrets. It can be said that Cavalcanti makes of memory a sepulcher and of death the cutting edge of vision: he broods over the severance death entails, and it thwarts his imagination. He is too much of a realist, too much of a philosopher to be able to soar above the dark abyss into which, nonetheless, he stares.

But the poet of the *Vita nuova* is impatient with this skepticism, this dead literalism, and from the start he seeks to rescue vision from the platitudes of the materialists. The figures of love are not irrelevant shadows or insubstantial phantoms in the theater of one's own mind, as Cavalcanti thinks when he ceaselessly beckons Dante to join him on the plain where the light of ideas endures. Nor are women part of an infinite metaphorization, always replaceable (hence never necessary), as the physician Dante da Maiano believes, who tells Dante that his dream of love is only lust that a good bath can cure.

The contrivance of the lady of the screen, related in chapter four, which literally makes a woman the screen on which the lover projects and displaces his own desires, is rejected because it casts doubt on Beatrice's own uniqueness. At the same time, chapter eight, which tells of the death of one of Beatrice's friends, allows Dante's sense of poetry in the *Vita nuova* to surface. Retrospectively, however, it is also another put-down of the materialists' belief that love is reducible to the mere materiality of bodies. Dante refers to the dead woman as a body without a soul—she is one "lo cui corpo io vidi giacere sanza l'anima" ("whose body I saw lying without the soul"). The poem he then proceeds to write is "Piangete, amanti, poi che piange Amore" (Weep, lovers, for Love himself weeps), which turns out to be, quite appropriately, a lament over the dead figure, "la morta imagine." But this poet can glance heavenward, "ove l'anima gentile gia locata era" (*Vita nuova*, 8.6, "where the gentle soul already had its home"). In short, Dante installs his poetry at the point where Cavalcanti's poetry—where most poetry, for that matter—stops: between the dead body and the soul's existence. Images are not *a priori*, mere simulacra of death, and the "stilo de la loda," which re-enacts the principles of epideictic rhetoric, strives for a definition of Beatrice's felt but unknown essence.

This concern with metaphysics, with the links between rhetoric and the soul, emerges in chapter twenty-five, where metaphor is said to be the trope that animates the face of the world. The meditation on metaphor, which is the burden of the chapter, is carried out as an attempt to grasp the nature of love. Here we see why Venus should be coupled to rhetoric. The question Dante raises has a stunning simplicity: is love a divinity, as the Notaro suggests, or is it a mere rhetorical figure, as Guido Cavalcanti states in his *pastorella*, "In un boschetto"? Dante defines love in only partial agreement with Cavalcanti, for whom love is "un accidente in sustanzia." The metaphoricity of Love is then discussed in terms of a movement from the animate to the inanimate and vice verse:

> Onde, con ciò sia cosa che a li poete sia conceduta maggior licenza di parlare che a li prosaici dittatori, e quei dicitori per rima non siano altro che poete volgari, degno e ragionevole è che a loro sia maggiore licenzia largita di parlare che a li altri parlatori volgari: onde se alcuna figura o colore rettorico è conceduto a li poete, conceduto è a li rimatori. Dunque, se noi vedemo che li poete hanno parlato a le cose inanimate, si come se avessero senso e ragione, e fattele parlare insieme; e non solamente cose vere, ma cose non vere, cioè che detto hanno, di cose le quali non sono, che parlano, e detto che molti accidenti parlano, si come fossero sustanzie e uomini; degno è lo dicitore per rima di fare lo somigliante, ma non sanza ragione alcuna, ma con ragione la quale poi

sia possibile d'aprire per prosa. . . . Per questo medesimo poeta parla la cosa che non è animata e le cose animate, nel terzo de lo Eneida, quivi: Dardanide duri. Per Lucano parla la cosa animata a la cosa inanimata . . . per Ovidio parla Amore, si come fosse persona umana. . . . (*Vita nuova*, 8.10)

Since in Latin greater license is conceded to the poet than to the prose writer, and since these Italian writers are simply poets writing in the vernacular, we can conclude that it is fitting and reasonable that greater license be given to them than to the other vernacular writers. Therefore, if we see that the poets have spoken to inanimate things, as if they had sense and reason, or have made them speak to one another (and they did this with real and unreal things—that is, they have said, concerning things that are not, that they speak, and they have said that many accidents speak as if they were substances and man), then it is proper that the vernacular poets do the same—but not without some reason; rather, with a reason that can later be glossed in prose. . . . This very same poet has an inanimate thing speak to animate things in the third book of *The Aeneid*: "Dardanide duri." In Luca the animate to the inanimate thing . . . in Ovid, love speaks as if it were a human person. . . .

It could be mentioned that "dicitori per rime" and "prosaici dittatori" are phrases that find their gloss in Brunetto Latini's *Rettorica*, which is defined as the science of two aims, one of which "insegna dire" and the other "insegna dittare. (*Rettorica* 8). More to the point, metaphor is given in the guise of *prosopopeie*, the orphic fiction whereby that which is dead is given a voice or, more correctly, a face.

With the actual death of Beatrice, related from chapter twenty-eight on, the fiction that poetry is capable of providing a simulation of life is no longer sufficient. To be sure, Beatrice was described as the living figure of love, but now that she is physically dead, the metaphors for her seem to be another empty fiction. If the question while Beatrice was alive was whether she is and how she is unique, now that she is dead the question is finding the sense of metaphors that recall her. Dante's imaginative dead-end at this point (it induces tears, but Dante records no poetry) narrows in the prose to a vast image of general darkness, the death of Christ. An analogy is established between Beatrice and Christ in an effort to invest the memory of Beatrice with a glow of material substantiality. Charles Singleton views this analogy as the exegetical principle of the *Vita nuova*, the aim of which is to portray the lover's growing awareness of the providentiality of Beatrice's presence in his life.[6]

But the tension between the Christological language, the status of which depends on the coincidence between the image and its essence, and the poetic imagination, which in this text comes forth in the shifting forms of memory and desire, is problematic. There is no doubt that the poetic imagination aspires to achieve an absolute stability which only the foundation of theology (which has its own visionariness) can provide. But Dante marks with great clarity the differences between his own private world and the common theological quest. The penultimate sonnet of the *Vita nuova* addresses exactly this predicament:

> Deh peregrini che pensosi andate,
> forse di cosa che non v'è presente.
> venite voi da si lontana gente,
> com'a la vista voi ne dimostrate,
> che non piangete quando voi passate
> per lo suo mezzo la città dolente
> come quelle persone che neente
> par che 'ntendesser la sua gravitate?
>
> Se voi restaste per volerlo audire,
> certo lo cor de'sospiri mi dice
> che lagrimando n'uscireste pui.
> Ell'ha perduta la sua beatrice;
> e le parole ch'om di lei pò dire
> hanno vertù di far pianger altrui.

Ah, pilgrims who pensively go your way, thinking, perhaps, of something far away, do you come from such a distant race (such as your appearance shows) that you do not weep when you traverse the middle of the sorrowing city, like those who understand nothing of the sorrow she bears?

If you would stop to listen, I know, from what my heart of sorrow tells me, that you would be weeping when you left this place. The city has lost its beatitude; and I know words which a man might speak of her with the affect of causing others to weep.

The sonnet is an apostrophe to the pilgrims who are going to Rome to see the true image—literally a prosopopoeia—Christ left on the veil of Veronica. The pilgrims are unaware of the lover's own heart-sickness, and the poet's mythology of love—that Beatrice is an analogy of Christ—comes forth as too private a concern. More precisely, the sonnet is built on a series of symmetrical correspondences: the pilgrims are going to see Christ's image and are caught in an empty space between nostalgia and expectation, away from their homes and not quite at their destination; the lover is in his own native place, but, like the pilgrims, away from his beatitude. But there is another contrast in the sonnet which unsettles the symmetries: the motion of the pilgrims, who are on their way, is in sharp contrast to the poet's invitation that they stop to hear the story of his grief.

In the canzone "Donne ch'avete intelletto d'amore," the heavens vie with the lover to have Beatrice; now the terms are reversed: the lover seeks to waylay the pilgrims, begs them to stop for a while, a gesture that is bound to remind us of the repeated temptations the pilgrim himself eventually will experience in *Purgatorio*.

The vision of the pilgrim's journey to Rome triggers the last sonnet, "Oltre la spera," which tells of the poet's own pilgrimage. This is an imaginative journey to the separate souls which the intellect cannot grasp, for the intellect stands to those souls, Dante says, "si come l'occhio debole a lo sole: e cio dice lo Filosofo nel secondo de la Metafisica" ("as does the weak eye to the sun: and so says the Philosopher in Book two of his *Metaphysics*"). At the moment when a revelation is at hand in this most visionary text, the eye is dazzled by the sun and the essences remain hidden behind their own inapproachable light. The perplexing quality of the image is heightened by the fact that it was used by both Averroes and Aquinas to describe the separate souls. Doctrinally, the text evokes and is posed between two opposite metaphysical systems. More poignantly, the phrase "'l sospir ch'esce del mio core" ("the sigh that comes out of my heart") echoes "sospiri, / che nascon de' penser che son nel core" ("sighs which come out of the thoughts that are in the heart"), which in turn is patterned on Cavalcanti's "Se merce fosse amica a' miei disiri" ("If mercy were a friend to my desires"). Cavalcanti restates the absolute separation of desire and its aim; Dante yokes rhetoric to metaphysics, makes of rhetoric the privileged imaginative path to metaphysics, though rhetoric can never yield the spiritual essence it gropes for.

The *Convivio* picks at the very start the reference to Aristotle's *Metaphysics* on which the *Vita nuova* comes to a close. But Dante challenges, as hinted earlier, the traditional primacy of metaphysics and replaces it with ethics. The move is so radical that Dante dramatizes the shift to ethics in the first song, "Voi che 'ntendendo il terzo ciel movete" ("You intelligences who move the third heaven"). Written in the form of a *tenso*, a battle of thoughts within the self, and addressed to the angelic intelligences that move Venus, the planet of rhetoric, the poem tells the triumph of the "donna gentile"— Philosophy—over Beatrice. With the enthronement of Philosophy, rhetoric is reduced to an ancillary status: it is a technique of persuasion, the cover that wraps the underlying morality within its seductive folds. The *envoi* explicitly confronts this issue:

> Canzone, io credo che saranno radi
> color che tua ragione intendan bene,
> tanto la parli faticosa e forte.
> Onde, se per ventura elli addivien

che tu dinanzi da persone vadi
che non ti paian d'essa bene accorte,
allor ti priego che ti riconforte,
dicendo lor, diletta mia novella:
"Ponete mente almen com'io son bella!"

Canzone, I believe that there will be few who are able to understand well your argument, so difficult and hard your speech. Wherefore, if by chance your words happen to go before those who, it may seem to you, are not well acquainted with your argument, then I pray you be comforted and say to them, my new and pleasing song, "At least take note of how beautiful I am!"

The confinement of rhetoric to a decorative role in philosophical discourse is not unusual. From Cicero to Brunetto Latini rhetoricians are asked to link rhetoric to ethics because of rhetoric's inherent shiftiness, its power to argue contradictory aspects of the same question (*Rettorica*, p. 7). In a way, it is possible to suggest that the voice of Dante in the *Convivio* is a Boethian voice, for like Boethius, who in his *De consolatione Philosophiae* banishes the meretricious muses of poetry to make room for Lady Philosophy, under whose aegis poetry is possible, Dante, too, makes of poetry the dress of Philosophy.

This analogy with the Boethian text stops here, for unlike Boethius, Dante does not seek consolation for too long. Philosophy, says Isidore of Seville, is "meditatio mortis" (*Etymologia* 2.24.9). Dante has no intention of being trapped in the grief that the shadow of Beatrice's death caused in him. He turns his back on the past in the *Convivio* and ponders ethics, which is not the land of the dead, but the "ars bene vivendi" (*Etym.* 2.24.5). As a matter of fact, his voice is that of the intellectual, who, exiled and dispossessed, asserts the authority of his knowledge and seeks power by virtue of that knowledge. This claim for power by an intellectual obviously does not start with Dante. Its origin lies in the revival of another sphere of rhetoric, the *artes dictaminis* elaborated by Alberic of Monte Cassino and the Bologna school of law and rhetoric, where intellectuals shaped and argued the political issues of the day.

Yet Dante's project in the *Convivio* to cast the philosopher as the adviser of the emperor fails utterly. Many reasons have been suggested by Nardi, Leo, and others as to why the project collapsed.[7] The various reasons essentially boil down to Dante's awareness that a text expounding a system of values cannot be written unless it is accompanied by a theory of being. The text that attempts the synthesis is the *Divine Comedy*.

The point of departure of the poem is the encounter with Vergil, whose "parola ornata" (an allusion to the *ornatus* of rhetoric) has the power, in Beatrice's language, to aid the pilgrim in his quest.

But if rhetoric is unavoidably the very stuff of the text, rhetoric's implications and links with the other disciplines of the encyclopedia are explicitly thematized in a number of places. One need only mention *Inferno* 15, where rhetoric, politics, grammar, law, and their underlying theory of nature are all drawn within the circle of knowledge; of *Inferno* 13, the canto which features the fate of Pier delle Vigne, the counselor at the court of Frederick II, whose failure can be gauged by Brunetto Latini's reference to him in *La rettorica* as a master in the art of "dire et in dittare sopra le questioni opposte" ("to speak and to compose on opposite questions," *Rettorica*, p. 5).

I shall focus, however, on *Inferno* 27 because this is a canto that inscribes Dante's text within the boundaries of the thirteenth-century debate on the liberal arts and, more precisely, on the Franciscan attack against logic and speculative grammar. The canto is usually read in conjunction with the story of Ulysses that precedes it. The dramatic connections between the two narratives, however superficial they may be, are certainly real. It can easily be granted that *Inferno* 27 is the parodic counter to *Inferno* 26 and its myth of style. In the *De vulgari eloquentia*, in the wake of Horace's *Ars poetica* and the *Rhetorica ad Herennium*, Dante classifies the tragic, elegiac, and comical styles in terms of fixed categories of a subject matter that is judged to be sublime, plain, or low. In the canto of Ulysses, with its "verba polita," to use Matthew of Vendome's phrase, moral aphorisms and grandiloquence stage the language of the epic hero whose interlocutor is the epic poet Vergil. Ulysses' is a high style, making his story a tragic text, for Ulysses is, like all tragic heroes, an overstater and hyperbole is his figure: he is one who has staked everything and has lost everything for seeking everything.

As we move into *Inferno* 27, there is a deliberate diminution of Ulysses' grandeur. His smooth talk is replaced by hypothetical sentences ("S'i' credesse che mia risposta fosse" or "Se non fosse il gran prete," 61–70), ("If I thought that my answer were . . ." or "But for the High Priest"); parenthetical remarks ("s'i' odo il vero") ("If what I hear is true," 65), swearing, colloquialisms, and crude idioms. From the start, Guido's speech draws the exchange between Vergil and Ulysses within the confines of dialect:

> . . . "O tu, a cu' io drizzo
> la voce, e che parlavi mo Lombardo
> dicendo: 'istra ten va, piu non t'adizzo.' " (19–21)

"O you to whom I direct my voice and who just now spoke Lombard, saying, 'now go your way, I do not urge you more,' "

Vergil allows Dante to speak to Guido, "Parla tu, questi e latino" ("You speak, he is Italian," 33), because Vergil, too, observes the rhetorical rules of stylistic hierarchy. There is a great deal of irony in shifting from Ulysses' high ground to the specifics of the Tuscan Apennines or Urbino and Ravenna. But from Dante's viewpoint the irony is vaster: degrees of style are illusory values, and Ulysses and Guido, for all their stylistic differences, are damned to the same punishment of being enveloped in tongues of fire in the area of fraud among the evil counselors. Even though the image of the Sicilian bull within which its maker perishes (7–9) conveys the sense that we are witnessing the fate of contrivers trapped by their own contrivances, it also harks back to Ulysses' artifact, the Trojan horse.

It could be said that Guido is the truth, as it were, of Ulysses. If the pairing of their voices, however, can be construed as a confrontation between the epic and the mock-heroic, style is not just a technique of characterizing their respective moral visions. Guido's municipal particularity of style introduces us to the question of political rhetoric—the rhetoric by which cities are established or destroyed—which is featured in the canto. What we are shown, to be sure, is an obsessive element of Dante's political thought: Guido da Montefeltro, the adviser of Pope Boniface VIII, counseled him how to capture the city of Palestrina, and this advice is placed within the reality of the temporal power of the papacy. From this standpoint *Inferno* 27 prefigures St. Peter's invective in *Paradiso* 27, and it also echoes *Inferno* 19, the ditch of the Simonists where Pope Boniface is expected.

As is *Inferno* 19, we are given the cause of the general sickness: just as Constantine sought out Pope Sylvester to cure his leprosy (94–99), so did Boniface VIII seek Guido da Montefeltro to cure his pride. If leprosy suggests the rotting away of the body politic, pride is the fever of the mystical body; the origin of both is the Donation of Constantine. The chiasmus that the comparison draws (Boniface is equated with Constantine) points to the unholy mingling of the spiritual and secular orders and to the role-reversal of the pope and his adviser.

But there is in the canto an attention to political discourse that goes beyond this level of generality. In a way, just as there was a theology of style, we are now allowed to face the politics of theology. We are led, more precisely, into the council chamber—behind the scenes, as it were—where "li accorgimenti e le coperte vie" ("I knew all wiles and covert ways," 76), the art of wielding naked political power, is shown. Here big deals are struck, so big that they focus on the destruction of cities and the salvation of souls. These are the terms of the transaction: by virtue of his absolute sovereignty (an authority that depends on the argument of the two keys, "Lo ciel poss'io serrare e diserrare, / come tu sai; pero son due le chiavi / che 'l mio antecessor non ebbe care" ["I can lock and unlock Heaven, as you know; for the keys are two, which my predecessor did not hold dear."] 103–05), the pope promises absolution for Guido's misdeed. Guido's advice is simply to make promises without planning to keep them, "lunga promessa con l'attender corto / ti fara triunfar ne l'alto seggio" ("long promise with short keeping will make you triumph on the High Seat" 110–11).

The advice, I would suggest, textually repeats and reverses Brunetto Latini's formulation in *La rettorica* (p. 19). Commenting on Cicero's statement that the stability of a city is contingent on keeping faith, on observing laws and practicing obedience to one another, Brunetto adds that to keep faith means to be loyal to one's commitments and to keep one's word: "e dice la legge che fede e quella che promette l'uno e l'altro l'attende" ("and the law says that faith is that by which one promises and the other expects what is promised"). The deliberate violation of the ethical perspective, which alone, as Brunetto fully knows, can neutralize the dangerous simulations that rhetoric affords, brings to a focus what the canto of Ulysses unveils: that ethics is the set of values rhetoric manipulates at will. From Dante's viewpoint, however, the arrangement between the pope and his counselor is charged with heavy ironies that disrupt the utilitarian calculus of the principals.

The pope begins by taking literally what is known as his *plenitudo potestatis*, the fullness of spiritual and temporal powers given to him by God, yet he is powerless to act and seize a town. He believes in the performative power of his words, that by virtue of this office his words are a sacramental pledge. Yet he takes advice to say words that do not measure up to his actions. There is irony even in Dante's use of the word "officio"—a term which for Cicero means moral duty; its appearance in line 91 only stresses the dereliction of duty. On the other hand, there is Guido, who knows that in the tough political games men play there is a gap between words and reality. Yet he believes in the pope's "argomenti gravi" ("weighty arguments" 106)—a word that designates probable demonstration according to logical rules—without recognizing that the pope does not deliver what he promises, which—after all—was exactly Guido's advice to him.

The point of these ironies is that Boniface and Guido thoroughly resemble and deserve each other. Both believe in compromises, practical gains, and moral adjustments, as if God's grace could be made adaptable to their calculus and to the narrow stage of everyday politics. And both are sophists of the kind St. Augustine finds especially odious in *De doctrina Christiana* (3.31), those who transform the world of political action to a world of carefully spoken words. As a sophist, Boniface entertains the illusion that he can control the discourse of others and ends up controlling Guido while at the same time being controlled by him. As a sophist, Guido is the character who is always drawing the wrong logical inference from his actions: he mistakenly believes Dante is dead because he has heard that nobody ever came alive from the depths of Hell (61–66); he becomes a friar, believing that thus girt he could make amends for his past (66–69).

What exactly does it mean to suggest, as I am doing, that Guido is portrayed as if he were a logician? And how does it square with the fact (to the best of my knowledge it has been investigated by commentators) that he is a Franciscan, or, as he calls himself, a "cordigliero" (67)? The fact that Guido is a Franciscan has far-reaching implications for the dramatic and intellectual structure of the canto. The tongues of fire in which the sinners are wrapped are an emblem more appropriate to a Franciscan like Guido than to Ulysses. The tongues of fire are usually explained as a parody of the Pentecostal gift of prophecy that descended on the apostles at the time of the origin of the Church. It happens, however, that the Constitution of the Franciscans established that the friars should convene at the Porziuncola every four years on Pentecost. The reason for this ritual is to be found in the Franciscans' conscious vision of themselves as the new apostles, capable of reforming the world.

Guido's language perverts the Pentecostal gift, and the perversion puts him in touch with the fierce enemies of the Franciscans, the logicians. The possibility for this textual connection is suggested by the canto itself. At Guido's death there is a *disputatio* between one of the "neri cherubini" ("black cherubs") and St. Francis over Guido's soul (112–17). The devil wins the debate and speaks of himself as a "loico" ("logician" 123). The debate between a devil and St. Francis is not much of a surprise, for as a fallen angel—one of the cherubim— the devil is the direct antagonist of Francis, who is commonly described in his hagiographies as "the angel coming from the east, with the seal of the living God" (Revelation 7.12). Furthermore, the reference to the devil as one of the cherubim, which means "plenitudo scientiae" ("fullness of knowledge") and is the attribute of the Dominicans, seems to be involved obliquely in Dante's representation of both orders of friars. But this is not the hidden allegory of a *quaestio disputata* between Dominicans and Franciscans. What is at stake, on the contrary, is the long debate in which the two fraternal orders were engaged in the thirteenth century—and in which they end up on the side of their opponents, as Dante implies. The debate centered on the value of the liberal arts at the University of Paris.[8]

In historical terms, the debate saw the preachers and the mendicants opposed by the secular masters of theology. The Dominicans, to be sure, adapted quickly to the pressures of university circles because they were founded with the explicit intellectual aim of combating heresies. The Franciscans, on the other hand, in response to the call for evangelical practice, believed that their homiletics had to retrieve the essence of the good news without any sophistry. St. Francis is an "idiota," given to the cult of *simplicitas;* Paris, the city of learning, is made to appear the enemy of Assisi.

This stress on simplicity did not mean that the Franciscans kept away for too long from the world of learning. There is in effect a strong Augustinian strand in their attitude toward academic knowledge. St. Augustine, it will be remembered, encourages Christians in *De doctrina Christiana* to make good use of pagan rhetoric in order to communicate the message of the Revelation effectively. Secular wisdom, which is crystallized in the liberal arts and which St. Augustine rejected in the *Confessions,* is not viewed as a treasure to be plundered by Christians the way the Hebrews plundered the "Egyptian gold" (2.40).

The Franciscans, figures such as Alexander of Hales, St. Bonaventure, and Duns Scotus, did move into the universities, but by virtue of their voluntarism they adhered to an essential anti-Aristotelianism. The formal edifice of Aristotelian logic was severely challenged, both as a theory of abstract reasoning and as a doctrine that the universe is a logical system of numbers and mathematically measurable order. In *Inferno* 27, as the devil is identified as a logician, logic comes forth as the art that deals with judgments about the consistency or contradictions within the structure of an argument, but radically lacks an ethical perspective. Appropriately, Guido, who has betrayed his Franciscan principles, is now claimed by one of the very logicians the Franciscans opposed.

But the debate between Franciscans and the secular masters is not left entirely on this academic level in the canto. There are political ramifications which Dante absorbs in his representation. Guillaume de Saint-Amour, a leader of the secular masters, had unleashed an attack in his *De periculis novissimorum temporum* against the Franciscans as the pseudo-apostles and heralds of the anti-Christ; in their purely formal observance of the externals of faith they are identified as the new pharisees, who connive with popes under the habit of holiness to deceive the believers. As Y. M.-J. Congar suggests, the polemic was a clear attempt to contain the power of the pope, for the mendicants, by being under the pope's direct jurisdiction, weakened the *potestas officii* of the local bishops. Largely at stake was the issue of confessions, a source of controversy between local priests and friars, which ironically was given a firm solution in the bull *Super cathedram* by Boniface VIII.

In *Inferno* 27, Boniface is "lo principe d'i novi Farisei" ("the Prince of the new Pharisees" 85); he makes a mockery of confession, "tuo cuor non sospetti; / finor t'assolvo" ("let not your heart mistrust.

I absolve you here and now" 100–1), and his *potestas* appears as only temporal power. By the same token, Guido, who as a Franciscan should believe in the power of confession, settles for a pharisaic formula, "Padre, da che tu mi lavi / di quel peccato vo'io mo cader deggio" ("Father, since you do wash me of that sin into which I now must fall" 108–9), and seeks absolution before the commission of sin—an act that makes a mockery of his prior contrition and confession (83). And finally, he is the pope's conniver throughout.

In effect, Guido da Montefeltro never changed in his life. The emblem he uses for himself, "l'opere mie / non furon leonine, ma di volpe" ("my deeds were not those of the lion, but of the fox" 74–75), gives him away. The animal images, to begin with, are consistent with the unredeemed vision of the natural world in terms of mastiff, claws, and young lion (45–50). More to the point, the metaphor of the lion and the fox echoes Cicero's *De officiis* (1.13.41), and it may be construed in this context as a degraded variant of the *Topos* of *sapientia et fortitudo*. But the fox, Guido's attribute, has other symbolic resonances. In the *Roman de Reynard*, the fox goes into a lengthy confession of his sin and then relapses into his old ways; for Jacques de Vitry, more generally, the fox is the emblem of confession without moral rebirth. More important for *Inferno* 27 is the fact that Rutebeuf, who wrote two poems in support of Guillaume de Saint-Amour, uses the fox as the symbol of the friars; in *Renart le nouvel* the fox is a treacherous Franciscan.[9]

These historical events and symbols are brought to an imaginative focus in the digression on the deceits of False Seeming in the *Roman de la Rose* of Jean de Meung. Absorbing the anti-fraternal satire of Guillaume, Jean presents Faussemblant as a friar, a "cordelier," who has abandoned the evangelical ideals of St. Francis and lives on fraud. Reversing Joachim of Flora's hope that the fraternal orders were providentially established so that history would hasten to a close, Jean sees the mendicants as symptoms of decay: "fallacious is the logic of their claim: religious garment makes religious man" (*Roman de la Rose*, 1.11200). This sense of the friars' deceptiveness ("now a Franciscan, now a Dominican," as Jean says) reappears in *Il fiore*, where Falsembiante's steady practice of simulation comes forth as metaphoric foxiness:

'I' sì so ben per cuor ogne linguaggio
le vite d'esto mondo i' ho provate;
ch'un or divento prete, un'altra frate,
or prinze, or cavaliere, or fante, or paggio.
Secondo hed i' veggio mi vantaggio.
Un'altra or son prelato, un'altra abate:
molto mi piaccion gente regolate,
che co llor cuopro meglio il mi' volpaggio' (Sonnet 101).

I well know by heart every language; I have so tried the lives of this world that at one hour I become a priest, at another I turn into a friar, then into a prince, then a knight, footsoldier and page. I seize the advantage whenever I see it. At another hour I become a prelate, then an abbot: I much like people who follow the Rule, for with them I cloak better my foxiness.

If "ogni linguaggio" hints at and perverts the apostles' knowledge of all tongues under the power of the Spirit, the sonnet also conveys Jean's insight: namely, that the only fixed principle in False Seeming's shifty play of concealment (which the technique of enumeration and the iterative adverbs of time mime in the sonnet) is falsification itself.

To turn to the anti-fraternal satirists such as Guillaume and Jean is not equivalent, from Dante's viewpoint, to granting assent to their statement or even giving them the seal of a privileged authority. In *Inferno* 27, Dante endorses the anti-fraternal rhetoric, for Guido da Montefeltro has clearly betrayed the paradigm of Franciscan piety. But Dante also challenges, as the Franciscan intellectuals did, the logicians' categories of knowledge. When the devil, at the triumphant conclusion of his dispute with St. Francis, appeals to logic's principle of noncontradiction ("ne pentere e volere insieme puossi / per la contradizion che nol consente" ["nor is it possible to repent of a thing and to will it at the same time, for the contradiction does not allow it."] 119–20), he is using logic only rhetorically: it is a sophistic refutation by which he sways the opponent. But logical conceptualizations, as has been argued earlier, are delusive because they are not moored to the realities of life and because they establish a *de facto* discontinuity between the order of discourse and the order of reality. More importantly, the devil is claiming Guido da Montefeltro as his own, whose very experience in the canto unveils exactly how the principle of noncontradiction is a fictitious abstraction: like Faux-Semblant, the pope, and the devil himself, Guido is Proteus-like (to use Jean de Meung's metaphor for the friars), shifty, and always unlike himself.

This rotation of figures and categories of knowledge is the substance of a canto in which, as this paper has shown, prophecy is twisted into rhetoric, theology is manipulated for political ends, politics and ethics are masks of the desire for power, and logic is deployed rhetorically. From this perception of how tangled the forms of discourse are comes Dante's own moral voice, both here and in his attacks against the sophistry of syllogisms immediately after the Dominican St. Thomas Aquinas celebrates the life of St. Francis (*Paradiso* 11, 1–3).

Because of this movement from theory to practice and back again to theory, and from one order of knowledge to another, it appears that the liberal arts can never be fixed in a self-enclosed autonomous sphere: each art unavoidably entails the other in a ceaseless pattern of displacement. Ironically, what Dante condemns in Guido da Montefeltro from a moral point of view becomes, in Dante's own poetic handling, the essence of knowledge itself, whereby the various disciplines are forever intermingled. The idea that the arts cannot be arranged in categorical definitions is not only a poet's awareness of how arbitrary boundaries turn out to be. Medieval textbooks and compendia are consistent, so to speak, in betraying the difficulty of treating each of the liberal arts as crystallized entities. If Isidore views dialectic as logic, John of Salisbury's *Metalogicon* considers *logica* an encompassing term for "grammatica" and "ratio disserendi," which in turn contains dialectic and rhetoric. For Hugh of St. Victor, who follows St. Augustine's *City of God, logica* is the name for the *trivium.*

These references are valuable only if we are ready to recognize that what is largely a technical debate never loses sight of the spiritual destination of the liberal arts. What the technicians may sense but never face, however, is that which rhetoricians and poets always know: that knowledge may be counterfeited. Small wonder that in the *Convivio* Dante would repress rhetoric—in vain. But in the *Vita nuova* and the *Divine Comedy,* we are left with the disclosure that rhetoric, in spite of its dangerous status and, ironically, because of its dangerousness, is the only possible path the poet must tread on the way to metaphysics and theology respectively. Whether or not the poet delivers genuine metaphysical and theological knowledge or dazzles us with luminous disguises is a question which lies at the heart of Dante's poetry.

Notes

1. General studies on rhetoric include Charles H. Haskins, *The Renaissance of the Twelfth Century* (Cambridge, 1927), 138–50, which surveys the revival of "oratio" in the Roman political and judicial fields as well as the renewed importance of the epistolary style in the Middle Ages. This art of drafting official letters and documents, identified in the Bolognese *dictatores,* finds its authority in Alberic of Monte Cassino, *Breviarium de dictamine,* and Boncompagno of Signa, *Antiqua rhetorica.* See C. H. Haskins, "The Early 'Artes Dictandi,' " in *Studies in Medieval Culture* (Oxford, 1929), 170–92; also Robert L. Benson, "Proto-humanist and Narrative Technique in Early Thirteenth-Century Italian 'Arts Dictaminis,' " in *Boccaccio: Secoli di vita* (Atti del Convegno internazionale Boccaccio 1975), ed. M. Cottino-Jones and E. F. Tuttle (Ravenna, 1977), 31–48; Ronald Witt, "Medieval 'Ars Dictaminis' and the Beginnings of Humanism: A New Construction of the Problem," *Renaissance Quarterly* 25 (1982): 1–35. Cf. Brunetto Latini, *La rettorica,* ed. F. Maggini (Florence, 1915), 5.

2. Brunetto Latini writes: "Rhetoric is the science of speaking well; that is, rhetoric is that science through which we can say and write ornately" (*Rettorica,* 4). The quote echoes the conventional definition of rhetoric. Cf. Isidore of Seville, "Rhetorica est bene dicendi scientia in civilibus quaestibus; ad persuadendam iusta et

bona," *Etymologiae* 2.1.1., ed. W. M. Lindsay (Oxford, 1966). The theory of the *ornatus* in Dante is tied to the principle of linguistic *convenientia*. Cf. *De vulgari eloquentia* 2.1.2–10, ed. A. Mariog, rev. P. G. Ricci (Florence, 1968). See Francesco Tateo, *"Retorica" e "Poetica" fra Medioevo e Rinascimento* (Bari, 1960), 209–11. For the *ornatus* and degrees of style, see Geoffrey of Vinsauf, *Poetria nova*, in *Les Arts poetiques du XIIe siecle*, ed. E. Faral (Paris, 1923), lines 830ff. Useful are the remarks by C. Grayson, "Dante e la prosa volgare," *Il verri* 9 (1963): 6–26, and A. Schiaffini, *Tradizione e poesia nella prosa d'arte italiana dalla latinita medievale al Boccaccio* (Rome, 1969).

3. The tension between the liberal arts—and rhetoric chief among them—has been neglected by Dante studies, although medieval scholarship has probed the issue. See, for instance, P. Delhaye, "Grammatica et Ethica au XIIe siecle," *Recherches de theologie ancienne et medievale* 25 (1958): 59–110; H. de Lubac, "St. Gregoire et la grammaire," *Recherches de science religieuse* 48 (1960): 185–226; J. A. Weisheipl, "Classification of the Sciences in Medieval Thought," *Medieval Studies* 27 (1965): 55–90.

4. Etienne Gilson, "Philosophy in the *Banquet*," in *Dante and Philosophy*, trans. D. Moore (New York, 1963), 83–161. But see the review by Bruno Nardi, "Dante e la Filosofia," in *Nel mondo di Dante* (Rome, 1944), 209–45.

5. Here are the main bibliographical items on Cavalcanti's poem: Mario Casella, "La canzone d'amore di Guido Cavalcanti," *Studi di filologia italiana* 7 (1944): 97–160; J. E. Shaw, *Guido Cavalcanti's Theory of Love: The Canzone d'Amore and Other Related Problems* (Toronto, 1949); B. Nardi, "L'averroismo del 'primo amico' di Dante," in *Dante e la cultura medievale*, 2d ed. (Bari, 1949), 93–129; see also by Nardi, "Dante e Guido Cavalcanti," and "L'amore e i medici medievali," in *Saggi e note di critica dantesca* (Milan-Naples, 1966), 190–219; Maria Corti, "Guido Cavalcanti e una diagnosi dell'amore," in *La felicita mentale: Nuove prospettive per Cavalcanti e Dante* (Turin, 1983), 3–37.

6. Charles S. Singleton, *An Essay on the "Vita nuova"* (Cambridge, Mass., 1949) 20–24.

7. Ulrich Leo, "The Unfinished *Convivio* and Dante's Rereading of the *Aeneid*," *Medieval Studies* 13 (1951): 41–64; Bruno Nardi, "Tre momenti dell'incontro di Dante con Virgilio," in *Saggi e note di critica dantesca*, 220–37.

8. The debate has been much examined. See Maurice Perrod, *Maitre Guillaume de Saint-Amour, l'Université de Paris et les ordres mendiants au XIIIe siecle* (Paris, 1895); Christine Thouzellier, "La place du 'Periculis' de Guillaume de Saint-Amour dans les polemiques universitaires du XIIIe siècle," *Revue historique* 156 (1927): 69–83; Decima L. Douie, *The Conflict Between the Seculars and the Mendicants at the University of Paris in the Thirteenth Century*, Aquinas Paper 23 (London, 1954); Yves M.-J. Congar, "Aspects ecclesiologiques de la querelle entre mendiants et séculiers dans la seconde moitie du XIIIe siècle et le début du XIVe," *Archives d'histoire doctrinale et littéraire du moyen age*, Année 36, Tome 28 (1961): 35–151.

9. Ernst Martin, *Le Roman de Renart* (Strasburg, 1882), I:13; *The Exempla of Jacques de Vitry*, ed. T. F. Crane (London, 1890), 125; *Roman du Renart*, ed. D. M. Meon (Paris, 1826), IV:125–461. More generally, see P. Glorieux, "Prelats français contre religieux mendiants," *Revue d'histoire de l'Eglise en France* 11 (1925): 480–81; cf. also Rutebeuf, *Poemes concernant "université de Paris,"* ed. H. H. Lucas (Manchester, 1952).

CHRONOLOGY OF
IMPORTANT DATES

1265	Dante is born under the sign of Gemini (middle of May–middle of June).
1283	Dante becomes of age and shortly thereafter is married to Gemma Donati, who bears him three children (Jacopo, Pietro, and Antonia), and perhaps a fourth, Giovanni.
1289	Battle of Campaldino (near Bibbiena) fought between Arezzo and Florence. Dante, who took part in this battle on 11 June, remembers it in the encounter with Bonconte da Montefeltro (*Purgatorio* V, 11, 88ff.).
1290	Beatrice dies 8 June.
1290–1293	Dante undertakes philosophical studies and writes *Vita Nuova.*
1294	Dante meets Charles Martel who is visiting Florence. Already the king of Hungary, he was the heir to the Kingdom of Naples and the country of Provence. Dante recounts their encounter in *Paradiso* VIII.
1295	Dante enters political life.
1300	Dante is prior for two months (15 June–15 August). Pope Boniface VIII proclaims the Jubilee Year. This is the fictive date (Eastertime) of the journey of the *Divine Comedy.*
1301	Dante goes on an embassy to Boniface VIII as Charles of Valois approaches Florence.
1302	The first sentence of exile reaches Dante while he is in Siena (27 January). He is sentenced to death 10 March.

1302	Birth of Francesco Petrarca.
1305	Clement is the new pope. Papacy moves to Avignon.
1304–1307	*De Vulgari Eloquentia* and *Convivio* written.
1308	Henry of Luxembourg crowned new emperor.
1310	Henry descends to Italy. Dante writes epistle to Henry. Possible date of the *Monarchia*.
1313	Henry dies near Siena. Birth of Giovanni Boccaccio.
1314	The *Inferno* is completed. Dante writes letter to Italian cardinals.
1315	Florence offers to pardon Dante; he refuses the conditions attached to the pardon. He moves to Verona in the household of Can Grande della Scala.
1319	Dante is in Ravenna. *Purgatorio* is completed. Correspondence with the Humanist Giovanni del Virgilio.
1320	Dante lectures in Ravenna on *De Quaestio de aqua et terra*.
1321	Dante dies in Ravenna on 13 or 14 September.

SELECTED BIBLIOGRAPHY

PRIMARY WORKS

The *Vita Nuova*, which tells the story of the poet's poetic apprenticeship and of his love for Beatrice. It is written in poetry and prose.

Rime. They comprise (1) poems taken from the *Vita Nuova;* (2) the *Tenzone* or debate in poetry with Forese Donati: (3) *Rime Petrose* ("Stony Verses"), a series of love poems that recount the unrequited love for a "lady of stone"; (4) various verses written during Dante's exile; and (5) allegorical or doctrinal poems, including the three *canzoni* of the *Convivio.*

The *Convivio*, an unfinished philosophical work whose primary concern is ethics. It consists of four parts: an introductory book and three books written as allegorical expositions of three long *canzoni.*

De Vulgari Eloquentia, an unfinished work on grammar, rhetoric, and the vulgar tongue.

Monarchia, a treatise on the world empire and its relationship to the church.

Epistles, Ecologues, and the *Quaestio de aqua et terra* (a scientific treatise on the specific weight of land and water).

The *Divine Comedy*, which consists of *Inferno, Purgatorio,* and *Paradiso.*

SECONDARY WORKS

Auerbach, Eric. *Scenes from the Drama of European Literature*. Trans. Ralph Manheim. New York: Meridian Books, 1959. Reprint, Theory and History Literature Series, no. 9. Minneapolis: University of Minnesota Press, 1984.
Barbi, Michele. *Life of Dante*. Trans. and ed. Paul G. Ruggiers. Berkeley and Los Angeles: University of California Press, 1954.

Bergin, Thomas G. *From Time to Eternity: Essays on Dante's "Divine Comedy."* New Haven and London: Yale University Press, 1967.

Bosco, Umberto, ed. *Enciclopedia dantesca.* Rome: Istituto dell'Enciclopedia italiana, 1970.

Charity, A. C. *Events and Their Afterlife: The Dialectics of Christian Typology in the Bible and Dante.* Cambridge: Cambridge University Press, 1966.

Corti, Maria. *Dante a un nuovo crocevia.* Florence: Libreria Sansoni, 1981.

Cosmo, Umberto. *A Handbook to Dante Studies.* Trans. David Moore. Oxford: Blackwell, 1950.

D'Entreves, Alessandro Passerin. *Dante as Political Thinker.* Oxford: Clarendon Press, 1955.

Freccero, John. *Poetics of Conversion.* Cambridge, Mass.: Harvard University Press, 1986.

Gilson, Etienne. *Dante the Philosopher.* Trans. David Moore. London © 1948, 1978 by the Pontifical Institute of Mediaeval Studies, Toronto.

Hollander, Robert. *Allegory in Dante's Commedia.* Princeton: Princeton University Press, 1969.

Kantorowicz, E. H. *The King's Two Bodies: A Study in Medieval Political Theory.* Princeton: Princeton University Press, 1957.

Kaske, Robert E. "Dante's 'DXV' and 'Veltro.' " *Traditio* 17 (1961): 185–252.

MacLennan, Luis Jenaro. *The Trecento Commentaries on the Divine Comedy and the Epistle to Cangrande.* Oxford: Clarendon Press, 1974.

Mazzotta, Giuseppe. *Dante, Poet of the Desert: History and Allegory in the Divine Comedy.* Princeton: Princeton University Press, 1979.

Reade, W. H. V. *The Moral System of Dante's Hell.* Oxford: Clarendon Press, 1909.

Schnapp, Jeffrey. *Dante's Transfiguration of History.* Princeton: Princeton University Press, 1986.

Shoaf, R. A. *Dante, Chaucer and the Currency of the Word.* Norman, Okla.: Pilgrim Books, 1983.

Singleton, Charles S. *Journey to Beatrice.* Dante Studies II. Cambridge, Mass.: Harvard University Press, 1958. Reprint. Baltimore: Johns Hopkins University Press, 1977.

Toynbee, Paget. *A Dictionary of Proper Names and Notable Matters in the Works of Dante.* Oxford: Clarendon Press, 1898.

SUGGESTED READINGS

The following journals are useful for their periodic bibliographies: *Studi danteschi, Dante Studies,* and *Deutsches Dantejahrbuch.*

The most impressive Dante commentary available is Hermann Gmelin. *Kommentar.* Stuttgart: E. Klett Verlag, 1954.

The standard edition of the *Divine Comedy* is *La Divina Commedia secondo l'antica vulgata.* Ed. Giorgio Petrocchi. 4 vols. Societa Dantesca Italiana. Milan: Mondadori, 1966–67.

For traditional (and partial) commentaries on the *Divine Comedy,* see *La Divina Commedia nella figurazione artistica e nel secolare commento.* Guido Biagi, ed. 3 vols. (Inferno, Purgatorio and Paradiso). Turin: Unione Tipografico-Editrice Torinese, 1924–29.

The translations from the *Divine Comedy* are taken from *the Divine Comedy.* Trans., with commentary by, Charles S. Singleton. Bollingen Series LXXX. Princeton: Princeton University Press, 1970–76.

INDEX

215

NOTES ON THE
EDITOR AND CONTRIBUTORS

Giuseppe Mazzotta, the editor of this volume, is Professor and Chairman of Italian at Yale University. He is the author of *Dante, Poet of the Desert* and several essays on Dante.

Dante's Epistle X is addressed to Can Grande della Scala. The authenticity of the letter is still contested.

Guido da Pisa was a Carmelite friar. His commentary is one of the earliest written on the *Divine Comedy*.

Giovanni Boccaccio (1313–75), author of the *Decameron*, gave a series of public lectures on Dante in 1374.

Benevenuto da Imola (?–+1388), a friend of Coluccio Salutati, heard Boccaccio's lectures in Florence.

Francesco Petrarca (1304–74) is one of the "Three Crowns of Florence" and remaker of the canon of literature.

Cristoforo Landino (1424–98) was a member of the Florentine Academy and the author of several Neoplatonic works. His commentary of the *Divine Comedy* was illustrated by Botticelli.

Benedetto Varchi (1503–65), Florentine humanist known as philosopher, grammarian, and poet.

Iacopo Mazzoni (1548–98) was a Neo-Aristotelean philosopher. He strenuously opposed the anti-Dantist ideas of Ridolfo Castravilla.

Gianvincenzo Gravina (1664–1718) was the disciple of the Cartesian philosopher Caloprese and one of the founders of the Academy of Arcadia.

Giambattista Vico (1668–1744) is the author of *The New Science*. His views on Dante as a mythmaker and sublime visionary are the watershed in the contemporary understanding of the *Divine Comedy*.

Francesco de Sanctis (1817–83) is the most authoritative historian and critic of Italian literature.

Benedetto Croce (1866–1952) is most noted for his theories of literature. His essay on Dante influenced a whole generation of critics.

Bruno Nardi (1884–1968) is a historian of medieval philosophy and the author of many books that aim to show the influence of the Averroistic interpretation of Aristotle on Dante.

Etienne Gilson (1884–1978) was a neo-Thomist historian of medieval philosophy. In his work on Dante he tempers Busnelli's Thomism.

Erich Auerbach (1892–1957), the author of *Mimesis* and the essay *Figura*, revived De Sanctis' views on Dante in our time.

Charles S. Singleton (1909–1985). His *An Essay on the Vita Nuova* and his *Dante Studies* I and II have established him as the foremost American critic of the *Divine Comedy* in our time.

Gian Roberto Sarolli is a noted medievalist who has laid the basis in his monumental *Prolegomenon alla Divina Commedia* for a reading of Dante in terms of political theology.

John Freccero is Rosina Pierotti Professor of Italian at Stanford University. He has been an influential Dante teacher, and his brilliant readings are collected in *Dante: The Poetics of Conversion*.

Giuseppe Ungaretti (1888–1970) is Italy's poeta-theologus in our time.

Jorge Luis Borges (1899–1986) was Argentina's seer and maker of poetic mythologies.